Profiles of Dual Language Education in the 21st Century

D1736716

CAL SERIES ON LANGUAGE EDUCATION

Series Editors: Joel Gómez, Terrence G. Wiley, M. Beatriz Arias and Joy Kreeft Peyton, *Center for Applied Linguistics*, *Washington, DC, USA*.

Current and aspiring education professionals need accessible, high-quality, research-based resources on language learning, instruction, and assessment. This series provides such resources, serving to inform teachers' classroom practice, enhance teacher education, and build the background knowledge of undergraduate and graduate students in applied linguistics and other language-related fields.

The books in this series explore a broad range of issues in applied linguistics and language education and are written in a style that is accessible to a broad audience, including those who are new to the field. Each book addresses a topic of relevance to those who are studying or working in the fields of language learning, language instruction, and language assessment, whether in English as a second language or other world languages. Topic areas include approaches to language instruction and assessment; approaches to content instruction and assessment for language learners; professional development for educators working with language learners; principles of second language acquisition for educators; and connections between language policy and educational practice.

All books in this series are externally peer-reviewed.

Full details of all the books in this series and of all our other publications can be found on http://www.multilingual-matters.com, or by writing to Multilingual Matters, St Nicholas House, 31–34 High Street, Bristol BS1 2AW, UK.

CAL SERIES ON LANGUAGE EDUCATION: 3

Profiles of Dual Language Education in the 21st Century

Edited by
M. Beatriz Arias and Molly Fee

MULTILINGUAL MATTERS
Bristol • Blue Ridge Summit

DOI https://doi.org/10.21832/ARIAS1664
Library of Congress Cataloging in Publication Data
A catalog record for this book is available from the Library of Congress.
Names: Arias, M. Beatriz, editor. | Fee, Molly, 1986 – editor.
Title: Profiles of Dual Language Education in the 21st century/Edited by
    M. Beatriz Arias and Molly Fee.
Description: Bristol, UK; Blue Ridge Summit, PA: Multilingual Matters, [2018] |
Series: CAL Series on Language Education: 3 | Includes bibliographical
    references and index.
Identifiers: LCCN 2018020933| ISBN 9781788921664 (hbk: alk. paper) |
    ISBN 9781788921657 (pbk: alk. paper) | ISBN 9781788921671 (pdf) |
    ISBN 9781788921688 (epub) | ISBN 9781788921695 (kindle)
Subjects: LCSH: Education, Bilingual. | Multicultural education. | Education,
    Bilingual—Case studies. | Multicultural education—Case studies.
Classification: LCC LC3737 .P76 2018 | DDC 370.117/5—dc23 LC record available at
    https://lccn.loc.gov/2018020933

British Library Cataloguing in Publication Data
A catalogue entry for this book is available from the British Library.

ISBN-13: 978-1-78892-166-4 (hbk)
ISBN-13: 978-1-78892-165-7 (pbk)

Multilingual Matters
UK: St Nicholas House, 31–34 High Street, Bristol BS1 2AW, UK.
USA: NBN, Blue Ridge Summit, PA, USA.

Website: www.multilingual-matters.com
Twitter: Multi_Ling_Mat
Facebook: https://www.facebook.com/multilingualmatters
Blog: www.channelviewpublications.wordpress.com

Copyright © 2018 M. Beatriz Arias, Molly Fee and the authors of individual chapters.

All rights reserved. No part of this work may be reproduced in any form or by any means without permission in writing from the publisher.

The policy of Multilingual Matters/Channel View Publications is to use papers that are natural, renewable and recyclable products, made from wood grown in sustainable forests. In the manufacturing process of our books, and to further support our policy, preference is given to printers that have FSC and PEFC Chain of Custody certification. The FSC and/or PEFC logos will appear on those books where full certification has been granted to the printer concerned.

Typeset by Nova Techset Private Limited, Bengaluru and Chennai, India.
Printed and bound in the UK by the CPI Books Group Ltd.
Printed and bound in the US by Thomson-Shore, Inc.

Contents

Contributors

M. Beatriz Arias is a Senior Research Scientist at the Center for Applied Linguistics and is currently advancing the work of the National Dual Language Forum, a network of Dual Language organizations. Her scholarly interests center on educational language policy and programs for Emergent Bilinguals/English Language Learners. Her co-authored books include: *Implementing Educational Language Policy in Arizona: An Examination of Legal, Historical and Current Practices in SEI and Academic Language in Second Language Learning.* Beatriz is an Associate Professor Emerita at Arizona State University where she was the director of the Center for Bilingual Education and Research. Arias, a National Education Policy Fellow, has been a Court-appointed expert in school desegregation cases including Los Angeles, Denver, and Chicago, advocating for educational programs which promote equity for English Learners.

Igone Arteagoitia is a Research Scientist at the Center for Applied Linguistics. Her research focuses on the language and literacy development of Spanish-English bilingual children. Dr. Arteagoitia is currently Project Director on a grant funded by the U.S. Department of Education to document characteristics of successful dual language programs in Oregon. In addition to her research, she provides a range of support services for districts that serve emergent bilingual learners. Dr. Arteagoitia has presented on her work at a number of conferences and published her research in peer-reviewed publications, including *TESOL Quarterly*, *Bilingual Research Journal* and the *Journal of Bilingual Education Research and Instruction*.

Carol Bearse received her Ph.D. from Lesley University and she has over 30 years' experience teaching at various grade levels K-12. She has been a Dual Language and ESL coordinator for secondary students in Massachusetts and has recently retired as an Associate Professor of Education from Touro College in Manhattan. She has published widely in academic journals and texts and now divides her time between Boston and Tucson.

Donna Christian is a senior fellow at the Center for Applied Linguistics (where she previously served as president). Her research focuses on the role of language in education, with special attention to second language learning, dialect diversity, dual language education and public policy. She is a co-author of *Dialects at School: Educating Linguistically Diverse Students* (2017) and the editor of a special issue of the *International Multilingual Research Journal* on dual language education (2016).

Dr. Ester de Jong is a Professor in ESOL/Bilingual Education and the Director of the School of Teaching and Learning at the University of Florida, in Gainesville, Florida (USA). Prior to coming to the University of Florida, she worked with ESL and bilingual programs in Massachusetts, United States. Her research interests include two-way bilingual education, educational language policy, and teacher preparation for bilingual students. Her book, *Foundations of Multilingualism in Education: From Principles to Practice*, considers a principled approach to school, program and classroom decision-making for bilingual learners. Dr. de Jong is currently Past- President of TESOL International Association (2018–2019).

Molly Fee is a Ph.D. candidate in the Department of Sociology at UCLA. Her research interests focus on refugee resettlement, international migration, political sociology and language policy. She previously worked at the Center for Applied Linguistics in Washington, DC. Her work has been funded by the National Science Foundation, the UCLA Luskin Center for History and Policy, and the UCLA Center for European and Russian Studies. She holds an M.A. in International Affairs and an M.A. in Cultural Translation from the American University of Paris.

Ofelia García is Professor in the Ph.D. programs in Urban Education and Latin American, Iberian and Latino Cultures at the Graduate Center of the City University of New York. García has published widely in the areas of bilingualism and bilingual education, the education of emergent bilinguals, sociology of language and language policy. She is the general editor of the *International Journal of the Sociology of Language* and the co-editor of *Language Policy* (with H. Kelly-Holmes). Among her best-known books are *Bilingual Education in the 21st Century: A Global Perspective* and *Translanguaging; Language, Bilingualism and Education* (with Li Wei), which received the 2015 British Association of Applied Linguistics Award. In 2017 she received the Charles Ferguson Award in Applied Linguistics and the AERA Lifetime Career Award in Bilingual Education. She is a member of the National Academy of Education.

Fred Genesee is Professor Emeritus in the Psychology Department at McGill University. He has conducted research on alternative forms of dual language education, the academic development of at-risk students in bilingual programs. language acquisition in typically developing and at-risk pre-school bilingual children, and internationally adopted children. He has published numerous articles in scientific journals, professional books and magazines and is the author of 16 books on bilingualism. He is the recipient of the Canadian Psychology Association Gold Medal Award, Paul Pimsler Award for Research in Foreign Language Education, Canadian Psychological Association Award for Distinguished Contributions to Community or Public Service, California Association for Bilingual Education Award for Promoting Bilingualism and the le prix Adrien-Pinard.

Barbara Kennedy, Ed.D has over 30 years' experience teaching and leading in multilingual classrooms, preschool through adult. Barbara is a co-author of the *Guiding Principles for Dual Language Education,* 3rd edition (2018) and is a national presenter and author. She has served as Director of Dual Language and Bilingual Education, Sponsored Projects, at the Center for Applied Linguistics in Washington, DC, where she assisted program directors across the country on program design, implementation, and evaluation. Barbara currently serves as Director of English Learner Support at the Texas Education Agency in Austin, Texas.

Kathryn Lindholm-Leary, Ph.D. is Professor Emerita of Child and Adolescent Development at San José State University, where she taught for 28 years. Kathryn has worked with many two-way and developmental bilingual programs (PreK-12) over the past 30 years and has written books, chapters and journal articles, and has given presentations to researchers, educators and parents. More recently, she worked with the National Academy of Sciences in their report on the development of English/Dual language learners. Kathryn has served on advisory boards or as consultant to federal and state departments of education, various professional organizations and other agencies, school districts and schools.

Patricia Makishima has held many positions in Illinois School District U-46 during the past 20 years. She has taught at the middle and high school levels, has chaired the high school ESL/Bilingual department and served for the last 11 years as a Coordinator for ELL Initiatives. She has been a key leader of the District wide implementation of the 80:20 DL Program. In addition, she is a contributing author in Collier and Thomas' *Creating Dual Language Schools for a Transformed World: Administrator's Speak.* She is an advocate for English learners who has committed her professional career to helping all students become bilingual and biliterate citizens of this global society.

Amy Markos Ph.D. is a teacher educator, specializing in preparing preservice teachers and in-service teachers to support linguistically and culturally diverse learners in educational contexts, from early childhood through high school. She has taught in the university settings for sixteen years and has spent the last twelve years working with educators and administrators through professional development opportunities in PreK-12 contexts. Her research interests include understanding teachers' dispositions and beliefs about English learners and the use of critical reflection in teacher learning.

Amy is also interested in education policies and pedagogical practices related to language learners' access to quality education.

Kate Menken is a Professor of Linguistics at Queens College of the City University of New York (CUNY), and a Research Fellow at the Research Institute for the Study of Language in Urban Society at the CUNY Graduate Center. Her books are *English Learners Left Behind: Standardized Testing as Language Policy* (Multilingual Matters, 2008), *Negotiating Language Policies in Schools: Educators as Policymakers* (co-edited with Ofelia García, Routledge, 2010) and *Common Core, Bilingual and English Language Learners: A Resource for Educators* (co-edited with Guadalupe Valdés and Mariana Castro, Caslon, 2015). Further information can be found on her website: http://katemenken.org.

Min-Chuan Tsai is currently a doctoral candidate in ESOL/Bilingual Education at the University of Florida and received her Master's in TESOL from Arizona State University in 2015. Min-Chuan is a UF Graduate School Fellow. Her research interests are dual language teacher preparation, Computer Assisted Language Learning, project-based learning, cross-cultural communication and distance education.

Wilma Valero is the former director of the ELL Program in District U-46. She developed and implemented district-wide coherent procedures for the identification, assessment and placement of emergent bilingual students in a program that validates and recognizes as invaluable assets their language(s) and culture. As the director, Valero led one of the nation's more ambitious and successful transitions of the traditional bilingual program into a nationally renowned 80:20 Dual Language Program, and in 2012, CABE awarded the district the notable title of the Promoting Bilingualism District of Distinction. In 2014 Wilma was awarded the Friends of the Teacher Mentoring Program (TMP).

Patricia Velasco started her career as a speech pathologist in Mexico City. She holds a MSC from the School of Human Communication Disorders, Mc Gill University and a doctorate from the Harvard Graduate School of Education (HGSE). In 1994 she established a Staff Development Institute (Casa de la Ciencia) that works with indigenous bilingual children and their teachers in San Cristobal de las Casas, Chiapas, Mexico. In 2003, Patricia came to New York City. She first worked for the Reading and Writing Project at Teachers College, Columbia University, as a staff developer supporting teachers all across New York City in addressing the literacy and language needs of English language learners. She was part of the faculty in the Bilingual/Bicultural Program at Teachers College, Columbia University. Currently, she is Assistant Professor of Education at Queens College, City University of New York, where she coordinates the Bilingual Program. Professor Velasco is the director Bilingual Language

Supports sponsored by the New York State Department of Education to create practices exclusive to bilingual learners facing the New York State Next Generation Language Standards.

Sara Vogel is a doctoral candidate in Urban Education at the Graduate Center of the City University of New York, interested in the intersection of computer science education, bilingualism, and social justice pedagogy. She is currently the lead research assistant on Participating in Literacies and Computer Science (PiLaCS), a National Science Foundation-funded project which aims to leverage the diverse language practices of bilingual youth as resources in their computer science learning. In the past, she worked as a research assistant for the City University of New York – New York State Initiative on Emergent Bilinguals.

Terrence G. Wiley is Professor Emeritus at Arizona State University and the former President of the Center for Applied Linguistics. Dr. Wiley's teaching and research have focused on educational and applied linguistics, concentrating on educational language policies; language diversity and immigrant integration; teaching English as a second and international language; bilingualism, literacy and biliteracy studies; and bilingual, heritage and community language education. He received his Ph.D. from the University of Southern California in Education with an emphasis in Linguistics, has two Master's degrees, in Linguistics and Asian Studies, and a B.A. in History. He has won numerous awards for scholarship, teaching, and service, including the American Association for Applied Linguistics (AAAL) Distinguished Scholarship and Service Award and the Joshua Fishman Award from the National Heritage Language Resource Center.

Preface

M. Beatriz Arias

About 20 years ago, the Center for Applied Linguistics (Christian *et al.*, 1997) published *Profiles in Two-Way Immersion Education*. This volume showcased three case studies of dual language education in public school settings and concluded that 'all three sites promote bilingualism, biliteracy and academic achievement.' (p. 3) At about the same time, the goals, or 'pillars' of Dual Language Education (DLE) programs were articulated as (1) Bilingualism and Biliteracy, (2) Academic Achievement and (3) Cross-Cultural Competence (Christian, 1996). The 1997 case studies did not attend very much to that third goal. In the interim, the definition of cultural competence has been refined and focused. Today, Dual Language Education programs strive to support the goals of equity within the context of Dual Language Education, recognizing the importance of the participation of minoritized communities. This has resulted in a more careful scrutiny of equity issues which underscore programmatic issues of language allocation and classroom language policy. This 21st-century volume of Profiles in Dual Language Education provides a more fulsome overview of the role that the third goal has played in DLE research and program planning.

The last two decades have witnessed a sea change in the field of DLE; the popularity of DLE has been validated through increased student enrollment and States have stepped up to support funding and legislation for the implementation of DLE programs. Today, DLE programs include many partner languages (with Spanish the most prevalent), they span the curriculum preK-12 and can culminate with graduation from secondary school with a Seal of Biliteracy.

In this volume, three case studies present DLE implementation at the school, district and city level. These case studies provide examples of how despite conflicts with the traditional DLE language allocation models, and struggles with the hegemony of English, collaborative and cooperative instructional staff can implement effective DLE programs. In view of the increasing demand for DLE programs to span the pre-K through 12 curriculum, we present two chapters addressing the expansion of DLE models to pre-school and secondary school. Finally, because DLE is at the nexus of education and language policies, we provide a chapter to review DLE teacher preparation and a chapter that elucidates the spaces that policy creates for DLE.

This volume begins with a short review of the research that has been conducted in the last 20 years which assesses the three goals: Bilingualism and Biliteracy, Academic Achievement and Cross-Cultural Competence. While there is substantial research on student achievement in DLE programs, the fact that many programs do not assess progress in the partner language, limits our understanding of student progress toward achieving bilingualism and biliteracy. Few scholars have attended to progress on the third goal, cultural competence. Studies addressing cultural competence are difficult to aggregate because of multifaceted definitions. A concern that has emerged in the last five years of DLE research is one for equity, equity in both access and instruction for the minoritized community and linguistic equity, where both languages and all the languaging has equal value and importance. Recently, concerns with the 'gentrification' of DLE programs have interrogated the positionality of minoritized communities.

The three Dual Language programs showcased in this volume highlight different contexts (school level, city level, district level) of Dual Language Program Implementation. The first case study focuses on a legacy Dual Language Program which has been in operation since 1966, highlighted in the 1997 volume, Key School in Arlington Virginia. This is a good example of how, over time, a program must adjust to the characteristics of a changing enrollment. This program was originally conceptualized as a gifted program and changes to meet the needs of the current community have been slow in coming. The lack of equity in serving the needs of all children is voiced by the teachers. 'The native English speakers in our school tend to be above grade level and our ELLs [English language learners] tend to be on or below. Despite our efforts at promoting Spanish and equity among groups, our native English students tend to dominate interactions and we are continually looking for ways to empower our ELLs and further challenge our highly-able students' (p. 33). The author, Dr. Arteagoitia, emphasizes that resisting the power of English as the dominant language is important both for pedagogical and social reasons.

The second case study highlights the role of policy and community in the development of Dual Language Education in New York City. It proposes reframing 'dual language' programs as dual language *bilingual* education (DLBE) which have the potential to empower communities building on the visions Puerto Ricans had for their children in the 1960s and 1970s. The authors highlight the tensions that exist between DLBE programs as traditionally defined and today's NYC multilingual communities. They provide a historical backdrop to dual language education in the Bloomberg and NCLB years noting that DLBE was beginning to lose the original intent of all bilingual education: that of providing bilingual communities with a meaningful and equal educational opportunity for their children. The authors interrogate the traditional Dual Language practice of language separation, noting that it does not represent how students use language. They call on DLBE programs to acknowledge the entire multilingual repertoire of most young people today, and establish a multilingual ecology that recognizes all the language practices of their students. With this in mind, the chapter calls for building bilingual programs that do not suffer from a monoglossic ideology that sees bilingualism as simply additive and does not understand its dynamics (García, 2009). Translanguaging may be a way to offer DLBE programs the flexibility they need to grow and expand and be made available in all communities that want it. The authors assert that beyond 'fidelity' to one type of bilingual programs, NYC needs to meet the needs of its very varied multilingual citizens in the 21st century. The rigidity of interpreting 'dual' as simply two autonomous languages for two different linguistic groups is simply not adequate for the complex multilingualism of NYC communities.

The third case study examines the implementations of a district-wide Dual Language Program in U-46, Elgin, in response to a desegregation consent decree. U-46 is the second largest school district in Illinois with 40 elementary schools, eight middle schools and five high schools. Its ELL program provides a continuum of services for more than 9000 emergent bilingual students in 41 schools. This chapter describes the journey of this district as it committed to equity and social justice through the implementation of an instructional program that is culturally and linguistically responsive to its diverse student population. Extensive planning was conducted, with feasibility studies which recommended to the superintendent an implementation of dual language education following the 80/20 design. The program began in 2011 at the pre-school and early elementary grades. By 2018 it has extended across all the middle and high schools. Professional development was key to a quality and consistent program implementation. An annual dual language academy was created to recognize and validate the vast knowledge of dual language teachers in the district and to recognize the partner language as an asset within both social and professional contexts. The authors, Wilma Valero and Patricia Makishima stress that a strong culture of collaboration was the most instrumental factor in the successful preK-12 implementation of the dual language program.

As Dual Language Programs have expanded across the grades, educators are challenged to determine how the instructional practices used in K-5 Dual Language programs apply to pre-schools and secondary schools. In Chapter 5, Dr. Kathryn Lindholm-Leary asks: Are standard dual language models that are used for K-5 appropriate at early childhood levels? Should student background factors impact the models that are used with young children? She notes that the position of The National Association for the Education of Young Children (NAEYC, 2009) recognizes the value of bilingualism at the federal level. Yet at the federal level there is no overall statement about the value of bilingualism, or the importance of learning a second language for native English-speaking (NES) preschoolers. Rather, the goal is to promote English language proficiency, possibly through building foundational support in the primary language.

Thus, at the pre-school level, the major language education program type is still *English mainstream*, which provides instruction only in English to both language minority and language majority students with the purpose of promoting English language development. Nevertheless, the research is very clear that there are distinct bilingualism and achievement advantages for school-aged children, both NES and DLL, who participate in a dual language program.

In summary, research from preschool and early elementary education levels support the advantages of dual language programs for both NES and DLL children. However, modifications of the models used in K-5 may be necessary for pre-schoolers, depending on the demographic and language backgrounds of the students.

Chapter 6 provides a synthesis of current research on secondary two-way immersion (TWI) program outcomes and some promising practices by teachers at the secondary level. The authors also maintain that the cultural dimension of TWI must take a more central place in research and practice in secondary TWI programs. In their review of the research, Drs. Bearse, de Jong and Min-Chuan Tsai found that most studies only consider outcomes in English and in particular English reading, writing and math. In contrast with studies at the elementary level, where student outcome in the partner language is usually considered, few studies at the secondary level assess or report on partner language performance. Importantly, the authors address the linkage between language use and identity development in adolescence. Program models at the secondary level are more diverse as TWI educators attempt to maintain 50% of instruction to be in Spanish. The authors state that researchers have begun to question the strict separation of languages called for in the TWI program structure and recommend that language in practice be used instead; i.e., forms of code-switching and multiple uses of discourses that highlight the rich cultural diversity that TWI students bring to the classroom. These practices would help to reinforce positive linguistic identity. Increasingly, studies have paid attention to the relationship between language and identity and how identities are constructed through classroom practices. A focus on identity and identity construction as an integral part of TWI program development is particularly important for adolescent TWI students given the central role that identity development plays for students at this age. Using and recognizing the validity of multiple discourses in the classroom are ways to address the inequities in a TWI classroom. There may, indeed, be a need to add a fourth goal to TWI programs. If TWI programs wish to meet their long-term language and academic goals, the authors argue, TWI educators need to pay attention to identity investment and its role in students' motivation to continue to learn and use the partner language in support of on-going bilingual development. Explicit attention to students' discourses and identities need to become part of successful and more equitable programs at the secondary level. Embracing multiple discourses and equitable programming are areas where additional research could pave the way for more innovative TWI programs at the secondary level.

Chapter 7 explores the state of teacher preparation for teaching in Dual Language settings. Noting the scant research available on Dual Language teacher preparation, Dr. Kennedy reviews bilingual teacher preparation in California, Minnesota, Oregon and Texas. In general she notes that state initiatives and state policy are important drivers in preparing teachers to deliver effective DL instruction. DL teachers can be certified in a variety of educational contexts including undergraduate or graduate degree, on-line or face to face. The majority of these programs are designed to prepare teachers at the elementary level rather than secondary. Standards for DL teacher preparation have not yet been developed. There is general agreement that it requires a comprehensive and coordinated effort among policy makers, university leaders, school district leaders and community stakeholders to effectively address the DL teacher shortage.

The final chapter examines the interaction between various policy contexts and DLE program implementation. Dr. Christian notes that Dual Language Education is at a unique nexus between education and language policies. Education programs respond to many state level policies including teacher preparation and graduation requirements. Language policies and politics are sometimes overt, such as those policies that restrict language use; and sometimes covert, embedded in the attitudes of educators and others regarding the legitimacy of second language learners. DLE program success is often linked to the sociolinguistic reality of 'attitudes, beliefs and ideologies about language and education that are sometimes independent of research-based evidence' (p. 115). This chapter provides an overview of how policy makes 'space' for the implementation of DLE. For example, the English language accountability required by the *No Child Left Behind Act* in 2001 and the *Every Student Succeeds Act of 2015* emphasize accountability in English achievement through program and assessment requirements. This would seem to discourage the space for DLE. On the other hand, states have begun to support DLE. The state of Utah has incentivized DLE including funding for the program and teacher professional development. Many states are incentivizing DLE by offering the *Seal of Biliteracy*, which validates that students possess academic proficiency in English and at least one other language. Thirty-three states and the District of Columbia currently offer the *Seal of Biliteracy*.

This volume on Dual Language Education would not have been possible without the support and guidance of staff at the Center for Applied Linguistics and at Multilingual Matters. I extend my sincerest appreciation to Ms. Molly Fee, associate editor, who efficiently reviewed and updated the manuscripts and facilitated contact with the authors and the publishers. Thanks also go to CAL's staff: Susan Gilson, Sophia Birdas and Jeannie Rennie. CAL's Multilingual Matters partner, Tommi Grover was supportive of the effort from the beginning and Laura Longworth helped guide the manuscript through the final publication processes. Finally, my deepest thanks go to the authors who contributed to this volume, scholars and practitioners alike, whose commitment to the field of Dual Language Education ensure its continuing improvement.

References

Christian, D. (1996) Two-way immersion education: Students learning through two languages. *The Modern Language Journal* 80, 66–76.

Christian, D., Montone, C.L., Lindholm, K.J. and Carranza, I. (1997) *Profiles in Two-way Immersion Education*. Washington, DC and McHenry, IL: Center for Applied Linguistics and Delta Systems Co. Inc.

García, O. (2009) *Bilingual Education in the 21st Century: A Global Perspective*. Malden, MA: Wiley-Blackwell.

National Association for the Education of Young Children (NAEYC) (2009) Where we stand. See http://www.naeyc.org/files/naeyc/file/positions/diversity.pdf

Foreword: The Re-emergence of Bilingual Education as Dual Language Education

Terrence G. Wiley

This important collection takes as its point of departure, recent developments in dual language education with a focus on the past two decades. The progress and warm embrace that dual language education has been experiencing represents a sharp break with the English-only era (Wiley, 2004) that proceeded it, when various forms of bilingual education came under wide-spread political attack, stigma and restriction.

Various forms of bilingual education have been ongoing in that portion of North America which was to become the United States long before the republic was founded (Fishman, 2014). In colonial times, missionaries sought first to learn the languages of American Indians so that they could proselytize among them and then promoted English among them. Various waves of immigrants and refugees attempted to educate their young both in their ancestral languages as well as in English. This was particularly true for German immigrants many of whose children attended bilingual schools throughout the 19th century and the first two decades of the 20th century (Toth, 1990), bilingual education also had thrived in states such as Texas (Blanton, 2004). All this changed dramatically in the World War I era when anti-German and anti-immigrant attitudes swept the country, with some 34 states restricting instruction in languages other than English by 1919. A challenge to one such restriction reached the U.S. Supreme Court in *Meyer v. Nebraska*, 262 U.S. 390 (1923). *Meyer* affirmed the rights of parents to allow their children to be able to learn languages in addition to English, but the legacy of the Americanization Movement (1914–1925) continued to have a lasting impact throughout the 20th century (Wiley, 1998, 2004).

During the Civil Rights era (1954–1968), language and literacy development became an area of increasing focus for minority children. For children whose first language was Spanish, bilingual education became of interest to address inequities in education. Noting the success of the Coral Way program in Miami, which began as a Spanish-English dual language program in 1963 for Cuban refugees and immigrants, there was increasing interest in bilingual education's promise to help language minority children build on their native languages as a bridge to instruction mediated through English. In 1967 Texas Senator Ralph Yarborough introduced the Bilingual Education Act (Title VII), which became law in 1968. It provided supplemental federal funding for developmental bilingual programs (San Miguel, 2004). While Title VII funding provided promise, it would take time to recruit and train teachers and develop sound programs. By the time the program concluded in 2001, it still only served a minority of the potentially eligible children. Early on, even with Title VII in place, in 1974, the Supreme Court in a landmark case, *Lau v. Nichols*, 414 U.S. 563, ruled against the San Francisco Unified School District for failing to adequately teach English to Chinese immigrant children. The school district remarkably had maintained that it was not obligated to teach the language that mediated instruction, and that it was incumbent on parents to do so, even if they did not speak the language. While mandating that schools must be proactive in teaching English, *Lau* did not mandate a bilingual education or a specific methodology (Arias & Wiley, 2015).

Progress was made during the late 1970s in establishing models for effective programs, but by the late 1970s there was also a growing backlash against bilingual education before it had been fully implemented. Under the Carter administration, the Office of Civil Rights (OCR) was proactive in supporting educational language minority rights, but during the Reagan years (1981–1989), there was a strong, resurgent English-only movement, lead at the federal level by Senator S.I. Hayakawa of California, which opposed bilingual education and sought to impose official English laws. Although this effort failed at the federal level, it was more successful among the states, with a majority passing largely symbolic official English laws.

Over time, at the federal level, the movement succeeded in chipping away at Title VII as well by allowing for the inclusion of English 'immersion' programs. Despite evidence of the effectiveness of many programs, bilingual education remained 'contested policy' (San Miguel, 2004). Bilingual education became a target in several high-profile state initiatives – most notably in California, with the passage of Proposition 227 in 1998, followed by Proposition 203 in Arizona in 2000, and Question Two in Massachusetts in 2001. With slogans such as 'English for the children' and steady stream of disinformation regarding the alleged negative effects of bilingual education by its opponents resulted in convincing a majority of voters to restrict access of language minority children to bilingual education and mandated English immersion.

Title VII was allowed to sunset with the implementation of No Child Left Behind in 2001. At the federal level, overt reference to bilingual education disappeared both in explicit legislation and in the renaming of the Office of Bilingual Education and Language Minority Affairs to the Office of English Language Acquisition (Wiley, 2005) and later as the U.S. Supreme Court surrendered authority back to the states in determining how best to teach language minority students in the *Horne v. Flores*, 557 U.S. 433 (2009), decision (see Moore, 2014 for elaboration). With federal retreat from bilingual education, the negative effects of restricting access for language minority students has been well documented (e.g., Faltis & Arias, 2012; McField, 2013; Moore, 2014).

Despite decades of opposition to federally supported bilingual education, where dual language programs have been available, as this volume provides evidence, a growing number of parents continued to see the value of giving their children the opportunity to become bilingual and biliterate. Even in states where there were restrictions on language minority children's access to bilingual education support has grown for 'seals of biliteracy.' Twenty-five states currently have laws in place, four are moving in that direction, with another ten considering the prospects (see http://sealofbiliteracy.org/ for current information). Meanwhile, in California, which became the first state in the contemporary era to restrict bilingual education, support grew to overturn proposition 227. In November of 2016, California overwhelmingly voted to do so with the passage of Proposition 58, which had widespread support from educators firm in the belief believe that dual language education should be available for all children (Wiley, in press).

The challenge going forward will be to ensure that the demand for dual language programs will be matched by strong programs of professional development with well-prepared teachers in programs based on sound, research-based principles. This important volume provides an excellent step in the right direction.

References

Arias, M.B. and Wiley, T.G. (2015) Forty Years after Lau: The continuing assault on educational human rights in the United States with implications for linguistic minorities. *Languages Problems and Language Planning* 39 (3), 227–244.

Blanton, C.K. (2004) *The Strange Career of Bilingual Education in Texas, 1836–1981.* College Station, TX: Texas A and M University Press.

Faltis, C. and Arias, M.B. (2012) *Implementing Educational Language Policy in Arizona: Legal, Historical and Current Practices in SEI.* Bristol: Multilingual Matters.

Fishman, J.A. (2014) Three hundred years plus of heritage language in the United States. In T.G. Wiley, J.K. Peyton, D. Christian, S.C.K. Moore and N. Liu (eds) *Handbook of Heritage and Community Language Education in the United States: Research, Policy, and Educational Practice* (pp. 36–44). London and Washington, DC: Routledge and Center for Applied Linguistics.

McField, G.P. (ed.) (2013) *The Miseducation of English Learners: A Tale of Three States and Lessons Learned*. Charlotte, NC: Information Age.

Moore, S.K. (2014) (ed.) *Language Policy Processes and Consequences: Arizona Case Studies*. Multilingual Matters.

San Miguel, G. (2004) *Contested Policy: The Rise and fall of Federal Bilingual Education in the United States, 1960–2001*. Denton, TX: University of North Texas State Press.

Toth, C.R. (1990) *German-English Schools in America: The Cincinnati Experience in Historical Context*. New York: Peter Lang.

Wiley, T.G. (2005) The reemergence of heritage and community language policy in the U.S. national spotlight. *Modern Language Journal* 89 (4), 594–601.

Wiley, T.G. (2004) Language policy and English-only. In E. Finegan and J.R. Rickford (eds) *Language in the USA: Perspectives for the Twenty-First Century* (pp. 319–338). Cambridge: Cambridge University Press.

Wiley, T.G. (1998) The imposition of World War I era English-Only policies and the fate of German in North America. In T. Ricento and B. Burnaby (eds) *Language and Politics in the United States and Canada* (pp. 211–241). Mahwah, NJ: Lawrence Erlbaum.

Wiley, T.G. (in press) The rise, fall, and rebirth of bilingual education in U.S. Educational Policy: The case of California. In T. Ricento (ed.) *Language Politics and Policies: Perspectives from Canada and the United States*. Cambridge: Cambridge University Press.

Part 1

Dual Language Programs

1 Recent Research on the Three Goals of Dual Language Education

M. Beatriz Arias and Amy Markos

Introduction

In the late 1990s two foundational articles on dual language education were published: Christian's 'Two way immersion education: students learning in two languages' (1996), defined and described dual language education programs and reported emerging results of dual language education at that time. Soon thereafter, Valdés (1997) published, 'Dual language education: a cautionary note concerning the education of language minority students,' problematizing the use of dual language education in meeting the needs of English learners (ELs). In this chapter, we review the last 20 years of research since those publications to report on the progress of research on the three goals of dual language education as defined by Christian (1996) and discuss the extent to which issues raised by Valdés (1997) have been addressed.

To begin, we offer an overview of the different types of dual language programs and the growth of these programs across the nation.

Overview of Dual Language Education

Dual language education has proven to be a successful program for both emergent bilinguals/English learners and native English speakers (NES), promoting the acquisition of a second language, sustaining academic achievement and developing cross-cultural competence (Lindholm-Leary, 2001; Thomas & Collier, 1997, 2002). Over the last 20 years, research indicates that several types of dual language education programs have developed, responding to local needs and communities. The differences across program types and the growth of programs are addressed below.

Types of dual language education programs

There are two main types of dual language education: two-way programs and one-way programs, see Figure 1.1 below for an overview of the various types (Boyle *et al.*, 2015). Whether two-way or one-way, dual language programs provide a full educational experience for students, supporting students' academic achievement and language development.

Dual language programs are primarily found in elementary schools, beginning in kindergarten and lasting through the end of 5th or 6th grade. Fewer programs extend into the middle and secondary years, and when they do, tend to shift from a focus on instruction and learning in two languages to a focus on maintaining proficiency in the partner language through foreign language courses. Many dual language programs at the secondary level are limited to a single class period (Bearse & de Jong, 2008). Presently, states and dual language advocates are exploring ways to promote the continuation of dual language education into the secondary years. One approach to encourage and support student's second language acquisition is to award a special certification to students upon graduation based on their demonstrated course work and communicative proficiency in a second language. This award, which is given upon graduation from high school, appears on the student's transcript as a Seal of Biliteracy. As of this date, 33 states and the District of Columbia offer the Seal of Biliteracy, a certification indicating that the student has attained grade level proficiency in a second language (Lead with Languages, n.d.).

Number of dual language programs in the U.S.

It is difficult to determine the actual number of dual language programs currently in place, but we do know that with increased parental interest and support at the state and community levels, the number of programs in the U.S. is on the rise. One of the difficulties in the identification of dual language programs is the reliability to which each program adheres to a common definition of 'dual language.' In 2004, the Center for Applied Linguistics (CAL) conducted an inventory of dual language programs across the nation. At that time, over 450 programs were identified across 32 states and the District of Columbia. For the 2004 inventory, CAL vetted each program with regard to student make-up (at least 30% native speakers of the partner language), the percentage of language allocated to the partner language (50/50 by 3rd grade), the instruction of content areas in the partner language (language arts taught in both the partner language and English) and the extent to which the program was articulated across the grades (Center for Applied Linguistics, n.d.).

CAL recently conducted another search of dual language programs across the nation. While this update did not attempt to validate that the

	Two-way Dual Language	One-way Dual Language Programs		
		Developmental Bilingual	Heritage/Native Language	One-way Immersion
Population Served	ELs and non-EL, ideally 50% from each group	ELs who share the same home language	English speakers who share a heritage or culture	English speakers
Languages	English and a partner language (the ELs' home language)	English and a partner language (the ELs' home language)	English and a partner language (the heritage language)	English and a partner language
Staffing	One teacher that is bilingual, or two teachers, one for each language	One teacher that is bilingual, or two teachers, one for each language	One teacher that is bilingual, or two teachers, one for each language	One teacher that is bilingual, or two teachers, one for each language
Time Allocation per Language	Usually 50:50, with some models using 90:10 (starting with 90% of instruction in the partner language) that transitions to a 50:50 model over a few years			
Language of Academic Subjects	Varies			
Language Allocation	Allocated by time, content area, and/or teacher			
Duration of Program	Kindergarten through the elementary grades. Some programs continue into secondary grades (middle and high school).			
Size of Program	Whole school, or a strand in a school			

Figure 1.1. Dual language education program models. Source: Boyle et al. (2015), *Dual Language Education Programs: Current State Policies and Practices* (p. 24)

programs adhered to a set of defining principles, the search found over 2500, self-identified dual language programs across 39 states and the District of Columbia. The U.S. Department of Education reported that of the states offering dual language programs in the 2012–13 school year, the most frequently identified partner languages were Spanish, Chinese, Native American languages and French (Boyle *et al.*, 2015: 30–31). A case study included in this same report noted over 900 dual language programs in just six states.

In summary, while it is currently difficult to specify the number of dual language programs in place, it is reasonable to say that the popularity of dual language programs and the number of programs has increased (Harris, 2015). Within the last ten years, we have witnessed an increase in state support for developing student's multilingual skills in order to enhance student's competitiveness in the global market. For example, Utah passed legislation in 2008 that established dual language programs throughout the state, providing funding for programs, teacher development and curriculum materials (Boyle *et al.*, 2015: 8). Utah is joined by Delaware, Georgia, New Mexico, North Carolina, Washington and the District of Columbia as states that are actively promoting dual language education for all students.

Research on Dual Language Education

For the remainder of this chapter, we use the term dual language education (DLE) to refer to two-way dual language education programs that serve emergent bilinguals: transnational English learners (ELs) and language majority students (NES) and provide instruction in and through two languages: English and the partner language. In DLE programs bilingual learners:

(1) develop high levels of proficiency in both languages;
(2) perform at or above grade level in academic areas in both languages; and
(3) demonstrate positive cross-cultural competence.

To determine the state of research on DLE programs, we reviewed the last two decades of research focusing on the three goals of DLE: bilingualism/biliteracy, academic achievement and cross-cultural competence. We are informed in this review by the recent publication '*Dual language education programs: current state policies and practices*' (Boyle *et al.*, 2015). This publication examines policies and practices of DLE across the states, including student eligibility and placement, standards and assessment used in DLE, teacher professional development and state policies toward bilingual programming. The report also reviews studies and research summaries on DLE programs published since 2004 (Boyle *et al.*, 2015).

We began with our review of the research included in the U.S. Department of Education's report (Boyle *et al.*, 2015), reading and coding studies based on those that addressed the 'quality' of DLE programs. This included literature describing both what constitutes a quality DLE program (student characteristics, instructional routines, etc.) and the effectiveness of DLE programs. We then further coded the 'quality' literature to note those that addressed each of the three goals of DLE (biliteracy/bilingualism, academic achievement and cross-cultural competence). Next, we coded the literature from the U.S. Department of Education's report to include those that attended to two concerns from Valdés (1997): the power differential between English and the partner language and challenges in promoting intergroup relations in DLE programs. In addition to reviewing the literature included in the government's report we expanded our search to include literature specific to DLE programs prior to 2004.

Research on Goal 1: Biliteracy and bilingualism

One of the major goals of DLE is the development of bilingualism and biliteracy. In order to determine if students are becoming bilingual and biliterate, it is necessary to make an assessment of their oral proficiency and literacy skills in the partner language and English. A range of assessments have been used to determine oral proficiency, there are instruments that assess overall Spanish proficiency such as the Language Assessment Scales (LAS), Woodcock-Johnson or Woodcock-Muñoz; teacher rating rubrics such as the FLOSEM and SOLOM; and student rating rubrics. For the assessment of literacy skills, usually a standardized test is used, relying on the reading and language sections and sometimes a Cloze reading test is used.

It is important to underscore that few DLE programs systematically assess student progress in both languages. Lindholm-Leary (2016) comments that, 'there are few studies that examine Spanish language development as most research focuses on English, especially the English language development of EL students' (2016: 3). She continues, stating that, 'While DL programs have a stated goal of biliteracy, there is often little accountability for demonstrating grade-level reading skills in Spanish' (2016: 20). As we review the research on biliteracy and bilingualism, we emphasize that the lack of accountability for the partner language proficiency (primarily in Spanish) has resulted in few research reports. That said, in this section we review research that has focused on the development of bilingualism and biliteracy in DLE programs, focusing on literacy and oral proficiency in the student's native language (L1) or partner language.

Two foundational research reports documenting the progress of ELs in DLE programs were published in 2001. The first report, 'A national study of school effectiveness for language minority students' Long Term Academic Achievement,' was authored by Thomas and Collier. This was a five-year research study from 1996–2001 of five urban and rural school districts across the U.S. including Houston ISD, Grant Community School in Oregon and two rural schools in Maine. While different assessment instruments were used across sites, a consistent evaluation was that native Spanish speaking (NSS) students in 90:10 or 50:50 two-way dual language programs continued their development in L1. For example, in the Houston DLE programs, Thomas and Collier concluded that, 'These analyses of Stanford 9 and Aprenda 2 results demonstrate that Hispanic students are staying on or close to grade level in both languages, and if continuing instruction is provided in both Spanish and English, the large majority will graduate proficiently bilingual' (2016: 130).

The second foundational research piece published in 2001 is Kathryn Lindholm-Leary's book, *Dual Language Education*, which brings together evaluation data from eighteen school districts across California and one in Alaska. Evaluation outcomes are provided for 4900 students and academic achievement for 6209 students. Most schools used three common Spanish Achievement tests: La Prueba, Aprenda, or SABE. To assess oral language proficiency teacher ratings were used in the SOLOM, FLOSEM. Language proficiency was also assessed using the LAS and the IPT (Idea Proficiency Test).

Lindholm-Leary found that in general, students made significant growth in their L1 reading across grade levels, and were on a par with their peers based on California state norms. 'Native Spanish speakers (NSS) and native English speakers (NES) in Spanish/English TWI programs performed at or above grade level in the contents areas in their first language, achieving standardized mathematics and reading tests scores on par with their state-wide peers by about grade 7' (2001: 180).

The research reported by Thomas and Collier and Lindholm-Leary has been the most comprehensive to date, including the largest numbers of students, documenting student bilingualism and biliteracy across grades K-8 and across various DLE program models, using standardized measures of Spanish and English proficiency, student self-report data and attitude assessment. Since the Thomas/Collier and Lindholm-Leary studies, there have not been longitudinal studies of student performance in DLE. Instead, the more recent research, reported below, focuses on DLE in specific grade levels, at the elementary, middle or high school but it consistently shows the academic benefits of DLE and underscores its benefits with English Learners and NES.

Small-scale studies reporting Spanish attainment

In 2004, Howard, Christian and Genesee reported a 3-year study following students in 11 DLE programs in grades 3–5. To address the question of NES and Spanish speaking student (SSS) progress in both languages, Cloze measures were designed to assess reading; writing skills were assessed using narrative writing assignments; and oral proficiency was measured with the Spanish Oral Proficiency Assessment (SOPA). While Spanish reading data were only available for 3rd grade, the results indicated that Spanish speaking students had high mean scores in their L1. The authors concluded, 'Overall both groups of students demonstrated mean growth in language and literacy ability in both languages' (Howard *et al.*,

2004: 33). In a longitudinal study of one DLE school site, Lindholm-Leary and Howard found that 'strengthening L1 vocabulary development in the early primary grades supports later achievement in L1 reading for Native English Speaking (NES) and Native Spanish Speaking (NSS) students, and for NSS students, L2 reading achievement also benefits' (2008: 183).

In 2010, Lindholm-Leary and Block reported on a study of 466 DLE students in grades 4–6 in one school. These students were administered the APRENDA, a norm-referenced achievement test assessing reading and math in Spanish. The researchers reported 'students exceeded the state average in both reading and math' (2010: 54).

In a study of DLE programs in five elementary or middle schools in California, Lindholm-Leary and Hernández focused on 763 students from 4th–8th grade. More than half of the students were in grades 4–5 and the rest were in grades 6–8. Using the APRENDA test, the FLOSEM (a teacher reflection of oral language proficiency) and a student question-naire the researchers reported on the student's proficiency in Spanish. On the reading portion of the Aprenda, students achieved slightly above grade level in reading/language arts measured in Spanish. On the FLOSEM, teachers rated the students with high levels of Spanish language profi-ciency and on the student questionnaires, the students rated themselves as 'very bilingual' and reported that they were able to read and write well in Spanish (Lindholm-Leary & Hernández, 2011).

Discussing the challenges of DLE instruction, Lindholm-Leary notes in 2012 that despite the fact that DLE programs have the stated goal of biliteracy, there is little accountability for demonstrating grade level skills in the partner language. 'In fact, and unfortunately, many DLE programs do not even assess literacy skills in the partner language. As a result, it is unclear whether students are making adequate progress in the partner language' (2012: 260).

Students' self-report of Spanish proficiency

There are several studies reporting student self-evaluations of their pro-ficiency in Spanish. Lindholm-Leary presented the results of a survey with 142 students from 9th–12th grade who had been enrolled in a dual lan-guage program since Kindergarten or first grade. Students included Hispanic Spanish Bilinguals and Euro American English bilinguals. The results were that students rated themselves at moderate levels of Spanish proficiency, had positive attitudes towards the benefits of bilingualism and continued to use Spanish frequently (Lindholm-Leary, 2003). In 2005, Lindholm-Leary and Ferrante report on a follow-up of 199 middle school TWI students. Using a self-rating scale of comprehension, fluency, vocabu-lary and grammar, students 'scored at or above grade level in Spanish read-ing' (p. 170). Similarly, Lindholm-Leary and Borsato (2005) reported on the attitudes of high school students who had attended DLE for over six years, noting students' self-reported positive attitudes toward bilingualism.

In contrast, some research indicates that at the high school level, many students report a loss of Spanish language proficiency (Potowski, 2007) or rate their Spanish skills at a fairly low level (Lindholm-Leary, 2003). The fact that there is less instructional time in Spanish at the high school level has contributed to student decrease in oral Spanish proficiency (de Jong & Bearse, 2014).

In summary, the most rigorous and longitudinal data on students acquiring bilingualism and biliteracy in the partner language were conducted in the late 1990s and published in 2001. Since that time, studies that assessed student oral proficiency and literacy in the partner language have focused on specific grade spans (Howard *et al.*, 2004; Lindholm-Leary & Block, 2010; Lindholm-Leary & Hernandez, 2011). At the secondary level, there are a few studies that have investigated student attitudes towards the partner language (Lindholm-Leary, 2003; Lindholm-Leary & Borsato, 2005; Lindholm-Leary & Ferrante, 2005). These studies found that DLE students acquired the partner language at or above grade level and at the secondary level, DLE students displayed positive attitudes toward the partner language. However, the research on the goal of bilingualism and biliteracy is in general not as robust as the research on student achievement. This is especially significant, in that we need more information on student development of partner language bilingualism and biliteracy. The next section will review the research on academic achievement in DLE programs.

Research on Goal 2: Academic achievement

When Christian (1996) first wrote about DLE programs and their goals, she noted at the time, that although the research was just emerging, there was evidence that DLE programs 'promoted academic achievement for both language minority and language majority students' (1996: 72). Over the last 20 years, the research base on DLE programs has grown. Through studies specifically on DLE (Gomez *et al.*, 2005; Lindholm-Leary, 2001; Lindholm-Leary & Block, 2010; Lindholm-Leary & Borsato, 2005; Steele *et al.*, 2017) or studies on the effects of various language programs for ELs, of which DLE programs have been included (August & Hakuta, 1997; Cheung & Slavin, 2012; Thomas & Collier, 1997, 2002; Umansky & Reardon, 2014; Valentino & Reardon, 2014), and most recently a study on ELs at varying levels of English proficiency in DLE programs (Lindholm-Leary & Hernandez, 2011) we now have a wider base of evidence to better assess the second goal of DLE: students will 'perform at or above grade level in academic areas in both languages' (Christian, 1996: 67).

Summary of research on academic areas assessed in English

Since 1996, there have been four, longitudinal, large scale comparative studies of ELs in DLE programs that include attention to academic achievement. In 2001, Lindholm-Leary presented the findings from a study of

9000 students in two-way immersion programs across 21 schools. For academic achievement data, results from students' standardized 7th-grade content area assessments in reading and math were collected. Thomas and Collier published two studies, one in 1997 and the other in 2002. Their 1997 study included 700,000 ELs and examined the long-term education outcomes for ELs in various language programs between 1982 and 1996. For academic achievement data, students' standardized test scores, given in English, across content areas were used. Thomas and Collier's 2002 report includes data on over 200,000 ELs in various programs, collected between 1996–2001. While the Lindholm-Leary report focuses on ELs in DLE programs, the two reports from Thomas and Collier examine effects of different language programs on ELs academic achievement, with DLE included in the program models examined. Most recently, in 2017, Steele and colleagues present findings of a study that included 3457 immersion lottery students participating in Dual Immersion programs in Portland, in which they investigated the effects of DLE on students reading, math, science and EL reclassification rates. Longitudinal data were collected from seven cohorts of students entering K between the years of 2004–2010, with outcome data measured through 2014 (Steele *et al.*, 2017).

Lindholm-Leary and Howard (2008) offered a review of three large-scale studies along with others (Christian *et al.*, 2004; Gomez *et al.*, 2005). A summary of the key findings related to academic achievement include:

- in the early years of a DLE program, from kindergarten through 3rd grade, ELs perform below NES and are on par or slightly below EL peers in other language programs;
- it takes 4 to 7 years of dual language instruction to close the achievement gap between ELs and NES; and
- by the end of elementary school or the beginning of middle school ELs in DLE programs are on par with NES and out-perform ELs in other language programs.

Key findings from the 2017 Portland study offer similar results: at 5th and 8th grade, DLE was shown to have a positive effect on students' reading performance as measured on the state assessment. At 5th grade, DLE students measured ahead of their non-DLE peers by 7 months. At 8th grade the effect was even larger, students in the DLE program were one academic year (9 months) ahead of their non-DLE peers in reading. The researchers found little benefit from DLE on math and science scores but noted that DLE also caused no detriment to the academic achievement of students in those programs (Steele *et al.*, 2017).

Along with Thomas and Collier (1997, 2002) and Steele and colleagues (2017), other researchers have reported on the effects of various language programs/language of instruction on the academic achievement of ELs. In 2012, Cheung and Slavin synthesized the 'research on outcomes of all types of programs likely to improve English reading outcomes for Spanish-dominant English language learners in elementary school' (2012: 389) reviewing 13 studies that encompassed 2000 ELs. While their report looked at two factors – language of instruction and approaches to reading instruction – only the first factor is discussed here, as the authors differentiated between the effects of bilingual (which includes DLE) and English only instruction on ELs reading achievement in English. The review found 'a positive, yet modest effect in favor of bilingual education' (2012: 357).

Umansky and Reardon (2014) examined the reclassification rates of ELs in different language programs, of which DLE was included. In their study, criteria for reclassification included language proficiency and academic achievement in reading. They found that while ELs in English-only program models showed higher reclassification rates in the early years, 'students in two-language programs catch up and surpass their English immersion peers in middle school. This pattern holds not only when looking at reclassification as an outcome, but also when examining academic ELA achievement' (2014: 903). Umasky and Reardon found that ELs in maintenance bilingual programs (which includes DLE programs) were 'most likely to reach the academic ELA threshold' (2014: 904). Findings from this study emphasize the importance of time in a bilingual educational setting and support the theory that academic benefits of DLE appear later in a student's educational career, middle school and beyond, reinforcing findings from other studies on the academic achievement of ELs in DLE programs (Steele et al., 2017; Thomas & Collier, 1997, 2002).

Valentino and Reardon (2014) studied the longitudinal outcomes of four different language programs for ELs (transitional bilingual, developmental bilingual, dual immersion and English immersion) on ELs academic achievement in ELA and math through middle school. The study included over 13,000 ELs, starting kindergarten between 2001–2002 and 2009–2010. Outcome data for ELA were collected in 2nd–8th grades and math outcomes in 2nd–6th grades. Results from this study indicate that when comparing the academic achievement of ELs in DLE to ELs in other programs (English immersion, transitional bilingual and developmental bilingual) while in the early years (2nd grade), ELs in DLE programs score the lowest on ELA assessments in English of all program groups. However, 'by fifth grade their test scores in ELA catch up to the state average, and on average by seventh grade ELs in DLE are scoring above their EL counterparts in in all of the other programs' (2014: 21). When it came to academic achievement in math, ELs in DLE programs (from 2nd through middle school) were the only ones 'whose test score trajectories are not slower than the state average, but rather mirror(ed) that of the average student in the state' (2014: 22).

Overall, the research on the second goal indicates that while there may be a lag in EL performances in the early elementary grades, by 5th grade, ELs had made up the difference and had closed the achievement gap with their native English-speaking peers.

Research on Goal 3: Cross-cultural competence

The third goal of DLE, cross-cultural competence, has received much less attention from scholars and practitioners (Parkes *et al.*, 2009). One potential reason is that DLE programs are not held accountable for cross-cultural outcomes in the same manner that they are accountable for achievement goals (Feinauer & Howard, 2014). Another contributing factor could be the varied definitions that have been attributed to cross-cultural competence. Originally conceptualized by Christian (1996) as the ability to 'demonstrate positive cross-cultural attitudes and behaviors and high levels of self-esteem' (1996: 67), this goal has been also defined as cross-cultural appreciation, cross-cultural competence, and cross-cultural understanding. Furthermore, the aspect of self-esteem has been accentuated in Lindholm-Leary's definition of cross-cultural competence (2001), which includes high self-esteem as a component of positive cross-cultural competence.

One of the hallmarks of DLE is its purposeful integration of immigrant Latinos, U.S. born Latinos and Anglo students in the same classroom (Scanlan & Palmer, 2009). In some DLE programs, cross-cultural competence is conceptualized as attitudes and skills between students from different linguistic backgrounds. Researchers in the late 1990s reported that dual-immersion students had more favorable attitudes toward children who were different from themselves (Cazabon *et al.*, 1993; Christian *et al.*, 1997; Lindholm-Leary, 2001). Most of the research that has been conducted on the 'third goal' of DLE has focused on students' attitudes toward themselves and the partner language community.

For example, in a case study of four DLE programs, Howard and Sugarman (2007) document how these programs were fostering the goals of positive cross-cultural attitudes and behaviors. They noted that these programs:

- foster an appreciation of and pride in the multiple cultures represented in the program;
- call attention to linguistic as well as cultural variation;
- use study of language and study of culture in mutually reinforcing ways; and
- promote integration of language and content instruction through cultural themes. (2007: 104)

Potowski (2007) reported positive attitudes toward Spanish among upper elementary school DLE students. de Jong and Howard (2009) found that two-way immersion programs offer the advantage of breaking down stereotypes and developing positive attitudes toward both languages and their speakers. Lindholm-Leary and Block (2010) report on two separate studies of Hispanic largely low-income schools with DLE programs in California. DLE students in 2nd and 5th grades had highly positive attitude scores in both studies, responding positively to items such as 'learning another language would help me to get along better with others' and 'I would like to become friends with someone who mostly speaks a non-English language' (2010: 55).

In a recent turn from attitude studies, there has been an emphasis on the sociocultural aspect of cross-cultural competence, more aligned with language socialization theory (Feinauer & Howard, 2014), with more studies using interviews, observations and focusing on identity development. As the definition of cultural competence has evolved, it has been suggested that understanding identity development is the first step in understanding the development of cross-cultural competence. According to Feinauer and Howard 'a strong sense of one's own cultural identity is a first important step in developing intercultural sensitivities and cross-cultural competencies' (2014: 261).

In summary, in comparison with the other two goals of DLE, Goal 3 has had the least attention from researchers, it has lacked clarity due to a variety of definitions and the sensitive issues of language status and power within the two groups of students in DLE programs have yet to be systematically addressed. The last decade's focus on testing and accountability has further marginalized the goal of positive cultural competence.

In the area of the third goal, we hear echoes of Valdés' (1997) concerns regarding the promotion of intergroup relations and the issues of language and power embedded in the process of bringing together two groups of students; one marginalized and one privileged. Scanlan and Palmer (2009) warn, 'Without directly addressing issues of race and class and explicitly serving children along all lines of diversity present in a community the program may end up serving the needs of those whose sense of entitlement most calls out to be served' (2009: 412). Valdés caution is for DLE educators to be 'sensitive to the realities of intergroup relations in the communities surrounding schools to the fact that teachers are products of the society with all of its shortcomings, and to the fact that mainstream and minority children live in very different worlds' (2009: 419).

Most recently, there has been a call for a need to develop a fourth goal for dual language programs, a 'critical consciousness' Cervantes-Soon et al. (2017). This arises from scholarly concern that dual language programs are not providing 'equal educational opportunities for transnational bilinguals or "English Learners" from immigrant families' (Cervantes-Soon et al., 2017: 404). Documented areas of inequality in DL programs are situated in three levels: the 'larger socio-political, teacher-focused and classroom/student contexts' (Cervantes-Soon et al., 2017: 408). In order to confront these inequalities a fourth goal of critical consciousness is proposed. 'Critical consciousness can be developed through expanding politically oriented curriculum and instruction that originate in the very knowledges and ways that students from marginalized communities experience language' (2017: 418).

Education Policy Shifts

To contextualize the research findings from the last 20 years on DLE, it is important to recognize that in the last two decades the U.S. has seen significant shifts in educational policy. Perhaps the most significant shift has been the emphasis on accountability and assessment ushered in with No Child Left Behind (NCLB). NCLB increased state accountability measures by introducing testing students, evaluating schools and teachers based on their scores, and required federal intervention on 'failing' schools not meeting federal standards. The increased attention on accountability and assessment frames the current state of knowledge surrounding DLE, affecting what we know about the effectiveness of the three program goals.

Since 2002, NCLB required districts across the country to account for student learning by assessing student's academic achievement in English. We assert that the required focus on English assessments has resulted in a limited amount of research on students' bilingualism and biliteracy. Although there is some current research on bilingualism, much of the performance data on student bilingualism are provided by student self-report and/or teacher observation; few current studies base assessments of biliteracy on standardized assessments. District resources (time, money, personnel) are dedicated to implementing and analyzing assessment measures in English. Similar dedication to assessment in the partner languages is limited.

Educational policy shifts have also affected what we know about the second goal of DLE: students will perform at or above grade level *in both languages*. English assessment data have become foundational in promoting the success of DLE programs. Therefore, when trying to understand how DLE students perform, most studies also compare how DLE students perform in relation to their peers in mainstream classrooms (non-language programs). Or, when comparing the academic achievement of ELs in DLE programs to ELs in other language programs (another research trend), assessments in English are used (Lindholm-Leary & Genesee, 2014). This focus on assessments in English limits the ability to analyze assessment *in both languages*.

NCLB is succeeded by the Every Student Succeeds Act (ESSA) signed in 2015 and scheduled to be fully implemented in the 2017–18 school year. In general ESSA seeks to maintain high standards set for states while cutting back on testing, increasing support for English Learners and low-income families and putting the power to determine standards and goals in state hands. John King, Secretary of Education noted, 'Under ESSA, states have the opportunity to broaden the definition of educational excellence to ensure that it is well-rounded and incorporates biliteracy and multiliteracy. States have the opportunity to invest in ensuring that all new teachers are ready to work in the diverse settings that characterize our schools, and to see the fact a child that speaks a language other than English at home as an asset rather than as a deficit' (Vander Ark & Lathram, 2016). Changes required by ESSA will give ELs a higher profile and reflect their growing importance in measuring overall student achievement. In the future, a schools' accountability for the progress that English-learners make in learning the language is now integrated into Title I. According to Pompa (2015) accountability for ELs will be more compelling under the requirement of Title 1. However, it is important to stress that this accountability will be for English language achievement and proficiency. Given that ESSA will be focusing more on states' leadership to develop accountability measures, those states which have already made DLE a priority such as Delaware, the District of Columbia, Illinois, Minnesota, Utah and Washington, will be in the vanguard to include assessment of the partner language and cross-cultural competence as a requirement in the state level assessments.

Concluding Thoughts: Valdés Concerns Revisited

At a time when DLE is witnessing unprecedented popularity and growth, it is important to revisit the concerns raised by Valdés in 1997. She pointed out that it is critical to examine how the language minority community is included in DLE and how issues of language and power are embedded in the process of bringing together two groups of students: one marginalized and one privileged. This caution is particularly relevant now, as we witness the 'gentrification' of DLE. As majority parents become aware of the benefits of bilingualism and DLE, they are eager to enroll their children in public DLE schools. For example, in the District of Columbia, local demand for DLE is unprecedented, with many schools listing 400–500 applications for 30 available slots (Garcia, 2016).

Dorner (2011) has pointed out that, 'Issues of power and politics are especially salient … where students and staff come from a mix of language, race and income backgrounds and where the demand for programs may flow from only one group of stakeholders: often middle-class, English-dominant parent and educators' (2011: 607). Owing to the fact that English is perceived as the language of prestige and power in the U.S., it has become challenging for teachers to assure linguistic and cultural equity in the classroom. Several studies have noted that teachers struggle to provide equal status for languages (Hernández, 2015; de Jong, 2006; Fitts, 2006; Palmer, 2007, 2008). These studies have indicated that English-speaking students dominate small group conversations or interrupt Spanish speaking students in whole group interactions. Palmer and Martinez (2013) ague that teachers need a more critical 'contextualized understanding of the power dynamics that operate in bilingual classroom context' (2013: 269). Similarly, Lucas and Grinberg (2008) note that teachers need 'an awareness of the sociopolitical dimensions of language use and language education' (2008: 612).

We have noted that several scholars are now calling for an examination of issues of race and class as they intersect with issues of language. We need research to help understand how we can counter the hegemony of English in the community, the school and classroom. The field needs to understand how we can support teachers to bring a critical consciousness into their practice. DLE research for the last 20 years has provided strong evidence for the efficacy of DL instruction in specific settings. Research is needed to address the growing concern that as DLE has been adopted by the white majority community, the efficacy of DLE is being denied to emergent bilingual students.

References

August, D. and Hakuta, K. (1997) *Improving Schooling for Language Minority Children: A Research Agenda.* Washington, DC: National Academy Press.

Bearse, C. and de Jong, E.J. (2008) Cultural and linguistic investment: Adolescents in a secondary two-way immersion program. *Equity and Excellence in Education* 41 (3), 325–340.

Boyle, A., August, D., Tabaku, L., Cole, S. and Simpson-Baird, A. (2015) *Dual Language Education Programs: Current State Policies and Practices.* Washington, DC: American Institute for Research. See http://www.air.org/resource/dual-language-education-programs-current-state-policies-and-practices

Cazabon, M., Lambert, W.E. and Hall, G. (1993) *Two-way Bilingual Education: A Progress Report on the Amigos Program.* Santa Cruz, CA: The National Center for Research on Cultural Diversity and Second Language Learning.

Center for Applied Linguistics (n.d.) Directory of two-way bilingual immersion programs in the U.S. See http://www2.cal.org/jsp/TWI/SchoolListings.jsp

Cervantes-Soon, C., Dorner, L., Palmer, D., Heiman, D., Schwerdtfeger, R. and Choi, J. (2017) Combating inequalities in two-way language immersion programs: Toward critical consciousness in bilingual education spaces. *Review of Research in Education* 41, 403–427.

Cheung, A.C. and Slavin, R.E. (2012) Effective reading programs for Spanish-dominant English language learners (ELLs) in the elementary grades: A synthesis of research. *Review of Educational Research* 82 (4), 351–395.

Christian, D. (1996) Two-way immersion education: Students learning through two languages. *The Modern Language Journal* 80, 66–76.

Christian, D., Genesee, F., Lindholm-Leary, K. and Howard, E. (2004) Project 1.2 Two-Way Immersion. Final Progress Report CREDE.

Christian, D., Montone, C., Lindholm, K.J. and Carranza, I. (1997) *Profiles in Two-way Immersion Education.* Washington, DC: Center for Applied Linguistics and Delta Systems.

de Jong, E. (2006) Integrated bilingual education: An alternative approach. *Bilingual Research Journal* 30 (1), 23–44.

de Jong, E.J. and Bearse, C.I. (2014) Dual language programs as a strand within a secondary school: Dilemmas of school organization and the TWI mission. *International Journal of Bilingual Education and Bilingualism* 17 (1), 15–31.

de Jong, E.J. and Howard, E. (2009) Integration in two-way immersion education: Equalizing linguistic benefits for all students. *International Journal of Bilingual Education and Bilingualism* 12 (1), 81–99.

Dorner, L. (2011) Contested communities in a debate over dual language education 'the import of "public" values on public policies'. *Educational Policy* 25 (4) 577–613.

Feinauer, E. and Howard, E.R. (2014) Attending to the third goal: Cross cultural competence and identity development in two way immersion programs. *Journal of Immersion and Content-Based Language Education* 2 (2), 257–272.

Fitts, S. (2006) Reconstructing the status quo: Linguistic interaction in a dual-language school. *Bilingual Research Journal* 29 (2), 337–365.

Garcia, A. (2015) *State Momentum Building in Support of Dual Immersion Programs.* Washington DC. New America Foundation. See https://www.newamerica.org/education-policy/edcentral/states-dual-immersion

Gómez, L., Freeman, D. and Freeman, Y. (2005) Dual language education: A promising 50–50 model. *Bilingual Research Journal* 29 (1), 145–164.

Harris, E.A. (8 October, 2015) Dual language programs are on the rise, even for native English speakers. *The New York Times.* See http://www.nytimes.com/2015/10/09/nyregion/dual-language-programs-are-on-the-rise-even-for-native-english-speakers.html?_r=0

Hernández, A. (2015) Language status in two-way bilingual immersion. *Journal of Immersion and Content Based Language Education* 25 (1), 102–126.

Howard, E. and Sugarman, J. (2007) *Realizing the Vision of Two-way Immersion: Fostering Effective Programs and Classrooms.* Washington, DC: Center for Applied Linguistics.

Howard, E.R., Christian, D. and Genesee, F. (2004) *The Development of Bilingualism and Biliteracy from Grade 3 to 5: A Summary of Findings from the CAL/CREDE Study of Two-Way Immersion Education.* CREDE.

Lead with Languages (n.d.) *The Seal of Biliteracy.* See http://www.leadwithlanguages.org/language-advocacy/the-biliteracy-seal/

Lindholm-Leary, K.J. (2001) *Dual Language Education.* Clevedon: Multilingual Matters.

Lindholm-Leary, K.J. (2003) Dual language achievement, proficiency, and attitudes among current high school graduates of two-way programs. *NABE Journal* 26, 20–25.

Lindholm-Leary, K.J. (2012) Success and challenges in dual language education. *Theory Into Practice* 51 (4), 256–262.

Lindholm-Leary, K.J. (2016) Students perceptions of bilingualism in Spanish and Mandarin dual language programs. *International Multilingual Research Journal* 10 (1), 55–70.

Lindholm-Leary, K.J. (in press) Developing Spanish in dual language programs: Preschool through twelfth grade. In K. Potowski (ed.) *Handbook of Spanish as a Minority/Heritage Language.* New York NY: Routledge.

Lindholm-Leary, K.J. and Borsato, G. (2005) Hispanic high schooler and mathematics: Follow-up of students who had participated in two-way bilingual elementary programs. *Bilingual Research Journal* 29, 641–652.

Lindholm-Leary, K.J. and Ferrante, A. (2005) Follow-up study of middle school two-way students: Language proficiency, achievement and attitudes. In R. Hoosain and F. Salili (eds) *Language in Multicultural Education* (pp. 157–179). Greenwich, CT: Information Age Publishing.

Lindholm-Leary, K.J. and Howard, E.R. (2008) Language development and academic achievement in two-way immersion programs. In T.W. Fortune and D.J. Tedick (eds) *Pathways to Multilingualism: Evolving Perspectives on Immersion Education* (pp. 177–200). Oxford: Blackwell.

Lindholm-Leary, K.J. and Block, N. (2010) Achievement in predominantly low SES/Hispanic dual language schools. *International Journal of Bilingual Education and Bilingualism* 13 (1), 43–60.

Lindholm-Leary, K.J. and Hernandez, A. (2011) Achievement and language proficiency of Latino students in dual language programs: Native English speakers, fluent English/previous ELLs, and current ELLs. *Journal of Multilingual and Multicultural Development* 32 (6), 531–545.

Lindholm-Leary, K.J. and Genesee, F. (2014) Student outcomes in one-way, two-way, and indigenous language immersion education. *Journal of Immersion and Content-Based Language Education* 2 (2), 165–180.

Lucas, T. and Grinberg, J. (2008) Responding to the linguistic reality of mainstream classrooms: Preparing all teachers to teach English language learners. In M. Cochran-Smith, S. Feiman-Nemser and D.J. McIntyre (eds) *Handbook of Research on Teacher Education: Enduring Questions in Changing Contexts* (3rd ed., pp. 606–636). New York, NY: Routledge.

Palmer, D. (2007) A dual immersion strand programme in California: Carrying out the promise of dual language education in an English-dominant context. *International Journal of Bilingual Education and Bilingualism* 10 (6), 752–762.

Palmer, D. (2008) Diversity up close: Building alternative discourses in the two-way immersion classroom. In T.W. Fortune and D.J. Tedick (eds) *Pathways to Multilingualism: Evolving Perspectives on Immersion Education* (pp. 97–116) Clevedon: Multilingual Matters.

Palmer, D. and Martinez, R. (2013) Teacher agency in bilingual spaces: A fresh look at preparing teachers to educate Latina/bilingual children. *Review of Research in Education* 37, 269–297.

Parkes, J., Ruth, T., Anberg-Espinoza, M. and De Jong, E. (2009) *Urgent Research Questions and Issues in Dual Language Education*. Albuquerque, NM: Dual Language Education of New Mexico. See http://www.dlenm.org/documents/Research%20Report.pdf

Pompa, D. (2015) *New Education Legislation Includes Important Policies for English Learners, Potential Pitfalls for their Advocates*. Washington DC: Migration Policy Institute. See http://www.migrationpolicy.org

Potowski, K. (2007) Characteristics of the Spanish proficiency of dual immersion graduates. *Spanish in Context* 4 (2), 187–216.

Scanlan, M. and Palmer, D. (2009) Race, power, and (in)equity within two-way immersion settings. *The Urban Review* 41 (5), 391–415.

Steele, J.L., Slater, R.O., Zamarro, G., Miller, T., Li, J., Burkhauser, S. and Bacon, M. (2017) Effects of dual-language immersion program on student achievement: Evidence from lottery data. *American Educational Research Journal* 54 (1S), 282s–306s.

Thomas, W.P. and Collier, V.P (1997) *School Effectiveness for Language Minority Students*. Washington, DC: National Clearinghouse for Bilingual Education. See http://www.thomasandcollier.com/assets/1997_thomas-collier97-1.pdf

Thomas, W.P. and Collier, V.P (2002) A *National Study of Effectiveness for Language Minority Students' Long-term Academic Achievement*. Center for Research on Education, Diversity and Excellence, (CREDE). See http://www.usc.edu/dept/educa tion/CMMR/CollierThomasComplete.pdf

Umansky, I. and Reardon, S.F. (2014) Reclassification patterns among Latino English learner students in bilingual, dual immersion, and English immersion classrooms. *American Educational Research Journal* 51 (5), 1–34.

University of Utah (n.d.) Utah dual immersion. See http://l2trec.utah.edu/ utah-dual-immersion/

Valdes, G. (1997) Dual-language immersion programs: A cautionary note concerning the education of language-minority students. *Harvard Educational Review* 67 (3), 391–430.

Valentino, R.A. and Reardon, S.F. (2014) Effectiveness of four instructional programs designed to serve English learners: Variation by ethnicity and initial English proficiency. See http://cepa.stanford.edu/sites/default/files/Valentino_Reardon_EL Programs_14_0326_2.pdf

Vander Ark, T. and Lathram, B. (2016, May 26). Supporting English language learners with next-gen tools. *Getting Smart*. See http://gettingsmart.com/2016/05/supporting-english-language-learners-with-next-gen-tools/

2 Legacy Programs: Key Elementary, Arlington, Virginia

Igone Arteagoitia

Introduction

Over 30 years ago, a small group of first-grade students and teachers inaugurated the dual language (DL) program at Escuela Key. The first decade of implementation of the program was documented in a chapter in *Profiles in Two-Way Immersion Education* published in 1997. This chapter is intended to provide an update on the program since that publication. The information provided is the result of interviews conducted with several people with a strong and long connection to the program, such as the principal and vice-principal, Marjorie Myers and Evelyn Fernández,[1] both of whom have been in those positions since 1995, when Escuela Key became a whole-school DL program. The author also interviewed the former World Languages (WLs) supervisor, Marleny Perdomo, who was a Spanish teacher at Escuela Key for a number of years before she moved to the district's central office, and Melissa Sen, WLs specialist and former teacher. Finally, she met with Matilde Arciniegas, a Spanish teacher with more than 22 years' experience in DL education who has taught at Escuela Key for over 12 years, and Deyanira López, the Spanish Lead Teacher and Math Coach and former teacher at Key, who has 17 years' experience in DL education, 15 as a teacher at Escuela Key. In addition to the interviews, the author has had the privilege to work with the DL program in a number of capacities over the past 15 years, including conducting research and professional development trainings for Spanish teachers, as well as the two most recent evaluations of the program.

Program Information

Program overview

Escuela Key, located in Arlington, VA, is a K-5 elementary school with a Spanish/English DL program that serves native Spanish- and native

English-speaking students (NES and NSS respectively), as well as a small number of children who speak another language at home. Escuela Key is one of two whole school elementary DL programs in Arlington Public Schools. The county offers a middle and high school program, both of them strands within a school, so that students at the two elementary DL programs can continue their education in the two languages.

True to its DL model, Escuela Key's goals are the attainment of bilingualism, biliteracy and cross-cultural understanding by all students attending the program. Because it is a neighborhood school, students who live in the area are automatically accepted into the program as are siblings of students in the program, even if they do not reside within the school boundaries. The rest of the spots are filled with students from Key feeder schools through a lottery system. Because the program requires a balanced number of NSS and NES, native language is used as a selection criterion for students residing outside of the school boundaries along with other commonly used variables (e.g., grade, gender) in order to maintain an appropriate balance. The school does not need to invest resources on student recruitment, as the popularity of the program in the county is such that every year they have several students on the waiting list. Because research has shown that learning a second language can take anywhere from four to seven years and the sooner a child starts learning a second language the better, parents are strongly discouraged from enrolling their children in the program after first grade. Some exceptions are made in cases in which students in higher grades can demonstrate some degree of bilingualism.

Brief history

The DL elementary program at Escuela Key was founded in 1986 as a gifted and talented program. Until then, APS offered two programs for emergent bilinguals: English to Speakers of Other Languages (ESOL) and High Intensity Language Training (HILT). Because APS does not have a Bilingual Office, the DL program is monitored by the district World Languages office. The program at Escuela Key started out as a strand within a mainstream program with one class of 18 first grade students. The Center for Applied Linguistics (CAL) worked closely with staff to provide technical assistance, Professional Development (PD) and annual evaluations during the first five years of the program. The program continued adding a grade level each subsequent year until it reached fifth grade in 1990. In 1991 the school added Kindergarten and became a full K-5 strand within the school. The popularity of the program in the district grew so quickly, that by 1989 there were not enough spaces to fill all of the applications to the program.

In the early years of the DL program, students classified as English learners (ELs) and those identified in need of special education services did not participate in the DL program and were in self-contained classrooms. In 1991, APS received a Title VII grant to increase Escuela Key's capacity to serve a larger number of students in the district, and enhance their professional development program and instruction. By the 1995–1996 school year the entire school became a DL program open to all students (not just gifted and talented students) under the leadership of Marjorie Myers. More details about the first ten years of the DL program at Key School can be found in the CAL publication *Profiles in Two-Way Immersion Education.*

The present

Thirty plus years after its inception, the DL program at Escuela Key has more than doubled in number and has an even more linguistically and culturally diverse population than it did in 1995 when it became a whole school program. With 730 students enrolled in the program in the school year 2015–2016, Hispanic students make up more than half the student body (53.7%, up from 48% in 1994–1995), while at the district level they represent less than 30% of the student population (see Table 2.1). Also, the number of Asian students and students from mixed backgrounds has increased in the past years, even though they still represent only a small portion of the whole student population. In terms of native language, the number of NES students has remained constant at 51.2%, but the number of NSS students has decreased somewhat (from 47% to 43.8%), while the number of speakers of a language other than Spanish or English has increased to 5%. Almost half of the students at Key (46.1%) are classified as English learners (ELs). Over 90% of NSS students and 85% of speakers of a language other than English and Spanish, and 42% of students in the program are eligible for free/reduced lunch.

When it comes to staff, even though hiring highly qualified bilingual teachers is a constant challenge, Escuela Key administrators do an exceptionally good job at hiring bilingual individuals. Currently 94% of classroom teachers are bilingual and biliterate in English and Spanish and so are 79% of resource teachers. Specials are taught in both languages. Art

Table 2.1 District and program characteristics

Student background	Escuela key (730 students)	District (25,678 students)
White	33.5%	46.7%
Hispanic	53.7%	28.2%
Black/African American	5.1%	10.3%
Asian	4.1%	9%
Amer. Indian/Alaskan Nat.	0.9%	0.5%
Multiple	2.7%	5.2%
Free/Reduced Lunch	42%	31.4%
English Learner	46.1%	Not available

is taught in Spanish, physical education in English, and music in both languages. The effort and success to hire bilingual staff goes beyond the teachers to include non-teaching staff, 91% of whom are bilingual in Spanish and English. While Virginia does not require DL teachers to have a bilingual certification, in order to teach Spanish language arts a K-12 Spanish Language certification is required. To fill this need, in 2004 Escuela Key hired a certified K-12 Spanish language teacher to support Spanish language instruction. Furthermore, in order to serve the needs of EL students, 10% of Escuela Key's staff have an ESL certification.

Over the past three decades the program has evolved to adapt to new circumstances and continues to do so as the federal and states policies change as do the demographics of the school. In the reminder of the chapter, I will describe the main program features including the curriculum and resources, instruction and assessment, program evaluation, staff professional development and parental involvement, highlighting changes that have taken place since the 1997 publication. I will conclude with reflections on lessons learned and how the program continues to adapt to new circumstances and some of the challenges in doing so.

Program Features

The DL program at Escuela Key is designed as a 50/50 model in which instruction is provided in Spanish half of the time and in English the other half by two different teachers. Additionally, different core subject areas are taught in Spanish (math and science) and in English (language arts and social studies). For years the program lacked a dedicated Spanish language arts block and Spanish language and literacy development was embedded within the math and science instructional blocks. More recently, and following the recommendations from an evaluation of the program conducted by CAL in 2004 (see Research and Evaluation section below), the program added 20–30 minutes of Spanish language arts instruction daily depending on the grade level.

Each class is built with a balance of Spanish and English speakers and a balance of ELs students. When it comes to support services for their students, Escuela Key provides English as a second language (ESL), Title I/Reading, special education, gifted and talented and response to intervention (RTI) services. Students receiving special education services and gifted services are clustered in some of the classes so as to facilitate the provision of targeted instruction. ESL instruction has traditionally been *pull-out*, with EL students receiving 1–2 hours of English language development instruction daily depending on their needs. Recently, however, the school has started adopting a *push-in* model to support EL students in the earlier grades. Special Education support is given in Spanish as well as English. The other services are provided in English only during English instruction. Students who have Individualized Educational Plan (IEPs) in math receive special education services in Spanish for math, since math is taught in Spanish. Even when there is no common planning time between the Spanish teacher and special education teachers due to scheduling constraints, special education teachers generally support and coordinate their services with Spanish teachers to help the students access the math curriculum in Spanish.

Curriculum

Escuela Key follows the same county-mandated curriculum as other (mainstream) programs in the county. For subjects taught in Spanish, the only difference is that the curriculum is in Spanish.

In the school year 2004–2005, Escuela Key got funding from the district to increase academic instructional time in Spanish. As mentioned earlier, following recommendations set forth in a program evaluation conducted by CAL in 2004, Escuela Key added a daily block (20–30 minutes) for Spanish language arts. Until that year, Escuela Key Spanish teachers had been in charge of teaching math and science and incorporating language instruction in those two content areas. Having to devote a daily block of time to explicit Spanish language instruction represented a challenge for many of the teachers. To facilitate their adjustment to this change, the school administration hired a specialist with a K-12 Spanish language certification to support the Spanish teachers. In the end, the specialist was asked to take over science instruction to alleviate the instructional load of the Spanish teachers so that they could strengthen the teaching of Spanish language arts. A change in priorities at the district level resulted in a reverse to the old model in which Spanish teachers were asked to focus their instruction on math and science and teach language through those two content areas.

A group of Spanish teachers and school administrators, under the guidance of the district's Foreign Language office and with the help of CAL, worked on the development of a stand-alone Spanish language arts curriculum and standards with end-of-year grade level expectations. The document has undergone several revisions, the most recent one in 2012. It is based on the English language arts curriculum but it takes into account structural differences between the languages and incorporates culture. Thus, for example, taking into account the progression of Spanish language development the Steering Committee created a list of language forms, grammar topics and key vocabulary per grade level. Furthermore, the school adopted a Spanish language reading series *Lectura* (Pearson/Scott Foresman), and passages from the series (and/or other more appropriate texts) were used to teach language (e.g., vocabulary and grammar) through them, and developed thematic units following the textbook. The school has also invested in supplemental Spanish language arts materials (i.e., Hampton-Brown Books) and more recently, has received classroom libraries in Spanish for first grade teachers (other grades are scheduled to receive them in the future) along with training in providing classroom reading time.

While teachers have been provided with resources in Spanish, the caliber of resources has been brought into question by many. Some teachers feel like the resources do not always reflect the cultures and values from Spanish-speaking countries that they can use to promote cross-cultural competence. As the first-grade teacher interviewed put it: 'we need more money and time to invest in this process at the school and county level. There are many books available (digital too) but it not only requires money but also time to choose the best quality. Some are poorly translated or too culturally specific.' The Spanish Lead Teacher agrees that there is inequality when it comes to the number of resources devoted to the two languages and the cultures associated with them and a great need to strengthen Spanish language arts instruction. Many times, teachers end up creating their own materials, even though it is a big time investment. For example, for Hispanic Heritage Month, each grade is assigned a country and students learn about that country through a combination of teacher-developed materials and authentic resources found online. Escuela Key students also celebrate 'El Día del libro' (The day of the book) on April 23rd, a Spanish festivity that remembers the death of the world-known Spanish author Miguel de Cervantes, through which students learn about the adventures of Don Quijote de la Mancha and that some books have passed the test of time by how many languages they have been translated into and how long their readers have enjoyed them.

While Escuela Key's efforts to develop a Spanish language arts program are commendable, due to pressure from the county and state to focus on English academic outcomes, the school's primary focus has been on English language and literacy development and math. As the first grade Spanish teacher put it: 'Our school-wide initiatives center around the scores of our students on county and state tests and in this context Spanish takes a back seat …' Similarly, the Spanish Lead Teacher expressed that the focus on English outcomes by APS has come at the expense of DL programs and 'has resulted in the deterioration of the vertical coherence of the Spanish language arts program.' In particular, the increased emphasis on testing and the use of test scores to make programmatic decisions has had an impact on the time dedicated to Spanish language arts and often times Spanish teachers fail to honor the 30 minute per day focus on Spanish language development and use that time for math instruction. English language arts instruction, on the other hand, has a dedicated 60−90 minute daily block (90 minutes in K-2 and 30 minutes in grades 3−5). The importance of a dedicated daily time in Spanish language arts instruction cannot be overstated. Through such instruction, NSS students have the opportunity to use their oral language skills to develop literacy skills in Spanish as well as English (as many literacy skills transfer), and further develop their oral language skills in their native language. NES students on the other hand, have the opportunity to build their vocabulary and sentence structure knowledge in Spanish.

Instruction

Escuela Key teachers use a variety of instructional techniques and supports that respond to different learning styles and proficiency levels, such as sheltering strategies, cooperative-learning and bridging between the languages. Instruction is student-centered providing learning opportunities that challenge students to develop language and literacy skills through prolonged engagement in challenging, authentic, interactive activities. For example, in a science unit in which students are learning about the planets, they will engage in a jigsaw activity where four or five children become the 'experts' on a planet and then present at our 'Congreso de Astrónomos' (Astronomers Conference). Similarly, in math, review questions are put around the room and students form groups to explain the answers to the rest of the class, the emphasis being on collaboration and team work beyond the specifics of the work.

Because of the limited time allotted for Spanish language arts, language development work is embedded in content area instruction. Teachers have multiple visual reminders in the classroom, such as sentence frames with phrases used frequently in the class. When students can only express their thoughts in one language, they are encouraged to seek help from a student who is bilingual. In an attempt to make content comprehensible to students who need the extra support, as they explain an idea, teachers use sheltering strategies (e.g., pictures and other visuals) and sketching, presenting the essence of a concept for children who have limited skills in the language of instruction.

For the most part, teachers are able to follow the program design in terms of language allocation (i.e., provide instruction exclusively in Spanish during Spanish instructional time). However, exceptions are made from time to time to help children meet the demands of standard testing in English. Since math and science county tests are in English, but taught in Spanish, in order to prepare students, in particular ELs, for these standardized county assessments, Spanish teachers will introduce some English terminology in their math and science instruction drawing on similarities with the Spanish terminology, as the majority of these terms are cognates in the two languages. English is also used to meet the needs of advanced math students in the early grades who do not have the Spanish language skills to complete open-ended, challenging math problems in Spanish. The Spanish teacher works with these students in English and at the same time introduces the terminology in Spanish and points out the similarities between the languages in an attempt to begin to build their metalinguistic awareness. Opportunities to compare and contrast between the languages are sought not only in math and science class through cognate awareness activities, but also during Spanish language arts instruction to build vocabulary and grammatical knowledge. For example, in first grade the teacher introduces concepts such as 'grammatical agreement' using student-friendly definitions ('matching') and brings attention to the fact that 'the' in English has four different forms in Spanish (two for the feminine and two for the masculine, singular and plural) that have to match depending on the gender and number of the noun.

While school language policies make a clear separation between Spanish and English instruction that is meant to protect Spanish, in practice the dominance of the English language is a constant challenge to these language policies. This challenge is fairly common in DL programs, especially when there is a disparity in the socio-economic status of the two groups of students. Despite teachers' efforts at promoting Spanish and equity among groups, the NES students tend to dominate interactions and teachers are continually looking for ways to empower EL students and further challenge students who are above grade level.

Assessment

Escuela Key's students' academic achievement in English language, math and science is measured annually via their performance on the Standards of Learning assessments (SOLs). All students in grades 3–5 take the SOLs. In addition to the state assessments, the school administers quarterly formative academic tests in those three core areas in English to students in grades 3–5. Students in the earlier grades take the English Phonological Screening Literacy Screening (PALS) twice a year (quarterly for those who are below grade level), which measures pre- and basic literacy skills in English. Some teachers also choose to administer the Developmental Reading Assessment (DRA), a standardized reading test used to determine a student's instructional level in reading in English, but the school does not mandate it. The school does not assess students' academic achievement in Spanish via a summative assessment. In the earlier grades, the school has on occasion used the Sistema de Evaluación de la Lectura (SEL), the Spanish counterpart of the DRA, to determine K-2 students' reading levels in Spanish.

In order to measure students' language proficiency in English, students classified as EL are administered the WIDA ACCESS English language proficiency test once a year. The students who score at level 5 are reclassified as Full English Proficient. Former EL students' English proficiency is monitored for two years as mandated by the county/state. While the school does not assess students' Spanish language proficiency using a standardized assessment, Spanish teachers have been monitoring their students' written language skills over the years through writing samples collected twice a year from students in all grade levels. The samples are scored by teachers using a rubric developed in collaboration with CAL researchers and the scores are used informally by the teachers to gauge their students' Spanish written skills, including vocabulary, grammar, spelling, punctuation and organizational skills. In the early years of the program, teachers also used the Student Oral Proficiency Rating to assess K-5 students' oral proficiency ability, including comprehension, fluency, grammar, vocabulary and pronunciation, on an annual basis (1995 scores can be found in *Profiles*). More recently and after piloting it with 3–5 grade students in 2010, Escuela Key started administering the Standards-based Measure of Proficiency (STAMP) to all students exiting the program. The STAMP assessment, originally designed for use in middle and high school foreign language programs, measures language proficiency in reading, writing, listening and speaking in nine languages including Spanish.

Professional development

Over the years, Escuela Key teachers and other staff have had extensive training in Sheltered Instruction Observation Protocol (SIOP) techniques and practices, which has helped with the integration of the teaching of language and content. For example, all new teachers receive SIOP training for a total of 18 hours during their first year at the school. Because Escuela Key leaders know that in order for PD to be effective it must be provided regularly and ideally with follow-up coaching, in the past two years all teachers have received 10 hours per year of PD from CAL staff on two-way SIOP strategies with a focus on lesson planning.

For a few years the county's World Languages office in collaboration with CAL provided exclusive training for Spanish teachers in Spanish on various topics related to the teaching of Spanish language and literacy skills. These trainings have not occurred in the past few years, which is unfortunate given that the explicit teaching of language and literacy in Spanish is still a work in progress for some of the teachers, who view themselves more like content specialists than language teachers. According to the Spanish Lead Teacher, students' Spanish language and literacy skills have been negatively impacted as a result of the lack of consistent Spanish language arts instruction in the past few years. As such, she firmly believes Spanish teachers at Escuela Key would greatly benefit from sustained PD in Spanish language arts instruction.

Parents and families

When you walk into Escuela Key's office, it is obvious that it is a bilingual school that welcomes families who speak Spanish, English, or both. The majority of the office staff speaks Spanish as do the principal and vice-principal. There is also a bilingual parent liaison dedicated to providing services to all families. Parent meetings in Spanish are offered for those families who have no or limited English language skills. Another indication that Escuela Key is a bilingual school is the fact that all of the signs, posters, banners and other environmental print found on the school walls are in both languages, and all the school-wide communication is conducted in the two languages (e.g., announcements, school-wide assemblies; parent-teacher conferences, etc.), as is the communication sent home.

Escuela Key's parents and community are very supportive of the DL program and are very engaged in the schools' various activities. The parent teacher association (PTA) at Escuela Key is very strong and it operates with NSS and NES parents. They sponsor fund-raising events and specials projects, such as book fairs and arts festivals. Parental input is valued by the school and parents are part of different committees in which important decisions about the program are made, such as the revision of the program's mission and goals every five years. All of the stakeholders interviewed agreed that Escuela Key's families and community are one of the greatest strengths of the DL program.

Program Evaluations

Research that has investigated the academic performance of students in DL programs has emphasized the importance of looking at long-term outcomes into middle and high school (e.g., Thomas & Collier, 2002; Valentino & Reardon, 2015). The English academic achievement data for the DL program in Arlington county are a good example. SOL data going back to the 2006–2007 school year have consistently shown that in third and fifth grade, NES in DL programs in the county perform as well or better than NES in other programs, but that is not the case for native speakers of other languages (which in APS are predominantly NSS), who perform not only below NES but also below their native language peers in other programs. However, by eighth grade native speakers of other languages are on par with native English speakers and above their language peers in other programs.

Unfortunately, APS does not administer a Spanish achievement test to students in the DL program. However, over the years CAL staff has worked with DL teachers and administrators at Key school in particular to conduct several evaluations of the program, the first one of which occurred during the first five years of the program and was discussed in the former publication. The second evaluation, also carried out by CAL, took place in 2004, almost a decade after the whole school adopted the dual program. The focus was on students' Spanish and English language and literacy outcomes as well as teachers' satisfaction with the program[2]. The second elementary program in the county, Claremont, and the middle school program, Gunston, a strand within a mainstream program, participated in the evaluation as well. Assessments of oral language proficiency and reading and writing ability in English and Spanish were administered to a stratified random sample of the DL students in third, fifth, and eighth grade during the 2003–2004 academic year, a total of 152 students (or 55% of the students in those grade levels) divided approximately evenly between NSS and NES. It is important to bear in mind that the eighth-grade sample ($n = 26$) was significantly smaller than the third ($n = 67$) and fifth grade ($n = 59$) samples, as at that point it's a strand within a school.

Oral language proficiency in English and Spanish was assessed using the Student Oral Proficiency Assessment (SOPA), a criterion-referenced assessment that measures speaking ability, including oral fluency, grammar, and vocabulary, and listening comprehension. Scores are assigned using a 9-point rating scale based on the Proficiency Guidelines of the American Council on the Teaching of Foreign Languages (ACTFL) (1999) that expands from Junior Novice-Low to Junior Advanced-High. CAL staff developed the SOPA in 1991 as an interactive listening and speaking assessment for children learning a foreign or second language in a school setting. Since 1991, the SOPA has been used widely to assess students in a variety of language programs, including DL programs (for an overview of the SOPA, see Thompson *et al.*, 2002). APS, with guidance from CAL, set expected end-of-year outcomes for oral production for students in third grade (Novice-High), fifth grade (Intermediate-Mid), and eighth grade (Advanced-Low), and a sublevel higher for listening comprehension for each of the grade levels (Intermediate-Low, Intermediate-High and Advanced-Mid respectively).

Reading and writing ability in English and Spanish was assessed using the norm-referenced Woodcock Language Proficiency Battery – Revised (WLPB-R). The WLPB-R is a battery of individually administered assessments of oral language, reading and writing ability. For the purposes of the evaluation, three subtests were administered: passage comprehension, dictation, and proofing. Because the evaluation focused on global literacy abilities, in addition to scores for all three subtests, the basic writing scores were calculated. Standard scores, normalized scores based on a mean of 100 points and a standard deviation of 15 points which can be used to compare APS students to the national norm for the WLPB-R, were used for analysis. A standard score between 90 and 110 points indicates grade-level performance (25–75 percentile rank range).

Findings from the 2004 evaluation are displayed in Tables 2.2–2.5 (see Appendix to this chapter). As shown in Tables 2.2 and 2.3, on average students for the most part exhibited grade level performance in English oral language and literacy measures, even if they were only getting 50% of their instruction time in that language. In fact, in oral language, the majority of students from both native language groups at all three grade levels scored in the advanced ranges of the SOPA rating scale and on average both native language groups exceeded APS expectations for oral language in English. Across the grade levels students performed at or above grade level on English reading comprehension. English writing outcomes were lower for all groups in general with eighth grade NSS students failing to reach grade-level performance, as a group.

The Spanish oral language results show more variability by native language group than the English oral language results. Students in both language groups met or exceeded APS guidelines for listening comprehension, and the NSS students did so in the three oral production domains as well (fluency, vocabulary and grammar), but the results for the NES students were more mixed especially in fifth and eighth grade (see Table 2.4). Spanish literacy skills are without a doubt the most challenging area for Escuela Key students across the board. NSS students' performance on Spanish reading comprehension was on grade level in third and fifth grade but in the low average range (80–89) for eighth grade students. NES students' performance on Spanish reading comprehension was below grade level across all grade levels. Just like we saw in English, performance on Spanish writing skills was lower than in reading comprehension, with both NSS and NES across the grades performing below grade level and NES eighth grade students in the low range (70–79).

Similar findings are reported in Howard and Sugarman (2007) from a longitudinal research study conducted in 2002–2005 with funding from the Institute of Education Sciences of the U.S. Department of Education. The study investigated biliteracy trajectories of Spanish-speaking students in grades 2–5 in different educational program types (DL and mainstream) nation wide. Escuela Key was one of the schools participating in the study. Results indicate that, while the English language and literacy mean scores of Key students' were higher than the mean scores for students in other DL programs, the opposite was true of the Spanish language and literacy mean scores.

A second evaluation of the county's DL program was conducted by CAL in 2011. The evaluation was much smaller than the one conducted in 2004 and included only Spanish oral language proficiency data from the SOPA assessment from 50% of fifth and eighth grade students. A stratified random sample of 136 students in grades 5 and 8 that comprised a balance of Spanish and English native speakers, ELs, former ELs and non-ELs, and students with disabilities was generated for the purposes of the study.

The results of the 2011 Spanish SOPA interviews were rather similar to those of the 2004 interviews (see Table 2.6). On average, NSS scored significantly higher than NES across grade levels, and the two domains in which the highest ratings occurred were listening comprehension and oral fluency and grammar and vocabulary the lowest. However, some differences can also be observed between the two cohorts. For example, the percentage of students who met or exceeded county expectations in 2011 was higher than that of 2004, and this was true across the two grade levels. This difference can be attributable to the fact that: (1) NES students on average performed higher in 2011 than in 2004; and (2) NSS students in fifth grade, while still exceeding the county's expectations, performed lower in 2011 than 2004. In other words, the gap between NSS and NES was larger in 2011 than in 2004.

Since the 2011 evaluation, the DL program at APS has been monitoring the Spanish language proficiency skills of students exiting the primary and middle school programs using the STAMP assessment. STAMP results are reported to the county's Board of Education and shared with DL program parents. Fifth and eighth grade students, as a group, exceeded APS grade level expectations on all four proficiency skills (speaking, listening, reading and writing). The county is reconsidering adjusting grade level expectations upwards in an attempt to capture a more accurate representation of students' Spanish language skills. Writing samples from students at all grade levels are also collected twice a year, at the beginning and end of the school year, and graded using a rubric developed by Escuela Key teachers in collaboration with CAL in 2002 and revised in 2012. The writing sample data are one of the criteria used for grouping students from year to year.

Conclusions

More than 20 years after the publication of *Profiles of Two-Way Immersion Education* and after 30 years in operation, Escuela Key's DL program has successfully educated hundreds of bilingual, biliterate and bicultural individuals. Over the years, the program has evolved to adapt to new circumstances and that flexibility has contributed to its success. Among the program's many attributes, some stood out in the interviews and the work that the author has carried out with the school's teachers, students and administrators over the years. First, the strong leadership provided by the principal and the vice-principal and their commitment to the program's mission, vision and goals. Second, the support and dedication of the former World Languages supervisor to the program and her belief in dual language education. Third, the staff, in particular the core of veteran teachers who have remained in the program in spite of the challenges faced and the changes required of them over the years. Fourth, the parents and families, their dedication to the school and their advocacy for the program which has remained strong over the years. Finally, the importance that the entire school community (administration, teachers, parents) places on continually assessing the effectiveness of the program and making any necessary changes in order to improve it.

By offering a K-12 dual language pathway, Arlington County provides students with the opportunity to receive their full mandatory educational experience through dual language programming. While more elementary programs around the country are expanding into secondary education, the majority of DL programs in the country are exclusively elementary programs. The importance of the continuation of a DL program into secondary cannot be overstated as research has shown that often times the impact of DL education is not evident until the middle school years (Valentino & Reardon, 2015). Moreover, the conscious effort made by the DL leadership, in particular at Escuela Key, to hire bilingual staff and not exclusively for the Spanish positions or the core academic areas allows the school to not only have 'a more unified staff,' as the principal put it, but to ensure that their program aligns with the 50/50 model language allocation plan they ascribe to. Finally, the fact that every year a large number of families are waitlisted to enroll their children in the DL program at Escuela Key is a testament to the wide community support that the school receives. The families that make it in 'are phenomenal partners with us in every school decision making ... and serve as outspoken advocates for the dual language immersion program that makes us all so proud,' as the principal, Marjorie Myers, put it.

In spite of all of the strengths of the DL program, demographic changes in the community have posed some challenges which the school is currently working on. According to the district administrator interviewed: 'the program was originally developed for gifted children and, while the population has changed tremendously (including newcomer students from Central America), appropriate adjustments to better serve the needs of the current population have not taken place.' This lack of equity in serving the needs of all children is echoed by the teachers. As one of them put it when discussing student participation in instructional activities: 'The native English speakers in our school tend to be above grade level and our ELLs [English language learners] tend to be on or below. Despite our efforts at promoting Spanish and equity among groups, our native English students tend to dominate interactions and we are continually looking for ways to empower our ELLs and further challenge our highly-able students.' Her concern regarding the lack of equity for the two groups of students extends to the emphasis on test scores which she fears may jeopardize the existence of programs like Escuela Key's that integrate speakers of both languages: 'The emphasis on test scores in our systems is making it difficult for inclusive immersion programs to exist and we risk only having programs for above-grade-level native English speakers which is the case in some of our neighboring school districts.'

The challenges that the DL program at Escuela Key faces in serving a linguistically and socio-economically diverse student body are not unique to the school or to inclusive DL programs for that matter. Yet, by definition DL programs have the potential to better serve the needs of students from Spanish and English-speaking backgrounds through the equitable use of students' native languages in school-wide activities, including instruction and assessment. In order for Escuela Key to better serve the needs of all the students and create a culture of equity, the status of the

Spanish language needs to be elevated to the level of the status of the English language in terms of instruction (the Spanish language arts block needs to be strengthened), assessments (the district needs to start assessing students' achievement in Spanish), and resources (the school needs to acquire more authentic instructional resources in Spanish). While running counter to the normative discourse in this country (Freeman, 1998), resisting the power of English as the dominant language is important both for pedagogical and social reasons. On the one hand, students need ample time to acquire the level of proficiency in the two languages that research has shown to result in academic and cognitive benefits of bilingualism and biliteracy (Bialystok *et al.*, 2010; Genesee *et al.*, 2006; Lindholm-Leary & Borsato, 2006; Lindholm-Leary & Genesee, 2010). On the other, when students experience inequality, they can feel alienated and this alienation can hinder their learning.

In order for the program to attain its core goals of bilingualism and biliteracy for all students, more instructional time and resources need to be devoted to explicit Spanish language instruction so that it is brought to the same level as English language arts instruction. Research has shown that in the long run doing so will have a positive impact on students' English outcomes. Moreover, Spanish language development needs to be monitored and measured on a regular basis (not just upon exiting the program) using multiple measures that are aligned with the school's Spanish language and literacy scope and sequence. Finally, in addition to extensive and ongoing PD in two-way SIOP strategies, Spanish teachers need PD that targets specific areas of the Spanish language instruction that are different from English language instruction and resources that reflect the linguistic characteristics of the language and the different cultures of Spanish speakers. Administrators and teachers alike are aware of these needs and are continuing to work on ways to fill them.

Notes

(1) In fact, Ms. Fernández was a teacher in the program prior to becoming the vice-principal and as such has been school staff since the inception of the DL.
(2) Only student outcomes will be discussed as the 2011 evaluation did not include teacher satisfaction data.

References

Bialystok, E., Barac, R., Blaye, A. and Poulin-Dubois, D. (2010) Word mapping and executive functioning in young monolingual and bilingual children. *Journal of Cognitive Development* 11 (4), 485–508.
Christian, D., Montone, C., Lindholm, K. and Carranza, I. (1997) *Profiles in Two-way Immersion Education*. Washington, DC: Center for Applied Linguistics.
Freeman, R.D. (1998) *Bilingual Education and Social Change*. Clevedon: Multilingual Matters.

Genesee, F., Lindholm-Leary, K., Saunders, W. and Christian, D. (2006) *Educating English Language Learners. A Synthesis of Research Evidence.* Cambridge, NY: University Press.

Howard, E. and Sugarman, J. (2007) *Realizing the Vision of Two-way Immersion: Fostering Effective Programs and Classrooms.* Washington, DC: Center for Applied Linguistics.

Lindholm-Leary, K.J. and Borsato, G. (2006) Academic achievement. In F. Genesee, K. Lindholm-Leary, W.M. Saunders and D. Christian (eds) *Educating English Language Learners: A Synthesis of Research Evidence* (pp. 176–222). Cambridge: Cambridge University Press.

Lindholm-Leary, K. and Genesee, F. (2010) Alternative educational programs for English language learners. *Research on English Language Learners* (pp. 323–382). Sacramento, CA: California Department of Education Press.

Thomas, W. and Collier, V. (2002) *A National Study of School Effectiveness for Language Minority Students' Long-term Academic Achievement.* Santa Cruz, CA and Washington, DC: Center for Research on Education, Diversity & Excellence. See http://www.crede.ucsc.edu/research/llaa/1.1_final.html

Thompson, L.E., Kenyon, D.M. and Rhodes, N.C. (2002) *A Validation Study of the Student Oral Proficiency Assessment (SOPA).* Washington, DC: Center for Applied Linguistics.

Valentino, R. and Reardon, S. (2015) Effectiveness of four instructional programs designed to serve English learners: Variation by ethnicity and initial English proficiency. *Educational Evaluation and Policy Analysis* 37 (4), 612–637. Stanford, CA: Center for Education Policy Analysis, Stanford University.

APPENDIX

Table 2.2 English SOPA average ratings, by component, grade and native language

		Grade 3		Grade 5		Grade 8	
		NSS	NES	NSS	NES	NSS	NES
Oral Fluency	Mean	6.90	7.63	7.59	7.96	7.41	8.11
	SD	0.790	0.731	0.756	0.649	1.121	0.601
Grammar	Mean	7.10	8.43	7.50	8.30	8.24	8.89
	SD	1.076	0.655	1.107	0.724	0.752	0.333
Vocabulary	Mean	6.87	7.74	7.47	8.19	7.35	8.11
	SD	0.846	0.657	0.761	0.736	0.862	0.601
Listening Comprehension	Mean	7.87	8.34	8.44	8.89	8.41	8.89
	SD	0.619	0.482	0.840	0.320	0.507	0.333
		$n = 31$	$n = 35$	$n = 32$	$n = 27$	$n = 17$	$n = 9$

Table 2.3 English WLPB-R standard score means, by subtest, grade and native language

		Grade 3		Grade 5		Grade 8	
		NSS	NES	NSS	NES	NSS	NES
Passage Comprehension	Mean	104.28	123.03	101.75	119.19	99.00	115.00
	SD	13.228	10.684	14.442	12.968	11.297	12.288
Proofing	Mean	101.50	116.94	95.84	116.74	92.59	106.89
	SD	17.856	14.414	17.009	18.476	7.771	14.979
Dictation	Mean	93.69	107.14	89.31	106.52	79.82	92.78
	SD	12.913	12.113	9.872	13.796	8.897	12.112
English Basic Writing	Mean	96.50	112.69	91.19	112.67	85.47	99.44
	SD	16.379	13.519	13.653	17.072	6.838	13.305
		$n = 32$	$n = 35$	$n = 32$	$n = 27$	$n = 17$	$n = 9$

Table 2.4 Spanish SOPA average ratings, by component, grade and native language

		Grade 3		Grade 5		Grade 8	
		NSS	NES	NSS	NES	NSS	NES
Oral Fluency	Mean	7.03	4.50	7.63	5.33	7.76	6.33
	SD	1.402	1.462	1.185	1.441	0.664	1.323
Grammar	Mean	7.19	4.29	7.69	4.96	8.47	6.11
	SD	1.401	1.338	1.306	1.400	0.717	1.453
Vocabulary	Mean	6.88	4.32	7.56	5.00	8.00	6.22
	SD	1.264	1.319	1.294	1.301	0.612	1.302
Listening Comprehension	Mean	7.78	5.68	8.16	6.48	8.82	8.22
	SD	0.941	1.296	1.051	1.014	0.393	0.441
		$n = 32$	$n = 34$	$n = 32$	$n = 27$	$n = 17$	$n = 9$

Table 2.5 Spanish WLPB-R standard score means by subtest, grade and native language

		Grade 3		Grade 5		Grade 8	
		NSS	NES	NSS	NES	NSS	NES
Passage Comprehension	Mean	94.47	84.69	90.00	80.63	86.29	76.22
	SD	9.762	8.940	8.504	9.422	10.528	8.028
Proofing	Mean	86.91	85.40	85.78	80.78	93.47	80.22
	SD	16.765	12.098	16.783	16.390	9.938	7.775
Dictation	Mean	91.44	89.03	86.63	84.63	80.00	79.78
	SD	9.524	9.439	9.973	8.139	7.399	8.700
Spanish Basic Writing	Mean	87.09	85.14	84.69	81.07	85.71	78.33
	SD	13.446	10.669	13.630	12.582	8.723	6.837
		n = 32	n = 35	n = 32	n = 27	n = 17	n = 9

Table 2.6 Average SOPA ratings by native language and year

		Grade 5				Grade 8			
		NSS		NES		NSS		NES	
		2004 n = 32	2011 n = 54	2004 n = 27	2011 n = 42	2004 n = 17	2011 n = 20	2004 n = 9	2011 n = 20
Oral Fluency	Mean	7.63	7.07	5.33	6.10	7.76	8.35	6.33	7.00
	SD	1.19	0.64	1.44	1.03	0.66	0.59	1.32	0.79
Grammar	Mean	7.69	6.94	4.96	5.62	8.47	8.35	6.11	6.90
	SD	1.31	0.76	1.40	1.06	0.72	0.59	1.45	0.91
Vocabulary	Mean	7.56	6.61	5.00	5.69	8.00	8.25	6.22	6.90
	SD	1.29	0.86	1.30	1.05	0.61	0.72	1.30	0.79
Listening Comprehension	Mean	8.16	7.37	6.48	6.60	8.82	8.75	8.22	8.00
	SD	1.05	0.62	1.01	0.89	0.39	0.44	0.44	0.56

3 Dual Language Bilingual Education in NYC: A Potential Unfulfilled?

Ofelia García, Kate Menken, Patricia Velasco and Sara Vogel

Introduction

In the past two decades, bilingual education programs of the type named 'dual language' have grown throughout the United States. New York City (NYC), with its large multilingual population, and especially its numerous Spanish speakers, has supported bilingual education programs since the early 1970s. In the recent past, what has been called the Multilingual Apple (García & Fishman, 1997) has also jumped on the bandwagon of the movement to implement what are termed 'dual language' programs. The press regularly reports on the achievements of these programs and portrays them as an asset for parents, children, communities and even the nation (see, for example, Harris, 2015a, 2015b; Veiga, 2018). But are these programs always fulfilling their potential? On the one hand, they offer a space to counter monolingual U.S. schooling, and we find examples of successful dual language bilingual education (DLBE) programs in NYC. On the other hand, many times these programs are implemented in ways that, in the long run, work against developing a bilingual American citizenry in the 21st century.

This paper outlines the history of DLBE programs in NYC, as well as their present situation. It contextualizes these programs against the backdrop of NYC's rich history of bilingual education and its present sociolinguistic and sociopolitical landscape. It proposes that reframing 'dual language' programs as DLBE has the potential to empower communities building on the visions Puerto Ricans had for their children in the 1960s and 1970s. But the paper also highlights the tensions that exist between DLBE programs as traditionally defined and today's NYC multilingual communities, showing how definitions and policies for DLBE which may have served their purpose well at the time have perhaps become dated now. We pay special attention to the ideological nature of language, bilingualism and education of bilinguals, as we point out the strict inter-pretations of a DLBE 'model' that have prevented it from reaching its potential for the city.

Bilingual Education in New York City: Beginnings

In this section, we overview the history of bilingual education in NYC, showing its close ties to local communities, and later in this chapter com-pare community ties of the past to policies and efforts aimed at bilingual education expansion today. Specifically, the history of bilingual education in NYC owes much to the struggles of the Puerto Rican community, who were U.S. citizens since the Jones Act of 1917, during the Civil Rights Movement. In 1966, Puerto Ricans comprised 21% of all students enrolled in NYC public schools (Castellanos, 1983), yet 87% dropped out before graduating from high school (García, 2011). ASPIRA, the Puerto Rican Civil Rights organization, decided to press for bilingual education to improve education for Puerto Rican children, while preserving the Spanish language and student identity (Del Valle, 1998). NYC's first bilingual elementary school, P.S. 25, opened in 1968 in the South Bronx in response to community demands (Pousada, 1987). P.S. 25's approach could be characterized as a maintenance or developmental maintenance bilingual education program.

From its beginnings, bilingual education in New York got caught in the political struggles over community control of education. The growth of such programs was very slow and the community became impatient, fueled by the actions of the newly formed Young Lords in 1969 (Reyes, 2006; Santiago, 1986). Shortly after the landmark *Lau v. Nichols* case had been decided,[1] ASPIRA and the New York City Board of Education (NYCBE) signed a Consent Decree in 1974, which stated:

> All children whose English language deficiency prevents them from effec-tively participating in the learning process and who can more effectively participate in Spanish shall receive: a) planned and systematic program designed to develop the child's ability to speak, understand, read and write the English language.... b) instruction in substantive courses in Spanish (e.g. courses in mathematics, science, and social studies)... [and] c) a planned and systematic program designed to reinforce and develop the child's use of Spanish. (Aspira v. Board, 1974a, para. 2, as cited in Santiago, 1986: 160)

Although the NYCBE agreed to provide only *transitional* bilingual education (TBE) under the Aspira Consent Decree, some of the programs utilized a *'maintenance approach* to educate the children through their school careers to be bilingual and bicultural' (Pousada, 1987: 20). By pro-viding what was later referred to as a 'late exit' TBE program, many bilin-gual education programs at this time had a maintenance ethos and were a source of community control. Policymakers in New York State passed Part 154 of the Regulations of the State Commissioner of Education in 1981, upholding the Aspira Consent Decree of 1974 by mandating that bilingual education be provided in all schools where there are 20 or more 'Limited English Proficient' students per grade who speak the same home language (Carrasquillo *et al.*, 2014; for more on this early history, see García, 2011).

In 1965, the Immigration and Naturalization Services Act lifted the quota that limited immigration to the U.S. to only 2% of the number of people who were already living in the U.S. in 1890. Because of this, by the 1980s, the city diversified and schools began serving recent immigrants from many countries in Latin America, Africa, Asia and Eastern Europe. Whereas Puerto Ricans were U.S. citizens, the new immigrants were often undocumented and lacked the political savvy to fight for the educational rights of their children. The city's increased linguistic heterogeneity also made TBE programs difficult to implement. At the same time, the country was beginning to change, with the election of President Ronald Reagan in 1980 and the introduction of the first constitutional amendment to make English the official language of the United States by Senator Samuel Hayakawa in 1981. The tide was turning, and bilingual education came under attack (for a historical account of this period, see, among others, Crawford, 2004; García & Kleifgen, 2018; Wiley, 1996).

Many bilingual education programs in NYC had become educational ghettos by the mid-1980s, segregating bilingual teachers and students from the rest of the school (e.g., by locating programs in basements; for more on this, see Flores & García, 2017). A few progressive educators started to clamor for bilingual education programs that were not remedial in nature. Among those was Sidney Morison, principal of P.S. 84 in Manhattan, which had offered TBE since 1969. As Latinx students became more bilingual, and the neighborhood attracted growing numbers of middle-class and white families, Morison changed the name of the program to 'Dual Language,' a label that was gaining traction around the country.

However, Morison's description of P.S. 84's transformed programming is indicative of what 'dual language' meant during that time, and differs markedly from what it means today, as discussed below. For Morison (1990), 'dual language' was an 'enrichment bilingual program… rooted in the principles of heterogeneity and inclusion of children's cultural backgrounds' (1990: 161). P.S. 84's 'dual language' program was open to all the children in the school community, especially to a Latinx community that was increasingly second and third generation and bilingual, and with growing numbers of children from mixed marriages. It did not engineer which types of students would enroll in each classroom. Because it had a progressive philosophy of enrichment, bilingual teachers built on the strengths of each individual child. There was one bilingual teacher per grade who alternated teaching one day in English and one day in Spanish, and who taught all subjects. But in keeping with its progressive philosophy, the teacher's attention to each individual child's emotional, cognitive, academic and linguistic needs meant that teachers' language use was flexible enough that children could engage with the lessons and make meaning, regardless of their proficiency levels. P.S. 84 was an island in an increasingly changing landscape.

Shifts in the Landscape: Dual Language Bilingual Education Rays of Hope[2]

In the late 1990s, bilingual education suffered its greatest national defeat when voters passed ballot measures seeking to abolish bilingual education in California in 1998,[3] Arizona in 2000 and Massachusetts in 2002. The word 'bilingual' was silenced in every piece of federal legislation and governmental office, substituted by 'English language acquisition' (Crawford, 2004; García, 2009; García & Kleifgen, 2018). The backlash against bilingual education also hit NYC, in spite of the support for bilingual education programs codified in the State Commissioner's Part 154 Regulations.

There were also rays of hope as some schools began to push the boundaries of the TBE programs found in most city schools. Some community-based organizations saw opportunities to start up developmental maintenance bilingual education programs, while simultaneously evading anti-bilingual education sentiment under the guise of the new label that did not in any way mention the word 'bilingual' – 'dual language.' The four 'dual language' schools that were founded in the late 1990s provided a different direction for bilingual education, one that encouraged developmental maintenance of children's bilingualism, while integrating children learning English with those who wanted to also develop literacy in Spanish or Chinese. With support from New Visions for Public Schools, the largest education reform organization in NYC, four dual language bilingual schools opened during this period – Amistad Dual Language School in Upper Manhattan (founded in 1996), Twenty-First Century Academy for Community Leadership in Upper Manhattan (founded in 1997), Cypress Hills Community School in Cypress Hills, Brooklyn (founded in 1997) and Shuang Wen School in the Upper East Side (founded in 1998). These four schools continue today to offer quality DLBE.

Despite the common ways in which they identify themselves as 'dual language,' these four schools are very different, adapting to the different lived experience of their children and their communities. Two of the schools – Twenty-First Century Academy and Cypress Hills Community School – came about through the organizing efforts of their respective communities, seeking to control their children's schooling. Asociación Comunal de Dominicanos Progresistas (ACDP) wanted a bilingual school for the growing Dominican population in Washington Heights. It attracted one of its educational leaders, Evelyn Linares, as principal of the school that became Twenty-First Century Academy. Cypress Hills was co-founded with the Cypress Hills Local Development Corporation. Its commitment to the community and bilingualism required a collaborative structure with two co-directors: a community activist, María Jaya, and a principal, Sheryl Brown, succeeded by Irene León. Approximately 95% of students in both schools are Latinos who fall along all points of the bilingual continuum. At Cypress Hills almost half the students (42%) of the students are categorized as 'English language learners' (ELLs), whereas at Twenty-First Century Academy, about a third of the students (33%) fall under the 'ELL' category. Many school officials and educators might consider these programs 'one-way' dual language bilingual programs, that is, programs for only one language group, since most of their students are Latinx. In reality, they are educational programs that support bilingualism and biliteracy as important in the education of children who happen to be mostly Latinx. Although they allocate languages to separate times, in reality educators at the schools adapt to the complex dynamic bilingualism of the community by providing students with support and scaffolding when students cannot make meaning of the language of instruction.

From its inception, Shuang Wen has followed a different model of DLBE, with the traditional school day in English, and the after-school until 5:00 pm conducted in Mandarin Chinese. Although the school is officially a 'dual language bilingual school,' it is more of a multilingual school, adapting to the many Chinese languages of the city, especially Fujianese. With the importance of Mandarin in the world today, the school receives more English-speaking children, but overall still largely serves a Chinese-origin population (71%). Seventeen percent of students in Shuang Wen are categorized as 'English language learners.'

The fourth school, Amistad Dual Language School is in Inwood, Upper Manhattan, a community that is undergoing gentrification and is starting to attract more white and Latinx middle-class families. Today, 91% of the students are Latinx and less than one-fourth (22%) are categorized as 'English language learners.' The school continues its commitment to the development of bilingualism and biliteracy in all children, but especially among Latinx students.

In an anti-bilingual education landscape, DLBE became the only way to offer hope to communities who wanted their children to become bilingual. Besides these four fully bilingual schools, many schools in the city started to shift from TBE programs to those that were now called 'dual language.' Despite their potential, the growth of these programs has been slow and offers some challenges.

The Unraveling of Bilingual Education: The Bloomberg Years

In 2002 when Mayor Michael Bloomberg took office, there were few dual language bilingual programs, and only 2.3% of the city's 'English Language Learners' were in such programs. The year 2002 witnessed two very important events that were to transform even further the direction of bilingual education in the city. One was the passage of No Child Left Behind, which repealed the Bilingual Education Act (Title VII) and put into place an accountability system measured by English-only assessments (see Menken & Solorza, 2014a, 2014b). The other was that Michael Bloomberg won mayoral control of schools in 2002, ending the system of decentralization that had been the hope of communities for political empowerment.

As the NYC school system was reorganized under Mayor Bloomberg's control, the Office of Bilingual Education was renamed the Office of English Language Learners. The silencing of the word 'bilingual' had now reached NYC. Late in 2009, and signaling the increased attention on student achievement scores and accountability, the Office was once more renamed the Chief Achievement Office: Students with Disabilities and English Language Learners.

As Menken and Solorza's research (2014a, 2014b) shows, the greater accountability of No Child Left Behind and the lack of institutional support for bilingual education has led to the closure of many bilingual education programs throughout the years of Bloomberg's administration and until today. Table 3.1 shows that ESL programs, where instruction is typically monolingual in English, have grown dramatically. Fifty-three percent (53%) of all students classified as English Language Learners were enrolled in ESL in 2002, as compared to 81% in 2016. In contrast, the number of students in TBE decreased considerably, from 37% when mayoral control became effective to 12% today. DLBE programs have grown very slowly since the start of Mayor Bloomberg's three terms in office. Two percent of all classified English language learners were enrolled in DLBE programs in 2002, and that number had only increased to 4.9% by 2016. Thus, while DLBE programs have grown, their growth has not been enough to counter the dramatic loss of TBE, which in most city schools were simply replaced by ESL programs.

Table 3.1 Enrollment of 'English language learners' in different types of programs*

	2002–3	2003–4	2004–5	2005–6	2006–7	2007–8	2010–11	2011–12	2012	2013–4	2014–5	2015–16
ESL	53.4%	59.7%	65.7%	66.8%	69.4%	69.2%	70.2%	76.0%	78.3	79.2%	80.0%	81.0%
TBE	37.4%	32.0%	29.8%	27.9%	25.6%	21.6%	18.5%	17.7%	15.2	15.4%	13.2%	12.1%
DLBE	2.3%	2.8%	2.6%	2.1%	3.7%	3.6%	3.8%	4.0%	4.1	4.5%	4.5%	4.91%

*Figures are compiled from the NYCDOE Demographic Reports annually from 2002–2016.

There were also important discursive changes during the Bloomberg times. The word 'bilingual' became associated only with 'transitional' remedial programs that were early-exit programs, and school authorities started talking about 'bilingual' programs and 'dual language' programs as if they were in opposition, silencing the potential of both DLBE and TBE to empower bilingual communities. The stage was set for confrontation. The label 'dual language' education soon took on characteristics that led it in another direction from its empowering possibilities, a path that became more and more associated with a neoliberal economic regime that proposed it as a way to attract more middle-class parents into public schools in the city. John B. King, New York State Commissioner of Education from 2011–15, stated that DLBE programs could be 'a vehicle to increase socioeconomic and racial diversity in schools by drawing more affluent parents' (Harris, 2015b). DLBE was beginning to lose the original intent of all bilingual education, that of providing bilingual communities with a meaningful and equal educational opportunity for their children. It is for this reason that we put forth the term 'dual language *bilingual* education' or DLBE (see also Sánchez *et al.*, 2017), and promote its use in this chapter as a better way to conceptualize DLBE for the 21st century, a point we return to later in this chapter.

In an effort to reconcile the two positions, strict guidelines were set for implementation of dual language bilingual programs. Fifty percent of the children had to be officially designated 'English Language Learners,' whereas the other 50% had to be 'Learners of the other language.' This 'model' reserved a space for 'English Language Learners,' ensuring that the programs did not become only an arm of powerful middle-class communities. It also was built on the possibility of integrating these two groups both linguistically and educationally. But where did this strict definition of student allocation leave the increasingly bilingual NYC communities? Where did it leave the many children growing up in bilingual homes? As noted above, significant numbers of second- and third-generation students and children from mixed marriages attend city schools today, and arrive in school at all different points along the bilingual continuum as a result; however, these students do not fit easily into the academic dichotomy that language allocation policies have created of 'English language learner' vs 'Target language learner' in 'dual language' programs. These bilingual students are also not given any priority in admissions to the small number of programs.

The dual language 'model' had been developed following a monolingual framework where students were seen as either monolingual in English or monolingual in a language other than English. At a time when policymakers were mainly trying to distance 'dual language' from TBE, the dynamic features of 21st-century bilingualism were ignored. The 'model' as defined by NYC school authorities left little room to be inclusive of the complex sociolinguistic characteristics of a changing multilingual city, and to view bilingualism as more than simply 'additive.' Today, although dual language bilingual programs could be an important resource for all communities who want their children to be bilingual and biliterate (the Puerto Rican 'dream' in the 1960s and 1970s for their community), the strict interpretation of these programs in the city makes the dream attainable only for very few, as we show in the next section.

Dual Language Bilingual Education Today: The Promise Unfulfilled

In an effort to reverse the trend of emergent bilinguals disproportionately being placed in ESL programs where they continued to fail, NYC Schools Chancellor Carmen Fariña, appointed by Mayor Bill de Blasio in 2014, made the annual expansion of DLBE programs a cornerstone of her leadership (Veiga, 2018). The Division of English Language Learners and Student Support was created in 2015, and Milady Baez was appointed to lead it.

Under Fariña and Baez, the New York City Department of Education (NYCDOE) announced the opening of 40 'new' DLBE programs in 2015–16 in the Bronx, 11 in Brooklyn, nine in Manhattan, eight in Queens and two in Staten Island (NYCDOE, 2015a). Not all programs were entirely new, however; fifteen of the schools were actually adding new languages or expanding grades of existing programs. In 2015, there were 162 public schools (out of a total 1665 schools in NYC) that offered DLBE. Most of these programs were English/Spanish DLBE programs (134 schools). The Spanish/English programs were located in Manhattan (39 schools), followed by Brooklyn (33), Queens (28), the Bronx (27), and Staten Island (7). There were also 10 DLBE programs in Chinese/English, nine in French/English, three in Haitian Creole/English, two in Russian/English and one each in Hebrew/English, Polish/English, Korean/English and Arabic/English.[4] Figure 3.1 displays a map that shows where these programs were located throughout the city in 2015, as Fariña and Baez's expansion efforts took effect. Clearly the distribution of languages and programs reflects the city's diverse neighborhoods – Spanish mostly in Manhattan, the South Bronx, and in the Elmhurst/Jackson Heights/Corona neighborhoods of Queens; Chinese mostly in the Lower East Side of Manhattan and in Flushing, Queens; French mostly in northwestern Brooklyn; Korean in Flushing, Queens; and Arabic, Haitian Creole, Hebrew, Polish and Russian in distinct neighborhoods of Brooklyn. Since 2015, further languages have been introduced into the dual language bilingual landscape, which do not appear on our map, including Italian, Japanese, and German. As this chapter goes to press, the city has committed funding to open 39 DLBE programs in the 2017–18 school year (NYCDOE, 2017).

These efforts to open new DLBE programs each year constitute a response by the current NYCDOE leadership to the claims that bilingual

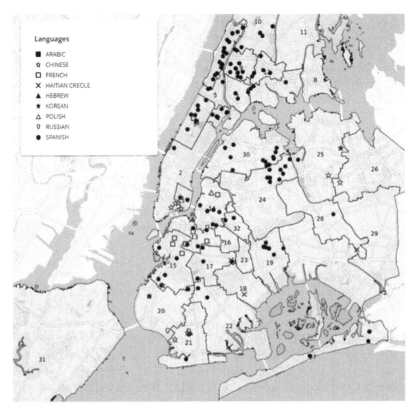

Figure 3.1 Dual language bilingual programs in New York City Community School Districts (2015–16)

education programs had been decimated by the prior administration. However, the NYCDOE has encouraged the new wave of DLBE programs to follow strict models and policies regarding student composition and language separation, orienting them as if the city had the same demographic and sociolinguistic characteristics as in the late 20th century. This stringency undermines efforts at bilingual education expansion and limits the potential of these programs. More than ever, DLBE programs are being used to do two contradictory things simultaneously – provide bilingual instruction for students classified as 'ELLs' and, at the same time, enable the language majority middle-class community access to programs for their children to become bilingual and biliterate. Many of the programs, although not all, are being promoted as 'gifted and talented' programs, serving to attract wealthier families back into local public schools, which they had abandoned. The availability of DLBE programs and the number of bilingual teachers is limited, thus many schools have long wait lists for admission and often screen students for selection, such that only students who show the most promise are selected. For 'English language learners,' this means that many are relegated to English as a Second Language programs (now known as English as a New Language in New York State) even in schools where a dual language bilingual program is available because schools have to maintain the 50/50 distribution of those classified as 'English language learners' vs 'Target language learners.'

Although what Fabrice Jaumont has called 'the bilingual revolution' (2017) is visible in NYC as DLBE gains popularity, the tension remains between privileged communities seeking further privilege for their children and those seeing these programs as a means of bilingual community empowerment. The most successful DLBE programs in the city continue to be those that build the program for their students and community, without attempting to socially engineer students as belonging to two entirely different, distinct groups. Since 2012 three schoolwide DLBE programs, where the entire student population is enrolled in bilingual education, were established – Castle Bridge (2014), Dos Puentes (2013) and the WHEELS school (2015) – all three in Upper Manhattan and at the elementary level. The longer standing schoolwide DLBE programs – Amistad, Cypress Hills, Shuang Wen, and Twenty-First Century Academy – have expanded to middle schools. But what makes these schools distinct from the many other schools that have recently opened up DLBE programs is their insistence that the programs serve the local community and take into account the dynamic bilingual continuum that exists. The difference then is that these DLBE programs are for the community, and respond to the educational needs of their students. This differs from an elitist vision of bilingualism in education that privileges only certain students or fails to take into account the complex and dynamic linguistic performances of bilingual children, thereby losing sight of the original aims of these programs to serve minoritized communities.

In late 2015, the NYCDOE issued a list of 15 schools which they stated offered 'model dual language programs' (NYCDOE, 2015b). Most were Spanish-English, one was Spanish-English and French-English, one was Chinese-English, one offered DLBE in four languages in addition to English: Chinese, Hebrew, Russian and Spanish. Deputy Commissioner Baez stated in a press release that these 'models' will *create uniformity* across the City on the essential components of Dual Language programs... Dual Language education is truly a game-changer that gives our students a *competitive edge* for college and career opportunities' (NYCDOE, 2015b, our italics). The mention of competitiveness responds to the economic interests of some communities, but not to the empowerment of others. It is interesting to consider the uniformity demanded by the school authorities. Only programs that were said to have a 'side-by-side' design (with one teacher speaking one language partnered with a teacher who speaks the other language) were considered 'model' programs by the NYCDOE, which then issued guidance on structuring DLBE programs only in these side-by-side arrangements. This arrangement is not always appropriate for elementary schools. For example, early childhood practices support the idea that young children are better served by having one teacher who can meet their emotional and developmental needs and get to know the child holistically. Furthermore, in order to get to totally understand the children's ability to use language, to make meaning, to understand content, to solve problems, to gain knowledge, it is easier for one teacher to view the child's abilities as a whole, and not through just one language or the other. In the side-by-side arrangements, it is imperative that time and space be set aside for meaningful and intense teacher collaboration. In codifying the uniformity of DLBE programs, the flexibility to establish programs that serve a community's needs and move their children toward bilingualism and biliteracy might be lost. Then there is the practical reality that running a side-by-side model means that schools must have enough designated 'ELLs' and 'Target language learners' to fill two entire classrooms. Many schools interested in offering bilingual education simply do not have the numbers to do so. Given that there is an ongoing bilingual teacher shortage, it is also easier to staff one class instead of two. Taken together, strict DLBE policies and guidelines can actually undermine the administration's aims of program expansion, when schools interested in starting programs or struggling to maintain them are discouraged from doing so because they cannot offer a side-by-side model program.

The challenges around supporting the development of bilingualism for all children within the DLBE 'model' became evident in the announcement made by the Chancellor on February 28, 2017 (NYCDOE, 2017). The Chancellor announced the opening of 39 new DLBE programs, but this time an additional 29 TBE programs are also slated to open, in spite of additional incentive funding aimed at DLBE expansion (schools were offered a $10,000 planning grant from the NYCDOE to start a transitional bilingual program, but $20,000 to start a dual language program). As the NYCDOE grapples with the tensions inherent in their strict requirements for linguistic 'purity' in developing DLBE programs, as well as the practical challenges, it has become easier for schools to open TBE programs for emergent bilinguals. But TBE programs do not aim to develop the minoritized students' bilingualism and biliteracy. The answer to this dilemma might be to insist on a more dynamic 'bilingual' reality for all programs. This would mean having more flexible guidelines for all bilingual programs – TBE and DLBE. Angélica Infante-Green, the Associate Commissioner for Bilingual Education and Foreign Language Studies in the New York State Education Department, recently said about the divisions between program models: 'There's a line in the sand; you can blur it.' (Infante-Green, 2016). Only by blurring lines between transitional and dual language *bilingual* programs, and focusing on bilingualism and biliteracy as a goal for all, will it be possible to forge a truly multilingual and multiliterate future for the Multilingual Apple. In the 21st century, bilingual schools throughout the world have had a major impact in making children bilingual and biliterate. NYC could learn from the flexibility afforded to schools all over the world that truly have set a plurilingual citizenry as their goal (Baker, 2011; García, 2009).

A Way Forward? Blurring the Line in the Sand and Fulfilling the Promise

For many schools and communities, the uniform guidelines given until recently by the NYCDOE reflect old understandings of language and bilingual education that limit their potential. In this chapter, we have shown how the advent of DLBE in NYC was reactionary against transitional programs of the time, and policies for these programs were aimed at providing bilingual education programs for the enrichment of all children, without getting mired in the debates over bilingual education of that time period. However, times have changed and we have seen how past policies have actually impeded DLBE programs from reaching their full potential in city schools. If DLBE programs are going to spread and grow throughout the city, some flexibility in implementation guidelines is needed. Furthermore, the programs need to work for children, to educate them deeply and meaningfully; and they need to work for communities, to empower them. The programs cannot simply work for named languages (either English or the language other than English). They cannot simply work for children who are at the beginning points of the bilingual continuum (whether they are English speakers or not), but must accommodate *all* children regardless of their linguistic or ability profiles. *Bilingual education of all types must work for all children.*

The guidelines offered by NYCDOE for DLBE programs engineer the program composition linguistically and simplify the complexity and dynamism of bilinguals' language practices by recognizing only two named languages. We know that increasingly students in the city grow up as simultaneous bilinguals or multilinguals, with homes in which multilingual language practices are common. We also know that the city's population is not simply bilingual. For example, Mexican immigrants are increasingly speakers of languages other than Spanish, like Mixteco (Velasco, 2014). DLBE programs need to acknowledge the entire multilingual repertoire of most young people today, and establish a multilingual ecology that recognizes all the language practices of their students. They must be careful not to create a double linguistic hierarchy, evaluating what is known as 'standard academic language,' whether English or a Language Other than English, as superior to all other linguistic practices. For language-minoritized populations, the interpretation of bilingualism as 'dual' ignores and stigmatizes their languaging practices which goes *beyond* the two named languages that are legitimized in schools (García, 2009; García & Kleifgen, 2018).

The demand that DLBE programs include 50% of 'ELL' students and 50% of 'Learners of a Language other than English' shows a lack of understanding of the social complexities of bilingual communities, who differ in socioeconomic status, race, nationality, and linguistic and cultural practices. While DLBE programs struggle to ensure that their programs maintain an artificial balance of linguistic groups and select the 'best' students to fill the programs, far too many who would benefit from bilingual instruction are left out. In engineering the balance of the student population only linguistically, programs remain blind to racial, socioeconomic, ethnic and gender differences. Programs are also then forced to ignore the linguistic development that is the by-product of schooling, and that will blur the lines between the two monolingual worlds on which DLBE guidelines are based. Furthermore, the DLBE guidelines ignore the flux and movement of students of all ages, created by an increasingly globalized world and a neoliberal economic regime. This population displacement brings into NYC schools students from different countries, of different ages, with diverse educational and literacy histories, with different capacities at different times – all deserving bilingual instruction. For DLBE programs to be truly successful, we would be building bilingual programs that do not suffer from a monoglossic ideology that sees bilingualism as simply additive and does not understand its dynamics (García, 2009).

The primary characteristics of dual language bilingual programs as defined by the NYCDOE appeared in a checklist that was made public in 2015. Most of the characteristics identified in the checklist are appropriate. However, some, as the three we identify below, present outdated notions of bilingualism and pedagogies to teach for bilingualism (our italics):

- *all* content areas are in *both languages*;
- the two languages are separated by time, space, or teacher and *are not used simultaneously;*
- translation by the teacher is *totally* prohibited.

From its early beginnings, sociolinguistic research in bilingual education has shown that not all subjects and content have to be taught in both languages to develop bilingualism and biliteracy (see Fishman & Lovas, 1970). Teaching *all* content areas in both languages does not recognize the sociolinguistic reality of language use, and the fact that speakers use language differently, depending on the context, content and interlocutors involved in the communicative event. Bilinguals never use the two languages for exactly the same purposes. Likewise, bilingual students do not have to learn the same content in two languages all the time. It is possible for one language to be used for some purposes and subjects, and not others, and for this to shift (or not) as the student moves through the grades, depending on societal goals. It is also possible for teachers to focus on learning subject matter deeply, and to allow students to use their two languages to gain further understandings. For example, it is possible for Latinx students in a class taught in Spanish on the science of hurricanes to use both Spanish and English as they search for information on the internet. This means that another period does not have to be added to teach the science of hurricanes in English.

The guideline about language separation and the prohibition of two languages being used simultaneously, and of translation, also needs some rethinking. We agree that there must be a language allocation policy that provides the affordances for one or another language to be heard and used, both orally and in writing. And we also agree that teachers should not be simply providing translations in the other language to students. But as Sánchez *et al.* (2017) have described, there must be flexibility and trans-formations in the strict language allocation policy advocated in many DLBE programs so that emergent bilinguals of all types are supported, their zones of proximal development expanded (Vygotsky, 1978), and their language practices legitimated.

The call for this more flexible language allocation policy is rooted in a different theory of language and bilingualism than that being used in the NYCDOE guidelines – a theory of translanguaging (for more on this, see, among others, García & Li Wei, 2014; Li Wei, 2017; Otheguy *et al.*, 2015, 2018). When considering bilingual/multilingual students, translanguaging theory distinguishes between named languages (i.e., English, Spanish, Chinese, French and so on) and the language of people. That is, the *trans* of translanguaging takes us *beyond* named languages (Li Wei, 2011), describing how these authorized named languages are sociopolitical and sociocultural constructions, and disrupting the idea that bilinguals develop, or 'do' language, with two language systems that are separate. Bilingualism is not simply the result of the addition of a 'second' named language to a 'first' named language. Bilingual students add new features, that is, phonemes, words, constructions, rules, etc., to their existing lan-guage system, as they interact with other speakers, in this way expanding their meaning-making capacities and their repertoire. Translanguaging views the language system of bilinguals as unitary, and unleashes it from the conceptual division and hierarchies imposed by named national languages.

The instructional spaces that bilingual schools provide for the two named languages are important because schools have an important role in helping bilingual students acquire the *social* understanding of when and how to use the many features of their repertoire. But good bilingual instruction must support bilingual students with a space where the stu-dents' own translanguaging is leveraged. This is important both for edu-cators to understand what students really know, as well as for bilingual youth to legitimize their own translanguaging practices as valid for their academic and social lives. In many ways, this translanguaging space in bilingual instruction would allow bilingual students to 'lift the veil' (to use W.E. Du Bois metaphor), to see (and hear) themselves not in relationship to the white monolingual gaze, but as bilinguals who can speak for themselves, and not simply for other monolinguals (Fanon, 1967).

Translanguaging does not negate the existence of bilingualism or multilingualism as a sociocultural concept, the importance of which especially in the lives of members of minoritized communities is most important. But it does negate the idea that named languages are linguistic objects that can be assessed separately. Translanguaging centers on the fluid and dynamic language practices of bilinguals who leverage their entire linguistic repertoire flexibly in order to make meaning. Rather than seeing fluid linguistic practices as interferences or errors, translanguaging is recognized as the discursive norm of all bilinguals when looked at from the point of the bilingual person rather than that of named languages.

The focus on language separation in the city's DLBE guidelines is rooted in notions of linguistic purism, monolingual norms, and an unfortunate understanding of bilingualism (Gort & Sembiante, 2015; Martínez et al., 2015; Menken & Avni, 2017; Palmer et al., 2014). Pedagogical practices based on translanguaging theory are beginning to be used in DLBE programs to support the development of bilingualism and biliteracy (see, for example, Celic & Seltzer, 2012/2013; García et al., 2016; García & Kleyn, 2016; Palmer et al., 2014). Translanguaging pedagogy works to ensure that emergent bilinguals appropriate all features as their own, and not as separate second languages, and that they develop a bilingual American identity that normalizes bilingualism in the United States.

DLBE programs need to grow, expand and serve all the many communities that desire it. At the same time, they need to keep the focus on the education of the growing number of bilingual and multilingual children in the United States. To do so, they will have to shed the strict and rigid policies that accompany the model with regards to who is monolingual and who is bilingual, and how bilingualism is conceptualized and developed.

New York City has never given up on the potential of bilingual education. But to meet the needs of the very varied multilingual New Yorkers in the future, and to expand DLBE programs, the NYCDOE will have to stop interpreting 'dual' as simply two autonomous languages for two different linguistic groups and recognize the multilingual practices, the translanguaging, of NYC students. The potential of DLBE programs is great, and we sincerely hope that the time for their transformation and growth is now.

Notes

(1) In Lau v. Nichols, the Supreme Court ruled in favor of the Chinese plaintiffs in San Francisco and ordered that something additional be done for language minority students.

(2) Many of the observations in this section and the following are based on our long-standing work in bilingual schools in New York City, some of us over 40 years.
(3) We note that in November 2016 voters in California passed Proposition 58, overturning the restriction of bilingual education programs in the state.
(4) These numbers are based on the NYCDOE report: Dual Language and Transitional Bilingual Education Programs, SY 2015–2016.

References

Baker, C. (2011) *Foundations of Bilingual Education and Bilingualism* (5 edn). Bristol: Multilingual Matters.

Blackledge, A. and Creese, A. (2010) *Multilingualism: A Critical Perspective*. London: Continuum.

Carrasquillo, A.R., Rodríguez, D. and Kaplan, L. (2014) *New York State Education Department Policies, Mandates, and Initiatives on the Education of English Language Learners*. New York, NY: CUNY-NYSIEB.

Castellanos, D.L. (1983) *The Best of Two Worlds: Bilingual-Bicultural Education in the U.S.* Trenton, NJ: New Jersey State Dept. of Education.

Celic, C. and Seltzer, K. (2013) *Translanguaging: A CUNY-NYSIEB Guide for Educators*. New York: CUNY- New York State Initiative on Emergent Bilinguals. See http://www.nysieb.ws.gc.cuny.edu/files/2013/03/Translanguaging-Guide-March-2013.pdf

Crawford, J. (2004) *Educating English Learners: Language Diversity in the Classroom* (5th edn). Los Angeles, CA: Bilingual Education Services, Inc.

Del Valle, S. (1998) Bilingual education for Puerto Ricans in New York City: From hope to compromise. *Harvard Educational Review* 68 (2), 193–217.

Fanon, F. (1967) *Black Skin, White Masks*. 'The Negro & Language' (pp. 8–27). London: Pluto Press.

Fishman, J.A. and Lovas, J. (1970) Bilingual education in sociolinguistic perspective. *TESOL Quarterly* 4 (3), 215–222. See http://doi.org/10.2307/3585722

Flores, N. and García, O. (2017) A critical review of bilingual education in the United States: From basements and boutiques to boutiques and profit. *Annual Review of Applied Linguistics* 37, 14–29. Doi: 10.1017/S0267190517000162

García, O. (2009) *Bilingual Education in the 21st Century: A Global Perspective*. Malden, MA: Wiley-Blackwell.

García, O. (2011) Educating New York's bilingual children: Constructing a future from the past. *International Journal of Bilingual Education and Bilingualism* 14 (2), 133–153.

García, O. and Fishman, J.A. (eds) (1997) *The Multilingual Apple. Languages in New York City*. Berlin, Germany: Mouton de Gruyter.

García, O. and Kleyn, T. (eds) (2016) *Translanguaging with Multilingual Students: Learning from Classroom Moments*. New York: Routledge.

García, O. and Kleifgen, J.A. (2018) *Educating Emergent Bilinguals: Policies, Programs, and Practices for English Learners (2nd ed.)*. New York: Teachers College Press.

García, O., Johnson, S.I. and Seltzer, K. (2016) *Translanguaging Classrooms: Leveraging Student Bilingualism for Learning*. Philadelphia: Caslon Publishing.

García, O. and Li W. (2014) *Translanguaging: Language, Bilingualism and Education*. London: Palgrave Macmillan Pivot.

Gort, M. and Sembiante, S. (2015) Navigating hybridized language learning spaces through translanguaging pedagogy: Dual language preschool teachers' languaging practices in support of emergent bilingual children's performance of academic discourse. *International Multilingual Research Journal* 9 (1), 7–25.

Harris, E.A. (2015a, January 14) New York City Education Department to Add or Expand 40 Dual-Language Programs. *The New York Times*. See http://www.nytimes. com/2015/01/15/nyregion/new-york-city-education-department-to-add-or-expand-40-dual-language-programs.html

Harris, E.A. (2015b, October 8) Dual-language programs are on the rise, even for native English speakers. *The New York Times*. See http://www.nytimes.com/2015/10/09/nyre gion/dual-language-programs-are-on-the-rise-even-for-native-english-speakers.html

Li, W. (2011) Moment analysis and translanguaging space: Discursive construction of identities by multilingual Chinese youth in Britain. *Journal of Pragmatics* 43, 1222–1235.

Li, W. (2017) Translanguaging as a practical theory of language. *Applied Linguistics* 2017: 1–23. doi:10.1093/applin/amx039

Infante, A. (2016, May) *Keynote Address*. Presented at the New York State Association for Bilingual Education Conference, Buffalo, New York.

Jaumont, F. (2017) *The Bilingual Revolution*. New York: TBR Books.

Martínez, R., Hikida, M. and Durán, L. (2015) Unpacking ideologies of linguistic purism: How dual language teachers make sense of everyday translanguaging. *International Multilingual Research Journal* 9 (1), 26–42.

Menken, K. and Avni, S. (2017) Challenging linguistic purism in dual language bilingual education: A case study of Hebrew in a New York City public middle school. *Annual Review of Applied Linguistics* 37, 185–202.

Menken, K. and Solorza, C. (2014a) No child left bilingual accountability and the elimination of bilingual education programs in New York City Schools. *Educational Policy* 28 (1), 96–125. http://doi.org/10.1177/0895904812468228

Menken, K. and Solorza, C. (2014b) Where have all the bilingual programs gone?!: Why prepared school leaders are essential for bilingual education. *Journal of Multilingual Education Research* 4 (1), 9–39. See http://fordham.bepress.com/jmer/vol4/iss1/3

Morison, S.H. (1990) A Spanish-English dual-language program in New York City. *The Annals of the American Academy of Political and Social Science* 508, 160–169.

New York City Department of Education (2015a, January 14) Chancellor Fariña to Launch 40 Dual Language Programs in September. See http://schools.nyc.gov/Offices/mediarelations/NewsandSpeeches/2014-2015/Chancellor+Fari%C3%B1a+to+Laun ch+40+Dual+Language+Programs+in+September.htm

New York City Department of Education (2015b, December 3) Chancellor Fariña Names 15 Schools Model Dual Language Programs – 2015–2016. See http://schools.nyc.gov/ Offices/mediarelations/NewsandSpeeches/2015-2016/Chancellor+Farina+Names+15 +Schools+Model+Dual+Language+Programs.htm

New York City Department of Education (2016, April 4) Chancellor Fariña Announces 38 New Bilingual Programs – 2015–2016. See http://schools.nyc.gov/Offices/mediar elations/NewsandSpeeches/2015-2016/Chancellor+Farina+Announces+38+New+Bi lingual+Programs.htm

New York City Department of Education (2017) Chancellor Fariña announces citywide bilingual expansion, bringing 68 new programs to schools this fall. See http://schools.nyc. gov/Offices/mediarelations/NewsandSpeeches/2016–2017/BilingualExpansion.htm

Otheguy, R., García, O. and Reid, W. (2015) Clarifying translanguaging and deconstructing named languages: A perspective from linguistics. *Applied Linguistics Review* 6 (3), 281–307. See http://doi.org/10.1515/applirev-2015-0014

Otheguy, R., García, O. and Reid, W. (2018) A translanguaging view of the linguistic system of bilinguals. *Applied Linguistics Review*, 1–27. See https://doi.org/10.1515/ applirev-2018-0020

Palmer, D.K., Martínez, R.A., Mateus, S.G. and Henderson, K. (2014) Reframing the debate on language separation: Toward a vision for translanguaging pedagogies in the dual language classroom. *The Modern Language Journal* 98 (3), 757–772. See http://doi.org/10.1111/modl.12121

Pousada, A. (1987) *Puerto Rican Community Participation in East Harlem Bilingual Programs*. New York: Research foundation of the City University of New York, Centro de Estudios Puertorriqueños, Hunter College.

Reyes, L.O. (2006) The Aspira consent decree: A thirtieth-anniversary retrospective of bilingual education in New York City. *Harvard Educational Review* 76 (3), 369–400.

Sánchez, M.T. García, O. and Solorza, C. (2017) Reframing language allocation policy in dual language bilingual education. *Bilingual Research Journal*. DOI: 10.1080/15235882.2017.1405098

Santiago, I.S. (1986) Aspira v. Board of education revisited. *American Journal of Education* 95 (1), 149–199.

Veiga, C. (2018, January 17) New York City will add dual language options in pre-K to attract parents and encourage diversity. *Chalkbeat*. See https://www.chalkbeat.org/posts/ny/2018/01/17/new-york-city-will-add-dual-language-options-in-pre-k-to-attract-parents-and-encourage-diversity/

Velasco, P. (2014) The language and educational ideologies of Mixteco-Mexican Mothers. *Journal of Latinos and Education* 13 (2), 85–106. See http://doi.org/10.1080/15348431.2013.821061

Vygotsky, L.S. (1978) *Mind in Society. The Development of Higher Psychological Processes*. Cambridge, MA: Harvard University Press.

Wiley, T.G. (1996) *Literacy and Language Diversity in the United States*. Center for Applied Linguistics, Washington, DC.

4 Elgin, Illinois: An Entire District Goes Dual. The Journey of a District Committed to Culturally and Linguistically Responsive Instruction

Wilma Valero and Patricia Makishima

Introducing School District U-46

School District U-46 is the second largest school district in Illinois, with 40 elementary schools, eight middle schools and five high schools. A major strength of the district is the cultural and linguistic diversity of its student population of over 40,000 in grades preK-12. Its English language learners (ELL) program provides a continuum of services for more than 9000 emergent bilingual students in 41 schools. There are over 97 languages represented in the district, with the major incidence languages being Spanish, Polish, Gujarati, Urdu and Lao. ELL program resources include ELL teachers, instructional coaches, bilingual para-educators, bilingual home–school liaisons, an in-house translator, a community outreach coordinator, a bilingual parent educator and other instructional support staff who provide services to help ensure the success of all students and families. In addition, the ELL Department operates the centrally located Family Welcome Center, which offers a variety of services, including but not limited to providing guidance to new families related to services and agencies within the community. One of the primary functions of the Family Welcome Center is ensuring that new students with a non-English background are placed in an appropriate instructional program.

To serve all segments of the district's demographics, and in compliance with federal and state regulations, U-46 offers appropriate programs for its emergent bilingual population. Prior to 2011, the district offered Transitional Bilingual Education and a Transitional Program of Instruction (better known as an English as a Second Language Program). In 2011, a dual language program was added to the options. This chapter will describe the creation and implementation of dual language in District U-46.

Investigating the Feasibility of Dual Language in U-46

Dr. José M. Torres was named superintendent of U-46 in 2008. Recognizing that English learners' native language is an asset, that the district could capitalize on this valuable resource, and that programs using more than one language offer value to both English learners and native English speakers, Dr. Torres convened a dual language committee during his first year in U-46. This committee was charged with conducting a feasibility study for the future development of dual language programs in the district. The ELL Department welcomed this endeavor and adopted the philosophy of the California Association for Bilingual Education that 'No child should lose a language to learn another language.' The dual language committee was composed of the ELL director, the ELL coordinator, a dual language consultant, ELL teachers, general education teachers, elementary school principals, district administrators (e.g., human resources, assessment and finance directors, curriculum and instruction coordinators), a former Elgin Teacher Association president, parents, the Bilingual Parent Advisory Council president and a representative from the National Education Association. Having the perspective and experience of all of these stakeholders gave this committee a powerful and well-informed voice to carry out its task.

The committee conducted an extensive review of the following to inform their work:

- the district's student demographics;
- data on the academic achievement and English language development of the district's emergent bilingual students;
- school practices supporting the district's emergent bilingual students;
- instructional programs that work for emergent bilingual students;
- current research on developing bilingualism and biliteracy in students;
- information from dual language programs across the nation with demographics similar to those of U-46;
- different program models for dual language education based on the allocation of the two languages for instruction (50/50, 80/20, 90/10);
- federal and state legal frameworks related to culturally and linguistically responsive instruction for emergent bilingual students.

With the knowledge they gained of demographics, research and legal considerations, the committee members felt confident they could make a well-informed recommendation concerning the feasibility of establishing a dual language program in U-46. The committee's recommendation to the district's superintendent was to implement dual language education following the 80/20 design. Their recommendation was based on research showing the effectiveness of dual language education for English learners. The superintendent accepted the committee's recommendation.

Planning and Implementation of the New Program

Once the decision about the program design was made, the planning phase began with an in-depth analysis of the resources and infrastructure available to proceed with the committee's recommendation. This analysis identified areas of strength to build upon and areas of need to work on. The superintendent charged the ELL Department with the development of the Dual Language Project Charter, a document that would reflect the results of this analysis. Titled *Accelerating Academic Achievement of English Language Learner Students*, the project charter became a framework for the scope, sequence, objectives and participants' roles in the implementation of the dual language program. The project charter comprised nine guiding milestones.

(1) Timeline of Implementation
(2) Identification of the Demographics of All Schools with Transitional Bilingual Education (TBE) Spanish Programs
(3) Determination of Program Model for Each School and Entry /Selection Criteria Specific to Each Program Model
(4) Creation of Dual Language Committees
(5) Development of Communication Plan
(6) Development and Implementation of a Professional Development Plan
(7) Alignment of Curriculum and Definition of Programmatic Features Specific to Dual Language Program Model
(8) Assessment Framework in English and Spanish
(9) Instructional Resources in English and Spanish

The superintendent presented the U-46 Dual Language Project Charter to the U-46 Board of Education in September 2010.

Next came an intense cycle of designing procedures and support systems. As a result of multiple hours of intense dialog, an integrated strategic plan was developed to bring structure and consistency to the district-wide implementation as well as to meet the expectations identified in the project's milestones. As part of building a strong infrastructure, nationally recognized dual language experts from Dual Language Education of New Mexico joined the ELL Department in the district's collaborative work. The Dual Language Project Charter was the blueprint for the work to be done. The milestones, discussed below, were the pivotal elements to build the infrastructure where emergent bilingual students would be at the center of the instructional program.

Milestone 1: Timeline implementation

A timeline was created to show how the dual language program would be implemented in phases. With the support of the superintendent, a decision was made to start the program in four grade levels the first year (2011–2012): grades preK, kindergarten, 1 and 2. An additional grade would then be added each year through 2017–2018, at which time the program would include grades preK through 8. Figure 4.1 represents the 80:20 dual language implementation timeline as well as language allocation. For the school year 2018–2019, the dual language continuum includes the high school level; 9–12 grade level language allocation was developed for the graduation requirement coursework. Students' linguistic profile was taken into consideration during the process as shown in Figure 4.2.

80:20 Dual Language Implementation Timeline			
School Year	Grade	Language of Instruction Spanish	English
2011- 2012	Pre-K	80%	20%
	Kindergarten		
	1st Grade	70%	30%
	2nd Grade	60%	40%
2012- 2013	3rd Grade	50%	50%
2013-2014	4th Grade		
2014-2015	5th Grade		
2015-2016	6th Grade		
2016-2017	7th grade	1. Spanish Language Arts Class 2. Social Studies	Course requirements by the Illinois State Board of Education taught by Bilingual and/or ESL teachers according to licensure requirements for emergent bilingual students
2017-2018	8th grade	1. Spanish Language Arts Class 2. Social Studies	

Figure 4.1 Dual language implementation timeline

DUAL LANGUAGE & ESL HIGH SCHOOL PROGRAM MATRIX

SCHOOL YEAR	GRADE LEVEL	LANGUAGE ALLOCATION	COURSE OF STUDY 1 Full-Time ELs	COURSE OF STUDY 2 Reclassified/English-dominant & Part-Time ELs	COURSE OF STUDY 3 Transitional Program of Instruction (TPI-ESL)
2018 - 2019	9th	SPANISH	1. ALE I Honors 2. Biology/Biology Honors 3. Math/Math Honors AP Spanish Language Test	1. ALE I Honors 2. Biology/Biology Honors 3. Math/Math Honors AP Spanish Language Test	1. ESL 2. Math*/Math Honors*/Trans. Math 3. Biology*/Biology Honors*/Trans. Biology 4. Elective/Trans. Elective 5. Elective/Trans. Elective 6. PE
		ENGLISH	1. ESL 2. PE 3. Elective/Trans. Elective 4. Elective/Trans. Elective	1. ELA/FLA Honors/ESL (PT ELs) 2. PE 3. Elective/Trans. Elective 4. Elective/Trans. Elective	
2019 - 2020	10th	SPANISH	1. AP Spanish Language/ ALE II Honors 2. Math/Math Honors 3. US History/AP US History 4. Salud (Health)* AP Spanish Language Test	1. AP Spanish Language/ ALE II Honors 2. Math/Math Honors 3. US History/AP US History AP Spanish Language Test	1. ESL 2. Math*/Math Honors*/Trans. Math 3. US History*/AP US History*/Trans. US History 4. Chemistry*/Chemistry Honors*/Trans. Chemistry 5. Elective/Trans. Elective 6. Elective/AP Elective*/Trans. Elective 7. Health*/Trans. Health/PE
		ENGLISH	1. ESL 2. Trans. Chemistry/Trans. Chemistry Honors 3. PE 4. Elective /Trans. Elective	1. ELA/FLA Honors/ESL (PT ELs) 2. Chemistry*/Chemistry Honors*/Trans. Chemistry/Trans. Chemistry Honors 3. Health*/Trans. Health/PE 4. Elective/Trans. Elective	
2020 - 2021	11th	SPANISH	1. ALE II Honors/AP Spanish Literature 2. Elective/AP Elective 3. Civics and Economics/AP Macro Economics and US Government* AP Spanish Literature Test	1. ALE II Honors/AP Spanish Literature 2. Elective/AP Elective 3. Elective/AP Elective AP Spanish Literature Test	1. ESL 2. Civics and Economics*/AP Macro Economics and US Government*/Trans. Civics and Economics 3. Math*/Math Honors*/Math AP*/Trans. Math 4. PE
		ENGLISH	1. ESL 2. Trans. Elective 3. Trans. Elective 4. PE	1. ELA/AP Language & Composition/ESL 2. Civics and Economics*/AP Macro Economics and US Gov.*/Trans. Civics and Economics 3. Math/Math Honors/Math AP*/Trans. Math 4. PE	
2021 - 2022	12th	SPANISH	1. AP Spanish Literature/ALE – Dual Credit 1 2. Elective/AP Elective 3. Elective/AP Elective AP Spanish Literature Test	1. AP Spanish Literature/ALE – Dual Credit 1 2. Elective/AP Elective 3. Elective/AP Elective AP Spanish Literature Test	1. ESL 2. PE 3. Elective/AP Elective*/Trans. Elective 4. Elective/AP Elective*/Trans. Elective
		ENGLISH	1. ESL 2. PE 3. Elective/Trans. Elective	1. ELA/AP Literature & Comp./ESL (PT ELs) 2. PE 3. Elective/Trans. Elective	
		SPANISH/ENGLISH	1. Elective	1. Elective	

* Based on student English Language Proficiency (ELP) Level

Figure 4.2 Dual language & ESL high school program matrix

Milestone 2: Identification of the demographics in all schools with a transitional bilingual education Spanish program

Following Illinois State Board of Education regulations, all non-English-background students are screened for English proficiency using state-prescribed language screening instruments. Those identified as emergent bilinguals must be enrolled in a program that will meet both their language and academic needs (e.g., transitional bilingual, English as a second language, dual language). Because the specific dual language program model (one-way or two-way) to be implemented at each school in district U-46 would be determined by the balance of Spanish-background emergent bilinguals and English-dominant students, demographic data were collected from every elementary school that was serving Spanish-background students in a transitional bilingual education program.

Milestone 3: Determination of program model for each school and entry/selection criteria specific to each program model

Based on the demographic data collected and on research related to effective dual language education, schools, where one third to one-half of the interested students were English dominant, were deemed appropriate for a two-way dual language program. All students identified as Spanish background emergent bilinguals in those schools would be eligible to participate. English dominant students whose parents were interested in the 80:20 Two-Way DL Program would be able to participate at their home school where the Two-Way DL was offered as long as space was available. In schools with not enough interest of English-dominant students, a one-way dual language program would be implemented for Spanish background emergent bilinguals. In addition, Two-Way DL Satellite schools were established to provide access to this opportunity to English-dominant students whose home schools did not offer Two-Way DL program. It is important to mention that both one-way and two-way programs would be guided by the same rigorous and relevant language and content, standards-based instructional principles and would provide instruction according to the grade level language allocation.

Milestone 4: Creation of dual language committees

Committees were created to ensure representation of all stakeholders in the implementation of the dual language program:

- Dual Language Implementation Advisory Committee;
- U-46 Dual Language Committee;
- High School Dual Language Committee.

The role of the Dual Language Implementation Advisory Committee, appointed by the ELL department director, was to advise, provide guidance and offer possible alternatives and recommendations to the superintendent on matters that directly concerned the effective implementation and instructional practices of the dual language program. Committee members, who represented general education teachers, ESL and bilingual education teachers, principals, curriculum administrators, assessment specialists, special education staff and the communications department, were selected for their experience, leadership and expertise. The intention was to benefit from committee members' expertise and ensure that all stakeholders had a voice in the process.

The U-46 Dual Language Committee, also strategically appointed by the ELL department director, provided another venue for gathering input and communication that was inclusive of the learning community. This committee included parents, teachers and administrators from various instructional programs in the district and provided instrumental support and feedback regarding the implementation of the dual language program. The two committees brought together a wide range of ideas, expertise and interests that were representative of the district and the community.

The high school dual language planning committee included members who were integral in outlining the high expectations for the high school dual language instructional program. In identifying the committee members, staff with high school background and expertise worked together to determine the coursework.

Milestone 5: Development of communication plan

A communication plan was created to gather input from and share information with all stakeholders regarding the planning and implementation of the dual language program.

Early communication involved several bilingual community informational meetings at all bilingual schools and other central locations in the community. In addition, informational meetings were conducted for instructional staff across the district, including middle and high schools. The year before the program was implemented, more than 100 dual language informational meetings were conducted simultaneously in Spanish and English. Information was also provided electronically in both languages on the district's website. To address the diverse demographics of the district, multiple communication strategies were used, including brochures, flyers, press releases, newsletters, television and radio broadcasts, social media outlets and posters. Many of these were disseminated through community centers, county agencies, libraries, childcare centers, churches and so forth.

Milestone 6: Development and implementation of a differentiated professional development plan

A professional development action plan was developed in compliance with federal and state regulations that require annual in-service training for all personnel involved in the education of English Learners. During 2010–2011, the year prior to the implementation of the dual language program, all bilingual schools were invited to select a team of general education and bilingual teachers, instructional coaches and principals to participate in a 3-day retreat facilitated by Dual Language Education of New Mexico and the U-46 ELL Department. The primary goal of the retreat was to gather input from all stakeholders to inform the design of the professional development plan for the dual language program. Professional development sessions were designed to address the goals of standards-based teaching and learning, biliteracy development, sheltered content and language instruction, and assessment within the framework of second language, bilingualism and biliteracy development.

As we all well know, research confirms that the most important factor contributing to a student's success in school is the quality of teaching (Mizell, 2010). Taking this into consideration, the year before the dual language program was implemented, grade-level educators participated in an intensive 3-day professional development session. This session addressed the imperative need for each school to develop a dual language learning community encompassing the entire school that shared the

SCHOOL DISTRICT U-46				
80:20 DUAL LANGUAGE PROGRAM PROFESSIONAL DEVELOPMENT ACTION PLAN				
BILINGUALISM-BILITERACY –POSITIVE CROSS CULTURAL ATTITUDES				
WHEN	HOW LONG	PARTICIPANTS	PURPOSE/GOALS	WHAT
SY 2010-2011 The 1st year previous to the district-wide implementation	2 days	ALL 80:20 dual language schools teams: Principal 4 Bilingual Teachers, 2 General Education Teachers	The retreat of all schools implementing the 80:20 DL Program. The retreat served as a need assessment, identifying each school needs in order to develop a differentiated professional development action plan based on schools' profile.	What is Dual language? • Research • Legal Framework • Demographics • One way /Two-Way 80:20 DL Program Design Language Allocation Instructional Resources
SY 2010-2011 1 year previous to the implementation of the 80:20 DL Program in grades: pre-k, kindergarten., 1 and 2	3 days	All pre-k, kindergarten., 1st and 2nd grade bilingual teachers and principals that will be implementing the 80:20 DL program the following year	The beginning of a dual language grade-level professional community. To develop the foundational knowledge about the essential components of the teaching and learning process in a Pre-k, kindergarten., 1 and 2 grade dual language classroom	Foundations of Dual Language Pre-k, kindergarten., 1st and 2nd grade language allocation Bilingual and Biliteracy Development DL Curriculum Alignment Plan-CAP DL Pre-k, Kindergarten., 1st and 2nd Grade Daily Routine DL Learning Environment Shelter Language Instruction
SY 2010-2011 1 year previous to the implementation of the 80:20 DL Program in grades: pre-k, kindergarten., 1 and 2	2 days	All bilingual teachers in grades 3, 4, 5, and 6	Introduction to Dual Language *Dual Language 101 – ELL Department Staff and 2 ELL Teachers*	What is Dual language? • Research • Legal Framework • Demographics • One way /Two-Way Standards-based Instruction ESL Curriculum Alignment
SY 2011-2012	1 day	All elementary schools dual language principals	Dual Language Classroom Observations 101	Reflection on practice - The DL Classroom
SY 2011-2012 1 year previous to the implementation of the 80:20 DL Program in 3rd Grade	3 days	All 3rd grade bilingual	The beginning of a dual language grade level professional community. Designed to develop the foundational knowledge about the essential components of the teaching and learning process in a third grade dual language classroom.	DL 3rd Grade Language Allocation Bilingual and Biliteracy Development DL CAP DL 3rd Grade Daily Routine DL Learning Environment Shelter Language Instruction
SY 2011-2012 Implementation Year of the 80:20 DL Program in grades: pre-k, kindergarten., 1 and 2	2 days	All bilingual teachers in grades pre-k, kindergarten., 1 and 2	Reflecting on the first year of the DL implementation. To continue developing and strengthening the dual language practice as well as increasing teachers' expertise in standards-based instruction in two languages.	Follow-up Bilingual and Biliteracy Development The Bridge Language Proficiency Levels Strategies to Scaffold and Differentiate Instruction
SY 2011-2012 Implementation Year of the 80:20 DL Program in grades: Pre-k, kindergarten., 1 and 2	2 days	All bilingual teachers in grades 4, 5 and 6	Dual language principles, shelter language instruction, the development of biliteracy skills. Culturally and linguistically responsive instruction for ALL students.	
SY 2012-2013	1 day	All elementary schools dual language principals	What Administrators Need to Know about Spanish Literacy Instruction	To explore how Spanish literacy instruction differs from English literacy instruction Understand the biliteracy development and its instructional and programmatic implications How word study-phonics, phonemic awareness, and spelling, is taught in Spanish Review of formative assessment in Spanish
SY 2012-2013 1 year previous to the implementation of the 80:20 DL Program in 4th grade	3 days	All 4th grade bilingual	The beginning of a dual language grade level professional community. Designed to develop the foundational knowledge about the essential components of the teaching and learning process in a fourth grade dual language classroom	4th Grade Language Allocation Bilingual and Biliteracy Development DL Curriculum Alignment Plan-CAP DL 4th Grade Daily Routine DL Learning Environment
SY 2012-2013 Implementation year of the 80:20 DL Program in 3rd grade	2 days	All 3rd grade bilingual	Reflecting on the first year of the DL implementation. To continue developing and strengthening the dual language practice as well as increasing teachers' expertise in standards-based instruction in two languages	Follow-up Bilingual and Biliteracy Development The Bridge Language Proficiency Levels Strategies to Scaffold and Differentiate Instruction
SY 2012-2013 Implementation Year of the 80:20 DL Program in 3rd grade	2 days	All pre-k, kindergarten., 1,2, 5 and 6 grade bilingual	Dual language principles, shelter language instruction, the development of biliteracy skills. Culturally and linguistically responsive instruction for ALL students.	

Figure 4.3 Professional development plan

mission of the dual language program. It is important to note that the professional development plan was aligned with the district's preK-12 initiatives, resulting in a cohesive and consistent message about expected instructional practices and outcomes for the dual language program. Figure 4.3 represents professional development offered for dual language educators to develop the understanding and skills needed to address the teaching and learning process in two languages.

SCHOOL DISTRICT U-46				
80:20 DUAL LANGUAGE PROGRAM PROFESSIONAL DEVELOPMENT ACTION PLAN				
BILINGUALISM-BILITERACY –POSITIVE CROSS CULTURAL ATTITUDES				
WHEN	HOW LONG	PARTICIPANTS	PURPOSE/GOALS	WHAT
SY 2013-2014 1 year previous to the implementation of the 80:20 DL Program in 5th grade	3 days	All 5th grade bilingual and ESL teachers	The beginning of a dual language grade level professional community. Designed to develop the foundational knowledge about the essential components of the teaching and learning process in a fifth grade dual language classroom	5th grade language allocation Bilingual and Biliteracy Development DL Curriculum Alignment Plan-CAP DL 5th Grade Daily Routine DL Learning Environment
SY 2013-2014 Implementation year of the 80:20 DL Program in 4th grade	2 days	All 4th grade bilingual and ESL teachers	Reflecting on the first year of the DL implementation. To continue developing and strengthening the dual language practice as well as increasing teachers' expertise in standards-based instruction in two languages	Follow-up Bilingual and Biliteracy Development The Bridge Language Proficiency Levels
SY 2013-2014 Implementation year of the 80:20 DL Program in 4th grade	2 days	All pre-k, kindergarten., 1,2, 3, 6, 7 and 8 grade bilingual and ESL teachers (3-8)	Dual language principles, shelter language instruction, the development of biliteracy skills. Culturally and linguistically responsive instruction for ALL students.	Strategies to Scaffold and Differentiate Instruction
SY 2014-2015 1 year previous to the implementation of the 80:20 DL Program in 6th grade	3 days	All 6th grade bilingual and ESL teachers	The beginning of a dual language grade level professional community. Designed to develop the foundational knowledge about the essential components of the teaching and learning process in a sixth grade dual language classroom	6th grade language allocation Bilingual and Biliteracy Development DL Curriculum Alignment Plan-CAP DL 6th Grade Daily Routine DL Learning Environment
SY 2014-2015 Implementation year of the 80:20 DL Program in 5th grade	2 days	All 5th grade bilingual and ESL teachers	Reflecting on the first year of the DL implementation. To continue developing and strengthening the dual language practice as well as increasing teachers' expertise in standards-based instruction in two languages	Follow-up Bilingual and Biliteracy Development The Bridge Language Proficiency Levels Strategies to Scaffold and Differentiate Instruction
SY 2014-2015 Implementation year of the 80:20 DL Program in 5th grade	2 days	All pre-k, kindergarten., 1,2,3,4,5,7 and 8 grade bilingual and ESL teachers in grades 3, 4, 5, 6, 7, and 8	Dual language principles, shelter language instruction, the development of biliteracy skills. Culturally and linguistically responsive instruction for ALL students.	Follow-up Bilingual and Biliteracy Development The Bridge Language Proficiency Levels Strategies to Scaffold and Differentiate Instruction
SY 2015-2016 1 year previous to the implementation of the 80:20 DL Program in 7th Grade	3 days	All 7th and 8th grade bilingual and ESL teachers	The beginning of a dual language grade level professional community. Designed to continue developing the foundational knowledge about the essential components of the teaching and learning process in a 7th grade dual language classroom	7th grade language allocation Bilingual and Biliteracy Development DL Curriculum Alignment Plan-CAP DL Learning Environment Spanish Language Arts
SY 2015-2016 Implementation year of the 80:20 DL Program in 5th grade	2 days	All 6th grade bilingual and ESL teachers	Reflecting on the first year of the DL implementation. To continue developing and strengthening the dual language practice as well as increasing teachers' expertise in standards-based instruction in two languages	Follow-up Bilingual and Biliteracy Development The Bridge Language Proficiency Levels Strategies to Scaffold and Differentiate Instruction
SY 2015-2016 Implementation Year of the 80:20 DL Program in 5th grade	2 days	All pre-k, kindergarten., 1,2, 3, 4 and 5 grade bilingual and ESL teachers in grades 3, 4, and -5)	Dual language principles, shelter language instruction, the development of biliteracy skills. Culturally and linguistically responsive instruction for ALL students.	
SY 2016-2017 Implementation year for 7th Grade 1 year previous to the implementation of the 80:20 DL Program in 8th Grade	3 days	All 7th and 8th grade bilingual	The beginning of a dual language middle school professional community. Designed to continue developing the foundational knowledge about the essential components of standards-based teaching and learning process in two languages at the middle school level.	4 Days - ALE Artes del Lenguaje en Español- Spanish Language Arts for Spanish Language Arts teachers Language Block 7 & 8th Grade Language Allocation Bilingual and Biliteracy Development DL Curriculum Alignment Plan-CAP DL Learning Environment
SY 2016-2017 Implementation year of the 80:20 DL Program in 7th grade	2 days	All pre-k, kindergarten., 1,2, 3, 4 and 5, 5, and 6 grades bilingual and ESL teachers in grades (3, 4, 5 and -6)	Instructional strategies and approaches that reflect the newest research and best practices in the field of DL education and biliteracy development for teaching Spanish and ESL.	Follow-up Bilingual and Biliteracy Development The Bridge Language Proficiency Levels Strategies to Scaffold and Differentiate Instruction
SY 2017-2018 1 year previous to the implementation of the 80:20 DL Program in 9th Grade	3 days	All 9-12 grades bilingual and ESL teachers	The beginning of a dual language high school professional community. Designed to continue developing the foundational knowledge about the essential components of standards-based teaching and learning process in two languages at the high school level.	4 Days - ALE Artes del Lenguaje en Español Spanish Language Arts for Spanish Language Arts teachers 9th-grade language allocation Bilingual and Biliteracy Development DL Curriculum Alignment Plan-CAP DL Learning Environment
SY 2017-2018 Implementation year of the 80:20 DL Program in 8th grade	2 days	All kindergarten., 1,2, 3, 4 and 5, 5, and 6 grades bilingual and ESL teachers in grades (3, 4, 5 and -6)	Instructional strategies and approaches that reflect Spanish language development standards in the field of DL education and biliteracy development for teaching.	Bilingual and Biliteracy Development Spanish Language Proficiency Levels Spanish standards-based language instruction

Figure 4.3 (*Continued*)

The professional development provided a learning dynamic cycle where participants were able to reflect, revisit and review instructional practices intended to engage emergent bilingual and English dominant students within a rigorous dual-language curriculum to increase student success. It also addressed the profile of new teachers to the district that hadn't been exposed to this instructional program. Summer and beginning of the year sessions were provided to newly hired and team teaching dual language teachers.

To ensure successful implementation of the dual language program at all dual language schools, ongoing support was provided to teachers and principals to help them implement the strategies, activities and best practices recommended at the professional development sessions. Professional development was key to a quality, consistent program implementation. An annual dual language academy was created to recognize and validate the vast knowledge of dual language teachers in the district and to recognize the partner language as an asset within both social and professional contexts. This academy served as another professional development venue conducted in the partner language, by dual language teachers for dual language teachers. To demonstrate that the value of the partner language extends beyond teaching and learning in the classroom, dual language teachers ensured that the partner language was validated throughout the school, the district and the community. Equal status of the languages of instruction supports the development of high academic proficiency in two languages (Thomas & Collier, 2012).

Dual language administrators also received specific professional development sessions having as a focus the Teacher Appraisal Plan (TAP) as well as observation practices that develop and support the work of bilingualism and biliteracy in the dual language classroom. The TAP is designed to meet the needs of certified staff at different points in one's career journey. One of the TAP purposes is to support and focus professional growth and development in a quest for distinguished levels of performance. It also includes as one of its goals to unify certified staff members and administration in its pursuit to maximize student learning ('School District U-46 Teacher Appraisal Plan', 2015). Professional development initiatives in other U-46 departments were also inclusive and designed for dual language teachers, practitioners and instructional support staff.

Milestone 7: Alignment of curriculum and definition of programmatic features specific to dual language program model

A critical piece of planning for dual language implementation was the creation of the Dual Language Curriculum Alignment Plan. This living document is aligned with the district's rigorous curriculum in the areas of biliteracy, science, social studies, mathematics, Spanish language arts and English language arts/English as a second language. Developed by the ELL Department in close collaboration with DLENM this plan describes the following:

- alignment of the dual language curriculum with the district's language and academic standards. Standards-based instruction established the rigor and relevance of the dual language instructional program;

- grade-level allocation of the languages of instruction for biliteracy development and content areas;
- district-provided and teacher-created instructional resources in English and Spanish that are authentic and reflect students' diverse backgrounds to ensure culturally and linguistically responsive instruction.

For the secondary level, in addition to a comprehensive CAP and matrix, rigorous Spanish Language Arts (ALE) curricula have been developed. These curricula come alive through an array of authentic resources from different Spanish speaking countries, including Latin America, Spain and the United States. These resources are relevant to the cultural and linguistic diversity of the students served in the U-46 community, elevating the status of the minority language. Additional procedures were strategically developed to facilitate the implementation across the district of culturally and linguistically responsive instructional practices. These included sample dual language program schedules reflecting the curriculum alignment plan and identifying essential practices within the daily classroom routine. All materials were created to be living documents that would be continually revisited and revised to reflect evolving curricular changes, knowledge, experience, practices and circumstances from the field.

Milestone 8: Assessment in English and Spanish

In response to the district's commitment to the implementation of the dual language program and consistent with standards-based instruction, a fair assessment framework was created in order to assess students' development of bilingualism and biliteracy. The district's assessment framework includes the Differentiated Literacy Battery, which was developed using Escamilla's 'biliteracy zone' (Escamilla *et al.*, 2007). At the elementary school level, a detailed biliteracy assessment framework was developed to measure students' literacy in both languages from year to year. The language of instruction used in each content area was taken into consideration in the design and administration of formative and summative assessments across the district. Teachers were trained in the administration of these assessments to ensure consistent administration, confidentiality, interrater reliability and appropriate use of the data to guide effective instruction.

Secondary level assessments continue with the district goal that assessment practices must reflect the languages of instruction.

The preK-12 district assessment framework is a live document to ensure that federal and state requirements are aligned with the local assessment practices. It is standard procedure for those involved to continuously revisit, review and revise these practices to ensure that collected language and academic data guides the teaching and learning process in two languages, while validating classroom instructional time.

Milestone 9: Instructional resources in English and Spanish

In keeping with a commitment to fiscal responsibility in the creation of the dual language program, U-46 conducted an inventory of available and needed instructional resources aligned with the grade-level thematic units. Needed resources were then either created or acquired from an external source. Thematic units were designed using the Understanding by Design framework (Wiggins & McTighe, 2011), which focuses on teaching for understanding. In addition, vertical and horizontal curriculum mapping was developed for grades K–6. Again, these were designed as living documents to be revisited and revised over time. Both documents were revisited at the end of the initial school year to ensure that recommendations from dual language teachers were valued and reflected in these documents.

Books selected for classroom libraries were chosen for their ability to engage students, promote critical thinking, present an array of ideas and provide exposure to an authentic variety of genres within the world of literature. These collections are designed to provide whole group and independent reading opportunities as well as access to resources that are conducive to deep investigation and research. These classroom libraries are intended to complement, enrich and support standards-based instruction district-wide and to promote and encourage biliteracy.

In addition, resources for the secondary level that address the two languages of instruction for Language Arts and content areas were selected.

Maintaining and Expanding the Program

During the whole implementation process, stakeholders had the opportunity to analyze and discuss research and data and to review dual language programs whose student demographics were similar to those of U-46. This active involvement resulted in a culture of trust in which stakeholders claimed ownership of the program and became well-informed advocates. These stakeholders represented the linguistic and cultural diversity of the district and the community and included parents, general education teachers, ESL teachers, school administrators and community leaders. This inclusive process allowed ongoing communication between the district and the community. All involved believed in the importance of using students' native language and culture as highly valued assets within the instructional program.

This culture of trust and shared ownership provided the foundation for what was to follow. Achievement of the original milestones was just the first leg of U-46's journey. Much work was needed to maintain the program, help it grow and support its future seamless expansion into high school. An essential component of these ongoing efforts was the establishment of school support visits.

Support visits are designed to maintain the rigor and high expectations of the dual language program across the district. They involve school visits from the assistant superintendent for elementary schools and the ELL director to observe dual language programs in action, particularly through the lens of equity and social justice. These visits provide an opportunity for in-depth conversations with administrators and teachers. A dual language protocol was developed to guide these conversations. The protocol includes indicators for and academic expectations in a dual language school. It also includes indicators for a welcoming and inclusive learning environment that promotes multiculturalism and biliteracy and for use of the partner language beyond the classroom – for example, on the playground, in the cafeteria, and in the front office. The assistant superintendent and the ELL director conduct school visits using the protocol as the basis for a collaborative dialog with principals. Input collected from these visits has been used to develop dual language support modules, such as the Dual Language Learning Environment support module and the presentation, *Understanding the ELL Standards-Based Thematic Units*. The DL learning environment module provides grade level guidance to teachers and administrators related to the linguistic spaces within the established language allocation, English, Spanish and the bridge. It includes examples of a student-centered relevant environment that reflects the languages and cultures of the students and the community represented in the district. It is intended to develop a deeper understanding of developmentally appropriate multicultural learning environment that supports the rigor of teaching and learning in two languages. On the other hand, a power point was developed explaining and giving examples of the major components of Understanding by Design framework used in the ELL Thematic Units.

Additional instructional approaches have been implemented to enhance and support the expansion of the dual language program. For example, team teaching has been promoted among all eligible interested teachers. Team teaching allows monolingual English teachers who have an ESL endorsement to partner with a bilingual teacher. Programs that use this teacher-pairing strategy frequently report fewer personnel changes and greater instructional effectiveness. Team teaching is a pragmatic way of utilizing the talents of participating teachers and increasing the cognitive level of instruction in both languages (Thomas & Collier, 2012).

Although team teaching was not intended as a recruitment approach, it helped to support the expansion of dual language into grades 3–6 and middle school. The ELL Department coordinated meetings with dual language principals and interested teachers to ensure that the daily schedule and instructional practices would meet with fidelity the language of instruction and program goals. Professional development was designed to address the needs of teachers participating in this professional partnership.

In 2014, showing their long-term commitment to the program, the U-46 Board of Education approved a preK through grade 12 dual language policy. This policy was instrumental in the expansion of the program into the secondary level. This created an opportunity to develop a standards-based curriculum for Spanish language Arts that is aligned with the ESL and the English Language Arts curriculum. The Spanish language arts curriculum reflects the richness of Latin American literature and the relevance of the Spanish language. In addition, it prepares students to obtain the *Illinois State Seal of Biliteracy* as well as the *Diploma de Español como Lengua Extranjera* (Diploma of Spanish as a Foreign Language) sponsored by the Consulate of Spain. Once the curriculum was developed, an exhaustive evaluation of resources was undertaken. The resource selection process entailed an in-depth review of an array of diverse fiction and nonfiction resources representing different Spanish-speaking countries. The rich dialogue during this review process served as a tool to revisit the dual language teaching and learning practices in the context of relevant resources in order to ensure students' engagement in learning. All these initiatives opened the doors of opportunities to dual language students, who more than ever, have immediate access to Honors and AP courses in both English and Spanish.

Parent and community involvement has also been vital to the implementation and continuation of the dual language program. In particular, they have been instrumental in recruiting English-dominant students to achieve the required balance of native Spanish and English speakers for the two-way dual language program. The ELL Department worked hard to develop a support system that would allow all parents to feel comfortable taking an active role in their children's bilingual, biliteracy development – welcoming, enhancing and promoting the development of two languages and cultures in their homes. The expected outcome was that their children would become successful bilingual, biliterate students and citizens of the world—true ambassadors of unity—respecting, enriching and appreciating cultural diversity.

Conclusion

This chapter has described the journey of a district committed to equity and social justice through the implementation of an instructional program that is culturally and linguistically responsive to its diverse student population. A strong culture of collaboration was the most instrumental factor in the successful preK-12 implementation of the dual language program. Throughout this amazing journey, the ELL Department recognized and valued the outstanding work of ALL stakeholders. Teachers, para-educators, home–school liaisons, parents, community leaders, principals, administrators, support staff, assistant superintendents, superintendent and the district CEO were all committed to the success of the dual language program. Thanks to their efforts, the first year of implementation was a successful one, with a total of 4194 students and 182 teachers in grades preK–2 across 29 schools. Every year since then has brought continued success. As the 2017–2018 school year was coming to an end, the number of participating students had increased to 10,064 and the number of teachers to 375, spanning grades preK–8 across 37 schools. The planning and preparation for a successful high school implementation have been done in collaboration with all stakeholders. The strategic planning was done having in mind a coherent consistent system for equitable access to emergent bilingual students to the only program that closes the achievement and opportunity gap.

As a committed journey for equity and social justice continues, U-46 will persist with the ongoing process of revisiting and reflecting on its comprehensive, research-based effective practices that close the opportunity gap. The district continues to ensure that the dual language program is taken into consideration since the inception of all district initiatives. Nationwide, U-46 is leading the way recognizing that the teaching and learning process must empower the voices and cultures of our diverse community. The mission of the district is to be a great place for all students to learn, all teachers to teach and all employees to work. Many languages, one message: Academic success for all. And in U-46, ALL means ALL. The results of the exemplary work done by all stakeholders in U-46 is clearly reflected in the well-known quote attributed to Margaret Mead: *Never doubt that a small group of thoughtful, committed citizens can change the world; indeed, it's the only thing that ever has.*

References

Elgin Teacher Association and U-46 (2015) School District U-46 Teacher Appraisal Plan. See http://theeta.org/wp-content/uploads/2010/09/TAP-2015.07.29.pdf

Escamilla, K., Hopewell, S., Geisler, D. and Ruiz, O. (2007, April) *Transitions to Biliteracy: Beyond Spanish and English.* Paper presented at the annual meeting of the American Educational Research Association, Chicago, IL. See http://www.colorado.edu/education/sites/default/files/attached-files/BeyondSpan%2BEngAERA07.pdf

Joint National Committee for Languages–National Council for Languages and International Studies (n.d.) *Dual Language Education Can Close Achievement Gap.* Washington, DC: Author. See http://www.thomasandcollier.com/assets/jncl-nclis-white-paper-on-dual-language-education.pdf

Mizell, H. (2010) *Why Professional Development Matters.* Oxford, OH: Learning Forward.

Thomas, W. and Collier, V. (2012) *Dual Language Education for a Transformed World.* Albuquerque, NM: Fuente Press.

Wiggins, G. and McTighe, J. (2011) *The Understanding by Design Guide to Creating High-quality Units.* Alexandria, VA: ASCD.

Part 2

Implementing Dual Language: Programmatic Issues

5 Implications of Research for Dual Language at the Early Childhood Level

Kathryn Lindholm-Leary

Dual language education has grown substantially over the past 30 years, though there is still little research on the implications for early childhood, ages 3–5. While there is a growing movement of parents who see the value in having their young children develop bilingual and biliteracy skills, more consideration of the best models and approaches for dual language development at early childhood levels is needed. Are standard dual language models that are used for K-5 appropriate at early childhood levels? Should student background factors impact the models that are used with young children? This chapter considers these issues in examining the implications of research for dual language at the early childhood level.

Child Background Factors that Impact Developmental and Schooling Outcomes

Children who grow up learning two languages concurrently are called 'simultaneous bilinguals' in the research literature. We know from research on these children that, given sufficient exposure in both languages, their language development in both languages is similar to that of monolinguals in that they typically follow the same stages in their acquisition of syntactic rules and structures as monolingual children do in each language (e.g., Baker, 2011; Gathercole, 2002; Lindholm, 1980, 1987; Paradis *et al.*, 2011). These children may be dominant in English, dominant in their primary language, or more balanced bilinguals in early childhood. For young children who are more balanced bilinguals, their high levels of bilingualism may be associated with enhanced social development as well (National Academy of Sciences, 2017).

Children who have acquired one language before school age and acquire an additional language in school are usually called *second-language learners* or *successive bilinguals* in the research literature (e.g., Baker, 2011). They are often referred to as *bilinguals* even though they may have minimal competence in their second language. These children include English language learners and may also involve native English speakers (NES) learning a second language.

According to the National Center for Educational Statistics, 11.7 million (or 22%) school-aged children spoke a language other than English at home (The Annie E. Casey Foundation, 2015); though it is not known how many preschoolers speak a language other than English at home, we can likely estimate that somewhere between a quarter and a fifth of preschoolers do so.

These children are typically referred to as language minority children, or dual language learners (DLL) in the preschool literature, and many of these children may be bilingual and proficient in English when they enter school. In 2007, about 26% of children enrolled in Head Start were DLL (U.S. Department of Education, 2015).

Preschoolers may differ in some other important ways that can impact decisions about language education models for these children; these issues may include socio-economic status or parent education and resulting potential exposure to academic language and literacy experiences in the home. Research shows that children from homes in which English is not spoken, or from economically disadvantaged and/or black or Hispanic families, and parents with low formal education achieve at lower levels on tests of academic achievement, though the most significant at-risk factors are low socioeconomic status – both low income and low maternal education (Halle *et al.*, 2009). These Socioeconomic Status (SES) differences can impact the kinds of schools that children attend, the kinds of educational and other experiences in which the children participate and the levels of language and literacy enrichment that students receive at home. According to U.S. Census Bureau statistics, Hispanic children are the largest group of children who are more likely to speak English with difficulty (2.1 million), and children who are poor are more likely to speak English with difficulty than non-poor children.

Furthermore, children enter school (preschool and/or kindergarten) with varying levels of English language proficiency (Hammer *et al.*, 2014) and that is true for NES children as well. In one recent study (California Department of Education, 2011) that examined the English listening, speaking, reading and writing proficiency of DLLs compared to NES, over half of DLLs start kindergarten at level 1 (Beginning) and 83% at levels 1–2 compared to NES, of whom 10% are at level 1 and 39% are at levels 1–2 in listening; only 1% of DLL and 23% of NES are at levels 4–5, defined as proficient. Speaking scores are similar for DLLs but much higher for NES. In reading and writing, about 85% of DLL and 60% of NES are at levels 1–2. These findings are important for two reasons. First, not all NES have full proficiency even in listening and speaking, and second, DLLs are far behind their NES peers in kindergarten and even more so in preschool.

These differences in English proficiency at school entry are highly problematic since research suggests that the language abilities of students in kindergarten are predictive of their academic achievement trajectories through at least fifth grade (Collins *et al.*, 2014; Halle *et al.*, 2012; Han, 2012). However, for young DLL students who speak Spanish in the home, Spanish language proficiency predicts the rate of English language growth; thus, students with low Spanish proficiency show slower growth than students with average or high Spanish proficiency (Jackson *et al.*, 2014; Lindholm-Leary, 2014). Yet, research shows that many DLLs enter preschool and kindergarten with low levels of proficiency in their primary language (Espinosa, 2014; Lindholm-Leary, 2014; Paez *et al.*, 2007). These findings have important implications for discussions of appropriate dual language models, especially for young at-risk second language learners.

Research and Dual Language Program Options

The National Association for the Education of Young Children (NAEYC, 2009) includes in its position statements some recommendations for working with young children who are linguistically diverse:

- *'Encourage home language and literacy development, knowing that this contributes to children's ability to acquire English language proficiency*: Research confirms that bilingualism is an asset and an educational achievement. When children become proficient and literate in their home language, they transfer those skills to a second language.'
- *'Help develop essential concepts in the children's first language and within cultural contexts that they understand*: Although some children can seem superficially fluent in their second language, most children find it easier to learn new, complex concepts in a familiar language and cultural framework. Once established, these concepts readily transfer into a second language and contribute to later academic mastery.'

In addition, Head Start clearly recognizes the value of promoting primary language development. In their Planned Language Approach (PLA), they state that among the key components of the PLA are (1) 'Home language support as a foundation for developing English language skills', and (2) 'Strategies to support DLLs to thrive in their home language(s) and English' (Head Start, 2015).

These position statements would suggest that there is some recognition of the value of bilingualism at the federal level. However, there is no overall statement about the value of bilingualism, or the importance of learning a second language for native English-speaking preschoolers. Rather, the goal is to promote English language proficiency, possibly through building foundational support in the primary language.

This overarching goal for English language development is evidenced by the services provided to DLL students at the elementary level. In one of the few nationwide studies on services provided to DLL students (Zehler *et al.*, 2003), results indicated that overall, 12% of students had English mainstream instruction with *no* DLL services; 24% received *some* service that was all in English; 8% *some* service that had some native language support (2–24% of instructional time); 3% *some* service that provided native language instruction for at least 25% of the instructional time; 23% received *extensive* service that was all in English; 12% received *extensive* service that had some native language support (2–24% of instructional time); and 17% received *extensive* service that provided native language instruction for at least 25% of the instructional time. In the ten years since that study, there has been a shift away from extensive DLL services and toward mainstream instruction and a shift toward more instruction in English (Goldenberg, 2008). However, while Spanish-speaking DLLs are more likely to be provided with instruction through their L1, there are very few dual language programs that provide instruction through the L1 for other language groups, which means that most of these students receive English-only programs (Asian American Legal Defense and Education Fund, 2008).

Thus, the major language education program type is still *English mainstream*, which provides instruction only in English to both language minority and language majority students with the purpose of promoting English language development. As noted previously, in some schools, there may be additional English language instruction through English as a Second Language classes or tutoring for the language minority students.

Most programs that use English and another language for instruction are referred to as dual language programs. The major types of dual language programs include:

- *Developmental bilingual education* – this is an enrichment form of dual language education that uses the primary language for instruction. The students in these programs are language minority students who speak the same primary language. These programs often vary in terms of the amount of instruction offered in the primary language vs English.
- *One-way immersion education* – enrichment forms of education specifically designed for native English speakers (NES); instruction is provided through a second language and English, with variations ranging from 50% to 100% in the second language at the early grade levels.
- *Two-way immersion education* – these programs integrate NES students and language minority students from a common native language background (e.g., Spanish, Mandarin) in the same classroom for instruction through both languages; these programs also vary in terms of the amount of instruction provided in the second language, typically from 50% to 90% at the primary grade levels.

Thus, while many educational organizations and educators recognize the value of at least some primary language instruction in preschool, there is considerable pressure to promote English proficiency over primary language proficiency, with some states developing English language arts standards, but no accountability or professional development for teachers instructing in the primary language. The accountability for English language development and lack of professional development in other languages means that many language minority or bilingual preschoolers experience English-only instructional approaches.

Yet, research clearly indicates that a strong first language can serve as an important foundation for the second language and can lead to stronger achievement and second language development at the preschool (Barnett *et al.*, 2007; Espinosa, 2007, 2014; Lindholm-Leary, 2014; Lopez & Greenfield, 2004) and elementary levels (Genesee *et al.*, 2006; Goldenberg, 2008; Lindholm-Leary & Genesee, 2010; Lindholm-Leary & Hernández, 2011; Lindholm-Leary & Howard, 2008). Such research would suggest the importance of primary language or bilingual instruction in preschool, as acknowledged in the NAEYC and Head Start position statements.

Lindholm-Leary and her colleagues (Lindholm-Leary & Borsato, 2006; Lindholm-Leary & Genesee, 2010), in large-scale reviews of the research literature on English Language Learners, also point out that research and evaluation studies conducted in the early years of a program (grades K-3) typically revealed that students in bilingual education scored below grade level (and sometimes very low) and performed either lower than or equivalent to their comparison group peers. In contrast, almost all evaluations conducted at the end of elementary school and in middle and high school showed that the educational outcomes of bilingually educated students were at least comparable to, and usually higher than, their comparison peers. These findings would suggest that it might be difficult to detect any advantages of bilingual education at early grade levels. Yet, there are a few studies that show differences favoring preschool DLLs educated in bilingual as opposed to English-only settings (Barnett *et al.*, 2007; Espinosa, 2007, 2014; Lindholm-Leary, 2014).

In one of the few studies of preschool two-way programs, Barnett *et al.*'s (2007) study comparing DLLs in 50:50 two-way immersion preschool programs vs English-only programs indicated that the DLL students demonstrated significant and larger gains in Spanish vocabulary and phonological awareness in English and Spanish compared to their peers in English-only instruction, though literacy skill results did not favor one instructional language over the other.

Similarly, in comparing students who received bilingual vs English-only programs in PreK-2, Lindholm-Leary (2014) reported two important findings. First, English language development was not negatively impacted by bilingual instruction; that is, children who were instructed bilingually across PreK-1 grade levels did not differ significantly in their English language development from children who received English during preschool or children who received English during kindergarten and first grade. Further, students who spent all three years in bilingual instruction made more growth across the grades than their peers who were instructed in English during preschool followed by bilingual in grades K-1. These results suggest for English language development that there is no disadvantage to being instructed bilingually and no significant advantage in English proficiency to being instructed through English. A second important finding was that among children who received bilingual instruction in preschool, those who were Mostly Proficient in Spanish scored significantly higher in English language development than children who were Mostly Limited in Spanish.

Though the topic of language loss or attrition has not received much investigative attention, researchers have consistently reported the loss and/or attrition of the primary language among potentially bilingual children who are instructed only or largely through English (Espinosa, 2007, 2013, 2014; Hammer et al., 2014; Jackson et al., 2014; Lindholm-Leary, 2014; Mancilla-Martinez & Lesaux, 2011). These results hold for young children in preschool through early elementary school, for Spanish and non-Spanish (e.g., Cantonese) speakers, and for oral and literate proficiencies. Furthermore, some researchers have even reported that some students who began as dominant or monolingual Spanish speakers suffered so much language loss that they were considered not proficient in their L1 (Lindholm-Leary, 2014; Mancilla-Martinez & Lesaux, 2011). As Mancilla-Martinez and Lesaux (2011) noted, 'at age 11, Spanish oral language skills had not reached the equivalent of a 4½-year-old monolingual speaker' (2011: 1555).

Numerous studies of NES in immersion programs in Canada and the U.S. demonstrate that NES students in immersion (both one-way and two-way) programs develop proficiency in the second language and they demonstrate the same competence in English as their NES peers in English mainstream programs, though they may score significantly lower than their NES peers in the primary grades. Further, these results hold whether the second language is Spanish or French, or typologically different such as Japanese or Chinese (e.g., Genesee & Lindholm-Leary, 2013; Lindholm-Leary & Genesee, 2014; Lindholm-Leary & Howard, 2008).

Furthermore, research on at-risk students also shows that NES in immersion and DLLs in two-way or Developmental Bilingual Education (DBE) programs demonstrate similar levels of achievement compared to their at-risk peers in English mainstream programs (Paradis et al., 2011), regardless of whether research defines at-risk in terms of special education, economic disadvantage, low levels of academic ability, or ethnic group membership (Lindholm-Leary & Howard, 2008; Paradis et al., 2011).

Issues and Challenges for Young Children in Dual Language Programs

The research is very clear that there are distinct bilingualism and achievement advantages for school-aged children, both NES and DLL, who participate in a dual language program. Though there is little specific dual language research with preschool-aged populations, there is some research at the preschool level, which is consistent with early elementary education findings for both NES and DLL students. Thus, this preschool and early elementary education research base is used to make the following recommendations regarding programmatic, instructional, language diversity and family involvement issues and challenges. Because the research on DLLs is largely focused on economically disadvantaged Spanish-speaking children, the issues and challenges presented below are more specific to these DLL children, though they may also be relevant to other DLLs with similar student characteristics (e.g., economically disadvantaged) as well.

Programmatic issues and challenges

DLLs

Collectively, the results presented previously indicate that DLLs, particularly low-income DLLs, come to school with poorly developed academic language skills in their primary language and English; they need considerable instruction through their primary language to build a strong primary language base, which will promote English language development. But research also shows that they need English language development so that they begin kindergarten with some English language proficiency. So, which program is best? Programmatically, both DBE and two-way dual language programs could be appropriate at the preschool level for DLLs, as both are additive bilingual models that could promote both L1 and L2-English language development. However, DBE programs with only DLL students may be advantageous over two-way programs in that DBE programs can target the specific English oral language development and Spanish preliteracy needs of young DLLs. Two-way programs may be beneficial in that DLLs will have access to NES models. However, with two-way programs, the needs of the DLL children must be clearly served so that they can develop a strong foundation in Spanish and appropriate academic oral language proficiency in English. If the second language development needs of NES students weaken the Spanish for DLLs, then the DLLs may not develop a sufficiently strong academic language and literacy base in their primary language.

There is no guidance as to how much of each language should be provided for young DLLs in either program. However, given the strong need for these children to maintain or further develop academic Spanish, a minimum of 50% of instruction through Spanish would be required.

Similarly, given the need to develop English oral language, the amount of English should be at least 20% so that students have sufficient exposure to some minimal English language development. Thus, programs of 50:50 or 80:20 would likely be effective for DLLs. In considering the amount of instruction in English, remember that research with preschoolers shows that a greater amount of instruction through English does not necessarily result in higher proficiency in English (Lindholm-Leary, 2014).

NES

Though there is little research on NES students who are enrolled in dual language programs as preschoolers, research on children who are English proficient, though language minority, demonstrates that these students show similar or higher growth in English language development compared to their peers in English-only instruction (Barnett et al., 2007). While normally developing middle class NES children may benefit from an immersion approach in preschool, there are some considerations that should be addressed for potentially at-risk NES children. This is not because immersion is not an appropriate program for such children per se, but we need to remember that NES preschoolers, like DLLs, are still in the early stages of learning their first language. As mentioned previously, research shows that many of these low-income NES children, like DLLs, come to school with poorly developed academic skills in their primary language. Thus, any language education program for preschool NES children *from low SES backgrounds* needs to *develop a strong English-L1 language and literacy foundation*. This means that a one-way program should not be a full immersion with 90–100% of the second language. Similarly, a two-way program that includes DLLs with no or little English proficiency needs to consider the English language development needs of the NES students as well. A beginning-level ESL program for DLLs will not provide the academic vocabulary and preliteracy skills and experiences that the at-risk NES student needs. That is not to say that these students should not participate in one- or two-way programs, since research clearly shows that there is an advantage for these students to learn a second language and they can develop bilingualism through such an experience; rather, the language development of their primary language needs to be carefully considered.

Further, though Barnett *et al*.'s (2007) study included alternating weeks of Spanish and English, I would strongly recommend using both languages every day for two reasons. First, children need to practice each language every day; short-term memory will disintegrate quickly, and there must be repetition and practice to move information into long-term memory. If students are alternating language by day or week, the lack of practice may lead to less long-term memory storage of the second language or even new concepts presented in the primary language. Second, young children should experience an additive bilingual environment in which they can feel safe in their primary language for at least some part of each instructional day. If they spend a full week in the second language, young children may not perceive an additive bilingual environment but a subtractive bilingual environment, which may hasten primary language loss and poorly developed English. Thus, unless children are bilingual, some may lose out on instruction in the L2 while they wait for the week in which their primary language is used and in which they feel more comfortable.

Instructional issues and challenges

While the program model may be designed effectively to meet the needs of preschool NES and DLL students, attention should also be given to the instructional strategies and approaches that may be most effective with these students. As various reviews of research (e.g., Espinosa, 2014; Genesee et al., 2006; Goldenberg et al., 2013; Howard et al., 2007) have indicated, there are a set of instructional practices and approaches that are more effective with second language learners, though these are not as well defined at the preschool level for dual language programs. In Genesee's (in press) examination of early childhood education issues for DLLs, he has clearly articulated many instructional modifications. Some of these include:

- Intentional focus on language teaching, and with an emphasis on oral language necessary for cognitive/academic purposes.
- Use of effective strategies to make comprehension more effective, including modeling, visuals and realia.
- Many opportunities for children to use and practice specific language skills.
- Group or pair work with carefully planned activities to promote higher levels of language skills.

Linguistic diversity issues and challenges

Many administrators say that they do not have the staff with the language proficiency necessary for a dual language program; either there is no access to trained staff with the language proficiency of a particular group (e.g., Spanish) or there are many different languages spoken in a classroom. If there is one language group, then it is incumbent upon the administrators to locate and train staff with the necessary language proficiency to provide parents with a bilingual option. If there are multiple languages, then a dual language program may not be feasible. However, in that case, there can be a policy of bilingualism and support for each language. That is, there should be books in each language, some signage in each language, recorded songs that children in the class could learn, and preferably an educational or community liaison that could use the language on some continuing basis with the child. These are minimal steps to help the child feel some value in his/her primary language and hopefully minimize primary language loss.

Family engagement issues and challenges

Family engagement has been reported as a significant factor in student success according to a large number of studies. Overall, research clearly shows that parents of DLL children are interested in their children's education and believe that parent involvement is important (Glick & White, 2004; Gonzalez *et al.*, 2005; National Academies, 2017; Sibley & Dearing, 2014). Yet, challenges to family engagement for culturally and linguistically diverse families may include a sense of alienation, distrust, and, for some families, a perception that their low educational skills or proficiency in English are not sufficient to assist in the classroom (Arias & Morillo-Campbell, 2008; Lindholm-Leary, 2001; Valdés *et al.*, 2015).

Home/school connections may be more effective when schools embrace a 'funds of knowledge' perspective to better understand the contributions of *all* parents to children's knowledge acquisition and sociocultural development, especially how family members may use their funds of knowledge in their lives and their children's lives (e.g., Gonzalez *et al.*, 2005). Thus, effective programs at the early childhood level tend to incorporate a variety of home/school collaboration activities, including those that honor and value the parents' home languages and cultures. Parents of DLLs can be encouraged to establish a sense of community by socializing their children in ways that preserve important features of their culture of origin (National Academies, 2017). For example, families can attend cultural celebrations to help children gain knowledge of and positive perceptions toward culture. Parents of NES children can utilize these approaches as well to promote cultural knowledge and identity.

Not surprisingly, parents' involvement in literacy activities with their young children results in stronger literacy development (August & Shanahan, 2006; Hammer *et al.*, 2009; Vera *et al.*, 2012). In dual language programs, it is important that DLL parents understand that talking and reading with their child is important and it is just as effective for them to do so in their primary language. One way that parents can promote stronger socio-cultural development is to ensure that children speak the home language and can engage with extended family members such as grandparents. Also, it is very helpful to provide parent workshops to help parents understand how to provide more enriched academic discussions and literacy development at home, especially for parents who have lower levels of formal education.

In summary, research from preschool and early elementary education levels support the advantages of dual language programs for both NES and DLL children. However, modifications of the models used in K-2 may be necessary depending on the demographic and language backgrounds of the students.

References

Arias, M.B. and Morillo-Campbell, M. (2008) *Promoting ELL Parent Involvement: Challenges in Contested Times.* Tempe, AZ, and Boulder, CO: Education Policy Research Unit and Education and the Public Interest Center. See ERIC database. (ED506652)

Asian American Legal Defense and Education Fund (2008) *Left in the Margins: Asian American Students and the No Child Left Behind Act.* New York: Author. See http://www.aaldef.org/docs/AALDEF_LeftintheMargins_NCLB.pdf

August, D. and Shanahan, T. (eds) (2006) *Developing Literacy in Second-Language Learners: Report of the National Literacy Panel on Language-Minority Children and Youth.* Mahwah, NJ: Lawrence Erlbaum Associates.

Baker, C. (2011) *Foundations of Bilingual Education and Bilingualism* (5th edn). Bristol: Multilingual Matters.

Barnett, W.S., Yarosz, D.J., Thomas, J.H., Jung, K. and Blanco, D. (2007) Two-way monolingual English immersion in preschool education: An experimental comparison. *Early Childhood Research Quarterly* 22, 277–293. doi: 10.1016/j.ecresq.2007.03.003

California Department of Education (2011) *A Comparison Study of Kindergarteners and Grade One English-Fluent Students and English Learners on the 2010–2011 Edition of the CELDT.* Sacramento, CA: California Department of Education.

Collins, B.A., O'Connor, E.E., Suarez-Orozco, C., Nieto-Castañon, A. and Toppelberg, C.O. (2014) Dual language profiles of Latino children of immigrants: Stability and change over the early school years. *Applied Psycholinguistics* 35 (3), 581–620. doi: http://dx.doi.org.libaccess.sjlibrary.org/10.1017/S0142716412000513

Espinosa, L. (2007) English-language learners as they enter school. In R.C. Pianta, M.J. Cox and K.L. Snow (eds) *School Readiness and the Transition to Kindergarten in the Era of Accountability* (pp. 175–196). Baltimore, MD: Paul H. Brookes.

Espinosa (2013, August) *Challenging Common Myths About Dual Language Learners.* Foundation for Child Development, Policy Brief No. Ten.

Espinosa, L. (2014) *Getting it Right for Young Children from Diverse Backgrounds: Applying Research to Improve Practice with a Focus on Dual Language Learners* (2nd edn). Englewood Cliffs, NJ: Prentice Hall.

Gathercole, V.C.M. (2002) Grammatical gender in bilingual and monolingual children: A Spanish morphosyntactic distinction. In D.K. Oller and R.E. Eilers (eds) *Language and Literacy in Bilingual Children* (pp. 207–219). Avon, UK: Multilingual Matters.

Genesee, F. (in press) Rethinking early childhood education for English language learners: The role of language. In V. Murphy and M. Evangelou (eds) *Early Childhood Education in English for Speakers of Other Languages.* UK: British Council.

Genesee, F. and Lindholm-Leary, K. (2013) Two case studies of content-based language education. *Journal of Immersion and Content-Based Language Education* 1 (1), 3–33. doi: 10.1075/jicb.1.1.02gen

Genesee, F., Lindholm-Leary, K.J., Saunders, W. and Christian, D. (2006) *Educating English Language Learners.* NY: Cambridge University Press.

Glick, J.E. and White, M.J. (2004) Post-secondary school participation of immigrant and native youth: The role of familial resources and educational expectations. *Social Science Research* 33 (2), 272–299.

Goldenberg, C. (2008) Teaching English language learners: What the research does – and does not – say. *American Educator* 32, 8–23, 42–44.

Goldenberg, C., Nemeth, K., Hicks, J., Zepeda, M. and Cardona, L.M. (2013) Program elements and teaching practices to support young dual language learners. In F. Ong and J. McLean (eds) *California's Best Practices for Young Dual Language Learners: Research Overview Papers.* Sacramento, CA: CDE Publications and Education Reviews.

Gonzalez, N., Moll, L. and Amanti, C. (2005) *Funds of Knowledge: Theorizing Practices in Households, Communities, and Classrooms.* Oxford: Routledge.

Halle, T., Forry, N., Hair, E., Perper, K., Wandner, L., Wessel, J. and Vick, J. (2009) *Disparities in Early Learning and Development: Lessons from the Early Childhood Longitudinal Study – Birth Cohort (ECLS-B)* Washington, DC: Child Trends.

Halle, T., Hair, E., Wandener, L., McNamara, M. and Chien, N. (2012) Predictors and outcomes of early versus later English language proficiency. *Early Childhood Quarterly* 27, 1–20. See http://dx.doi.org/10.1016/j.ecresq.2011.07.004

Hammer, C., Hoff, E., Uchikoshi, Y., Gillanders, C., Castro, D. and Sandilos, L. (2014) The language and literacy development of young dual language learners: A critical review. *Early Childhood Research Quarterly* 29, 715–733.

Hammer, C.S., Davison, M.D., Lawrence, F.R. and Miccio, A.W. (2009) The effect of maternal language on bilingual children's vocabulary and emergent literacy development during head start and kindergarten. *Scientific Studies of Reading* 13 (2), 99–121.

Han, W. (2012) Bilingualism and academic achievement. *Child Development* 83, 300–321. See http://dx.doi.org/10.1111/j.1467-8624.2011.01686.x

Head Start (2015) Cultural and linguistic responsiveness. See http://eclkc.ohs.acf.hhs.gov/hslc/tta-system/cultural-linguistic/planned-language-approach

Howard, E.R., Sugarman, J., Christian, D., Lindholm-Leary, K.J. and Rogers, D. (2007) *Guiding Principles for Dual Language Education* (2nd edn). Washington, DC: Center for Applied Linguistics.

Jackson, C.W., Schatschneider, C., Leacox, L., Schuele, C.M. and Davison, M. D. (2014) Longitudinal analysis of receptive vocabulary growth in young Spanish English-speaking children from migrant families. *Language, Speech and Hearing Services in Schools* 45 (1), 40–51.

Lindholm, K.J. (1980) Bilingual children: Some interpretations of cognitive and linguistic development. In K. Nelson (ed.) *Children's Language*, Volume II. New York: Gardner Press, Inc.

Lindholm, K.J. (1987) English question use in Spanish-speaking ESL children: Changes with English language proficiency. *Research in the Teaching of English* 21, 64–91.

Lindholm-Leary, K.J. (2001) *Dual Language Education.* Clevedon: Multilingual Matters.

Lindholm-Leary, K. (2014) Bilingual and biliteracy skills in young Spanish-speaking low-SES children: Impact of instructional language and primary language proficiency. *International Journal of Bilingual Education and Bilingualism* 17 (2), 144–159. doi: 10.1080/13670050.2013.866625

Lindholm-Leary, K.J. and Borsato, G. (2006) Academic achievement. In F. Genesee, K. Lindholm-Leary, W. Saunders and D. Christian (eds) *Educating English Language Learners* (pp. 176–222). New York: Cambridge University Press.

Lindholm-Leary, K. and Genesee, F. (2010) Alternative educational programs for English language learners. In California Department of Education (eds) *Improving Education for English Learners: Research-Based Approaches* (pp. 323–382). Sacramento: CDE Press.

Lindholm-Leary, K. and Genesee, F. (2014) Student outcomes in one-way and two-way immersion and indigenous language education. *Journal of Immersion and Content-Based Language Education* 2 (2), 165–180.

Lindholm-Leary, K. and Hernández, A. (2011) Achievement and language proficiency of Latino students in dual language programs: Native English speakers, fluent

English/previous ELLs, and current ELLs. *Journal of Multilingual and Multicultural Development* 32 (6), 531–545. doi: 10.1080/01434632.2011.611596

Lindholm-Leary, K.J. and Howard, E. (2008) Language and academic achievement in two-way immersion programs. In T. Fortune and D. Tedick (eds) *Pathways to Bilingualism: Evolving Perspectives on Immersion Education* (pp. 177–200). Clevedon: Multilingual Matters.

Lopez, L.M. and Greenfield, D.B. (2004) The cross-language transfer of phonological skills of Hispanic Headstart Children. *Bilingual Research Journal* 28, 1–18. See http://dx.doi.org/10.1080/15235882.2004.10162609

Mancilla-Martinez, J. and Lesaux, N.K. (2011) The gap between Spanish speakers' word reading and word knowledge: A longitudinal study. *Child Development* 82 (5), 1544–1560.

National Academies of Sciences, Engineering, and Medicine (2017) *Promoting the Educational Success of Children and Youth Learning English: Promising Futures.* Washington, DC: The National Academies Press. doi: 10.17226/24677

National Association for the Education of Young Children (NAEYC) (2009) Where we stand. See http://www.naeyc.org/files/naeyc/file/positions/diversity.pdf

Paez, M.M., Tabors, P.O. and Lopez, L.M. (2007) Dual language and literacy development of Spanish-speaking preschool children. *Journal of Applied Developmental Psychology* 28 (2), 85–102. doi: 10.1016/j.appdev.2006.12.007

Paradis, J., Genesee, F. and Crago, M. (2011) *Dual Language Development and Disorders: A Handbook on Bilingualism and Second Language Learning* (2nd edn). Baltimore, MD: Paul H. Brookes Publishing Company.

Sibley, E. and Dearing, E. (2014) Family educational involvement and child achievement in early elementary school for American-born and immigrant families. *Psychology in the Schools* 51 (8), 814–831.

The Annie E. Casey Foundation (2015) *The 2015 Kids Count Data Book: State Trends in Child Well-being.* Baltimore, MD: Author. See http://www.aecf.org/resources/the-2015-kids-count-data-book/

U.S. Department of Education, National Center for Education Statistics. (2015) The condition of education 2015 (NCES 2015-144) *English Language Learners.*

Valdés, G., Menken, K. and Castro, M. (2015) *Common Core Bilingual and English Language Learners.* Philadelphia, PA; Caslon.

Vera, E.M., Israel, M.S., Coyle, L., Cross, J., Knight-Lynn, L., Moallem, I., Bartucci, G. and Goldberger, N. (2012) Exploring the educational involvement of parents of English learners. *School Community Journal* 22 (2), 183–202.

Zehler, A.M., Fleischman, H.L., Hopstock, P.J., Pendzick, M.L. and Stephenson, T.G. (2003) *Descriptive Study of Services to LEP Students and LEP Students with Disabilities (No. 4 Special Topic Report: Findings on Special Education LEP Students).* Development Associates, Inc.: Arlington, VA.

6 Opportunities and Dilemmas for TWI Programs at the Secondary Level

Carol I. Bearse, Ester J. de Jong and Min-Chuan Tsai

Introduction

This chapter examines the current knowledge base related to secondary two-way immersion (TWI) programs, a growing segment within TWI. Although still only a small number nationwide, secondary TWI programs play an important role in sustaining high levels of language competence in more than one language. The purpose of this chapter is to provide a synthesis of current research on secondary TWI program outcomes and some promising practices by teachers at the secondary level. We also argue that the cultural dimension of TWI must take a more central place in research and practice in secondary TWI programs. We begin with a brief overview of the context of secondary TWI, followed by a review of language and academic program outcomes and end with an overview of the research concerning students' linguistic and cultural identities. The second part of the chapter focuses on the third goal, cultural outcomes which focus on identity construction and innovative practices to support this goal for adolescent students. We conclude with the challenges of implementing cultural goals as well as high achievement in TWI secondary programs.

Program Models

The TWI directory maintained at the Center for Applied Linguistics (CAL TWI Directory) listed a total number of 497 TWI programs in 2015. Out of these, about 20% ($n = 99$) are implemented at the middle or high school level; and 92% of these secondary programs use Spanish as the partner language for instruction. The significantly lower number of secondary than elementary TWI programs is not surprising. It takes

5–6 years before an elementary program is articulated into the secondary level. Moreover, the implementation of a secondary TWI program is more complicated due to scheduling, staffing and curriculum mandates (Cruz, 2000; Hsieh, 2007; Montone & Loeb, 2000).

Program models at the secondary level are more diverse as TWI educators attempt to maintain 50% of instruction in Spanish. Looking at the programs in the TWI directory, most middle school programs have 2 or 3 courses taught in Spanish (Spanish reading/Language arts, social studies and/or science). At the high school, practices vary greatly in response to high school requirements, an emphasis on English testing, competition with other student interests, and resources. Several educators have therefore looked for creative approaches that continue to emphasize the relevance of bilingualism that include, for example, offering medical interpreter courses in the high school (Cazabon, 2008). Kibler *et al.* (2014) found that an after-school high school program, entitled Language Across Borders, enabled dual language students to use both English and Spanish in activities that fostered intercultural communication. Cruz (2000) describes a suburban New York middle school language enrichment program that started in 6th grade. In this model students were exposed to the same grade level curriculum in the dominant language four days a week and the second language once a week.

Linguistic and Academic Outcomes

Two types of evaluation studies examine secondary TWI program outcomes. Some studies follow TWI students as they move from elementary to secondary TWI programs within the same school system and compare them to non-TWI students (Bearse & de Jong, 2008; Cazabon *et al.*, 1998; Cazabon, 2000; Hsieh, 2007; Lindholm-Leary, 2011; Lindholm-Leary & Ferrante, 2005; Lindholm-Leary & Hernández, 2011; McGee, 2012; Quintanar-Sarellana, 2004; Senesac, 2002; Stevenson, 2014). The other set of studies considers the impact of elementary TWI program participation on middle school or high school performance (Baralis, 2009; Cobb *et al.*, 2006; Kohne, 2006; Lindholm-Leary & Borsato, 2001, 2005; Porter, 2014; Vega, 2014). In the latter, students attended a TWI program as an elementary student but at the time of the study were in a regular, mainstream, non-TWI program. Except for performance in science (see below), the trends are similar in both sets of studies.

Regardless of design, most studies only consider outcomes in English and in particular English reading, writing and math. Only nine out of the 23 studies in our review included outcomes in the partner language and only four studies considered social studies or science as outcomes. This is in sharp contrast with studies conducted at the elementary level where assessment in both English and the partner language are not only more common but also expected (cf. Howard *et al.*, 2003; Lindholm & Genesee, 2014). A few studies considered alternative outcome measures than standardized tests, such as grade point average and advanced placement courses (Cazabon, 2000; Cazabon *et al.*, 1998; Kohne, 2006; Lindholm-Leary & Borsato, 2001, 2005).

Overall, the studies show that students who attend or attended a TWI program significantly outperform peers in English reading. For example, Quintanar-Sarellana (2004) found that middle school students in a TWI program in California, performed at or above the 50th percentile in reading on the SAT-9 Reading and Language Arts test. Moreover, scores increased as students moved up towards higher grade levels. TWI students also outperformed non-TWI students on standardized writing tests (Cazabon, 2000; Cobb *et al.*, 2006; Senesac, 2002; Vega, 2014). Studies that included measures of proficiency in the partner language show continued growth in partner language development on standardized tests as well as locally developed assessments (Cazabon, 2000; Cazabon *et al.*, 1998; Lindholm-Leary, 2011; Lindholm-Leary & Borsato, 2005; Lindholm-Leary & Ferrante, 2005; Lindholm-Leary & Hernández, 2011; Quintanar-Sarellana, 2004; Senesac, 2002; Stevenson, 2014).

In terms of subject matter learning, the majority of studies consider math outcomes and again confirm that TWI student perform similar or better than non-TWI students on standardized math achievement tests. Social studies and science outcomes are significantly less researched and, when examined, show a more complex picture than reading and math (Lindholm-Leary & Borsato, 2001, 2005; Lindholm-Leary & Ferrante, 2005; McGee, 2012; Senesac, 2002; Vega, 2014). Keeping the limited number of studies in mind, the studies seem to suggest a differential pattern between the two types of studies. Vega (2014), who looked at elementary TWI program participants, discovered that former-TWI students did not do better than their non-TWI peers on the ACT (Admissions College Test) science in high school. Yet, TWI students did outperform their peers in science in studies that considered TWI students who stayed in the TWI program (McGee, 2012; Senesac 2002). In social studies, Senesac (2002) found that TWI students achieved close to the same level or better than non-TWI students in the state.

Some studies include academic outcomes other than standardized test scores, such as graduate point average and advanced placement course selection. TWI students appear to be more likely to select more advanced placement courses than their non-TWI peers. More Hispanic Spanish-speaking bilingual students enrolled in both Algebra II (28% Hispanic Spanish-speaking bilingual students vs 0% comparison group of non-two-way Hispanic speaking students) and trigonometry/calculus (13% of Hispanic Spanish-speaking bilingual students vs 0% of non-two-way Hispanic speaking students) (Lindholm-Leary & Borsato, 2001, 2005; Kohne, 2006). On other hand, Kohne (2006) also found that both

Caucasian and Hispanic TWI students overall GPAs were lower than non-TWI students. Clearly more research is needed in these areas.

Cultural Outcomes

The third goal of TWI, cross-cultural competence, has received significantly less attention than the other two goals. In a recent review, Feinauer and Howard (2014) note that most studies have used the lens of student attitudes to analyze dual language program outcomes. Increasingly, however, studies have paid attention to the relationship between language and identity and how identities are constructed through classroom practices. A focus on identity and identity construction as an integral part of TWI program development is particularly important for adolescent TWI students given the central role that identity development plays for students at this age. Adolescence is a period of rapid physiological, psychological and social change (Erickson, 1968; Markus & Kitayama, 1991; Spindler & Spindler, 1989; Swanson et al., 1998). Personal identity develops within the context of role relationships situated within a community of individuals whose values become increasingly important to the growing adolescent. By extension, secondary bilingual learners face complex issues of forming new and multiple identities as they negotiate multiple worlds in and outside of school (e.g., Lima & Lima, 1998; McKay & Wong, 1996; Rodriguez & Trueba, 1998; Vega deJesús & Sayers, 2006).

Recent identity studies extend socially constructed notions of identity to include the concept of 'millennium' identities that are shaped by technology, media, and globalization (De Costa & Norton, 2016; Higgins, 2015; Norton, 2013). Higgins explores how these forces provide language learners with new identity options 'including in-between identities and transnational identities that are more closely tied to others who share their experiences' (Higgins, 2015: 379). This concept embraces linguistic varieties and dialects as well as hybrid language. The intersection of technology, media and globalization with language use create 'new millennial hybrid and alternative identities' (2015: 377). In addition, Darvin and Norton (2015) note that today's learners navigate online and offline identities in complex digital spaces. Language investment now occurs at the 'intersection of identity, capital and ideology' (De Costa & Norton, 2016: 588).

TWI students' attitudes

Similar to studies at the elementary level, students in secondary TWI programs display positive attitudes towards school, the TWI program, bilingualism, as well as diversity (Bearse & de Jong, 2008; de Jong & Bearse, 2011; Lindholm-Leary, 2011; Lindholm-Leary & Borsato, 2001).

Bearse and de Jong (2008) interviewed middle school and high school students as to their cultural and linguistic investment in their TWI experience. They found that the majority of the students enjoyed their experiences and valued their bilingualism. Even though both the Euro-Americans and the Latinos acknowledged the economic or instrumental use of becoming bilingual, the Latinos emphasized its cultural benefits as they could better connect with their families and friends through their Spanish language and through a study of Spanish literature. Furthermore, TWI students have high opinions regarding their global self-worth, displaying a positive outlook towards life in general (Cazabon, 2000).

Baralis (2009) found a significant difference in biculturation among New York middle school students in favor of TWI students than mainstream students as measured by the AHIMSA (Acculturation, Habits, and Interests Multicultural Scale for Adolescents) survey.

Language and linguistic identities

Learning languages has a significant impact on identity development. In a case study analysis of a Southwest TWI program, Arnot-Hopffer (2007) found that learning languages was a key element in the formation of three high school students' identity. As a result of their study of Spanish and English in a K-12 TWI program, these adolescent girls became confident in themselves as biliterates.

Merritt (2012) interviewed seven focal students from a fifth-grade class into high school and attended middle school policy review meetings. During the interviews, students expressed dissatisfaction with the experience of language learning and use in secondary school because the high school focus was on encapsulated forms of Spanish rather than a variety of language uses that they had experienced in elementary school. In high school, Spanish teaching was concentrated in passing the AP exam. Twelfth grade students expressed similar sentiments in de Jong and Bearse (2011) where students thought that AP Spanish classes concentrated more on language grammar rather than using the language for real purposes.

Dworin (2011) investigated language and literacy practices of five graduates of a Spanish-English K-12 program from a large metropolitan area of southern California. The participants included two Mexican-Americans, one African-American and two European-Americans, ages 19–25. Besides the finding that all the participants reported being bilingual/biliterate, Dworin found two distinct conceptualizations of linguistic identities associated with Spanish: a functional use of Spanish to accomplish specific kinds of communication and using Spanish to build linguistic and cultural affinities with native Spanish speakers. In contrast to Bearse and de Jong (2008), using Spanish in specific contexts was not limited to those of Hispanic ethnicity. Both Euro Americans and Latinos used Spanish interchangeably in their southern California context. Studies by Block (2012) and Dorner (2010) similarly found that being able to communicate effectively in Spanish was perceived as additional support for the development and growth of ethnolinguistic identities as well as the development of close family and community ties.

Constructing identities in the classroom

Feinauer and Howard (2014) conclude their review of the literature related to the cultural goal of TWI programs with a call for studies that help us understand better how students view themselves within the culturally diverse classrooms that TWI provides. Education plays a significant role in legitimizing or marginalizing students' linguistic and ethnic/racial identities. Through discursive practices, educators construct spaces where they and their students negotiate and construct meaning and apprentice to become competent language users. In the case of TWI programs, students are developing and constructing new language identities along with their specific home linguistic varieties. Despite the need for these classroom studies, very few exist.

McCollum (1999) is an exception. She investigated language as cultural capital in a Southwestern middle school program. This study is unique in its classroom-based focus and how linguistic identities and ideologies are constructed through student and teacher–student interactions. Noteworthy in this study is the finding that only 'high' Spanish, not ethnic varieties, was validated in the dual language classes, as well as in the school environment. She concluded that the elements of the hidden curriculum, instructional practices and assessment policy all served to devalue students' native linguistic capital. What students learned, in fact, was that English, not Spanish was the language of power.

Kibler *et al.* (2014) examined an after-school TWI program model and found students valued conversational dual language activities where they could appreciate each other's ethnolinguistic resources. Through formal and informal activities that encouraged oral communication, students developed confidence in speaking both Spanish and English. Through the creation of bilingual books for elementary students, peers consulted with each other when encountering writing or translation issues (see also Hernandez, 2008). One student declared, 'It's more than just being in a class...they do more than speak the language...they live the language' (2008: 263). In fact, they were ratifying their peers' ethnolinguistic identities.

Promising Practices in Secondary TWI

The importance of creating spaces where the negotiation of meaning, knowledge and identity construction can take place also emerges when considering what studies have noted about instructional practices in secondary TWI program (Conrad, 2000; Hernandez, 2008). Although research in this area is still emerging, secondary TWI teaching practices can be organized under four categories: (1) cooperative learning; (2) practices affirming students' identities; (3) bilingual curriculum development; (4) continuing bilingual development.

Cooperative learning

Cooperative learning and project-based learning are two strategies that meet the need to provide adolescent learners with opportunities for students to use their multiple discourses to construct identity and knowledge though discussion and negotiation of meaning. In a Texas study, Hernandez (2008) investigated the role of peer collaboration in dual language programs. She interviewed three high school students, two who were of Mexican background and one who was English dominant, observed their classes and participated in conference presentations with them. In addition, she administered a questionnaire to former TWI students, where 86% of the students made mention of the peer support that they received in dual language programs which fostered their learning and confidence of language learning. Peers become 'language teachers' as they negotiate meaning for one another and contribute their understandings to the whole class. Their ethnolinguistic identities become powerful tools for the creation of new knowledge. Like cooperative learning, project-centered activities work to encourage intercultural communication (Conrad, 2000; Hernandez, 2008) and to make conceptual connections across subject areas (de Jong & Bearse, 2014).

Rubinstein-Ávila et al. (2015) studied a 7th–8th grade mathematics classroom where mathematics discourse and biliteracy practices were observed. These practices encourage group problem solving using bilingual pairs where students use all their linguistic resources to make meaning of the world, and then present their solutions to a group of peers. Language is viewed, then, as fluid and dynamic. The use of sheltered instruction strategies that promote collaborative thinking (e.g. Chalk Talk, collaborative posters) and creative use of language that is both expansive and particular to mathematics discourse gives students the ability to use all their linguistic repertoires in support of solving a problem as well as supporting the literacy objectives in the Common Core.

Martin-Beltran (2014) investigated in an after-school Language Ambassadors program how high school students learning English and those learning Spanish in a Maryland high school used reciprocal teaching and learning to create autobiographical essays. Students acted as peer teachers and were guided by questions about their language-learning experiences.

Practices that affirm students' identities

Language Arts practices that expand the opportunities to explore one's identity are also important. The reading of Latino literature holds promise for TWI classrooms. For example, de Jong and Bearse (2011) found that the reading of identity literature from the Caribbean, Latin America and South America nurtured the development of bilingual and bicultural identity development in their middle school students. Bearse (2005) found that developing an identity curriculum for both a bilingual and a TWI middle school energized students to not only write well, but also to read authors that represented their cultural identity. The writing of poetry gave students confidence to write longer pieces, such as memoir and personal experience narratives. Similarly, a New Mexico high school enhanced literacy instruction through community connections (Stebner & Ruiz, 2012). Interestingly, they combined a Freirean method with writer's workshop in order for students to use their language skills to connect with their community. Freshman level AP Spanish, for example, focused on inquiry that focused on problems present in their immediate environment such as education, environment, health care, and immigration. Grammar was taught in context, evolving in a meaningful way for communicative competence. Research projects led to a final community action activity. The authors found a connection between these students' immersion in Spanish and high scores on the AP Spanish exam. Eighty-six percent of the students passed the exam with 80% passing with a 4 or 5.

Bilingual curriculum development

TWI high school educators have used creative curricular approaches to motivate their students. Ysleta ISD teachers in EL Paso, Texas (Sizemore & Graduates of Del Valle High School, 2008) had students lead the way in creating a dual language curriculum that included classes in Spanish that focused on the development of economic language in both English and Spanish. The students also requested that at least four of the eight credits earned in Spanish come from core academic subject areas. Student involvement encouraged student engagement with the program. Cruz (2000) similarly emphasized the importance of the structure of the middle school into a house system where interdisciplinary or thematic units could be planned.

Another El Paso teacher and TWI coordinator (Salcido, 2009) took the district's Algebra curriculum and translated into Spanish the academic language and the essential questions (the Big ideas), and connected the mathematics ideas to cross-cultural relationships in the real world. In the first lesson on Functions in Algebra, students were asked to write and reflect upon a real-life example in which algebraic functions were part of their world; they then shared these ideas during a Socratic seminar. These ideas build on the new Common Core curriculum in mathematics and apply them in a unique way to this school's particular context.

Continuing bilingual development

Przymus (2016) studied the use of an innovative model in an American Government class in a charter public high school in Tucson, Arizona. His model used a 2–1–L2 model, where in a 90-minute class the following structure was used: 30 minutes of immersion in English, 30 minutes of immersion in Spanish, and a final 30 minutes of hybrid language practices. In this model students were treated as bilingual content area users, and various levels of bilingualism were celebrated. He asserts that there is a need to create curricular 'third spaces' for bilingual practices, as well as separate spaces to develop strong academic skills in two languages.

García and Wei (2014) suggest that recognizing the use of hybrid languages is a useful pedagogy to apply to the many discursive practices of Latino students which are employed in U.S. high schools. She cites an example of this practice from an International High School in New York City. One of the English teachers, Camila, was working on the theme of literary conflicts. She used the rap, 'Si se Puede' by El Chivo of Quinto Sol to address issues of racism and discrimination against immigrants. Students translated the lyrics from Spanish into English and identified the types of conflict voiced in the rap and the key words to express this conflict in Spanish. She then played the rap 'Mosh' by Eminem and asked students to translate the lyrics from English into Spanish. This kind of practice builds extensively on critical thinking skills in order to implement a social justice curriculum.

Lindholm-Leary (2015) further recommends that secondary TWI programs give students a real purpose to use partner languages (i.e., internships, community service or study abroad posts) where multiple discourse practices are honored. Students who achieve high levels of literacy in two languages could be recognized for their language achievement with a 'Seal of Biliteracy,' thus encouraging secondary students to continue their study of two languages. She also suggests that using multiple discourses (i.e., code-switching) to find meaning could lead to higher levels of critical thinking that are more creative and complex (Lindholm-Leary, 2016).

Challenges

Many studies acknowledge that secondary TWI programs are rewarding but also bring challenges. These challenges include: institutional program integration, curricular alignment, the finding of qualified teachers who can meet the linguistic, cultural and academic demands of the program at this level, and the development of pedagogies that embrace multiple discourses which result in more equitable program solutions.

Institutional integration

Scheduling concerns have had a major impact on the development of TWI programs at the secondary level (Cruz, 2000; de Jong & Bearse, 2014; Forman, 2016; Hsieh, 2007; Montone & Loeb, 2000). To facilitate the scheduling of multiple content classes in both Spanish and English requires administrators to work effectively with teachers in a shared leadership framework (De Matthews & Izquierdo, 2017). Ideally, teachers and principals could work together to maximize the sharing of resources to promote equity for all students. They could help to solve the problems of scheduling multiple content area classes in two languages.

de Jong and Bearse (2014) in their study of a TWI middle school found that another hurdle to overcome was to provide mutual planning time for mainstream and TWI teachers. This was especially true in Language Arts where the teachers were on separate teams. TWI Spanish teachers of language arts were relegated to 'foreign language' teams, which were not part of the 'academic' teams. This amounted to the allocation of Spanish as a less prestigious course and undermined the TWI goal of providing equitable programming.

Curricular alignment and transition from elementary to middle school and then to high school is also mentioned by teachers as a concern (de Jong & Bearse, 2011; Sellards, 2015). Indeed, there is a need for more thoughtful planning of longitudinal curricular alignment to ensure high levels of bilingual development at all levels. Within this process, discussions of language variety, race, culture and class need to be taken into account. This requires a process of inquiry and reflection as well as broad stakeholder engagement (De Matthews & Izquierdo, 2017).

Forman (2016) discusses the challenge of balancing state testing in English with other student interests and resources in one middle school. She discovered that conflicting school interests influenced dual language policies at the district and local level. There was concern among teachers about the allocations of resources, increased work load and preferential hiring of teachers with bilingual backgrounds. Creating and sustaining TWI programs prove challenging at best and must include all stakeholders in creating successful TWI programs at the secondary level.

Teacher preparedness

Creating alternative pathways to teacher certification and teacher preparation are critical challenges in finding qualified teachers and leadership for TWI programs (De Matthews & Izquierdo, 2017; Garcia & New America, 2017). Cervantes-Soon et al. (2017) point out that bilingual certification is only available in 25 states and DC and only seven require TWI teachers to have this certification to teach in content area classrooms. This is clearly a stumbling block in creating more equitable teaching programs at both the college and the state level. Responding to the challenge of having more qualified dual language teachers in expanding their dual language programs (not only TWI) in the Portland (Oregon) Public schools, Amaya Garcia (2017) describes several pathways to help remove barriers to entering the teaching profession, in particular those that impact bilingual paraprofessionals. This program also supports recruitment of teachers from within their own community as proposed by the 'Grow Your Own' programs suggested by the Dual Language Teacher Partnership. The alternative pathways included a three-course teacher preparation syllabus and an intensive training that culminated in the teachers immediately teaching in dual language classrooms while finishing the required coursework. For secondary teachers, the pathways include a Master's degree plus a world language endorsement. These innovative programs helped to address the teacher shortages of qualified personnel. Likewise, DeMatthews and Izquierdo (2017) suggest the importance of principal preparation and support of TWI programs. They acknowledge that principals should understand the underpinnings of TWI research as well as a thorough knowledge of how language variety, race, culture and class affect the language planning process. Principals are in a position to promote school values that affirm diversity and linguistic assets of students as well as ensuring equitable use of school resources.

Embracing multiple discourses

TWI programs have traditionally endorsed the separation of languages when teaching two languages. However, in reality, students bring a variety of discourses to a classroom depending on their cultural and academic background. While not necessarily focusing on secondary schools (but see for example García et al., 2011), researchers have begun to question the strict separation of languages called for in the TWI program structure and recommend that language in practice be used instead; i.e., forms of code-switching and multiple uses of discourses that highlight the rich cultural diversity that TWI students bring to the classroom (e.g., Durán & Palmer, 2014; Sánchez et al., 2017). These practices would help to reinforce positive linguistic identity, in particular among marginalized communities that exist in urban areas where local 'dialects' and language practices are frowned upon in favor of 'pure' or 'high' academic Spanish.

García (2009) endorses the use of multiple language practices that students bring to the classroom as a challenge for TWI educators who need to acknowledge that monolingual bilingual practices are not sufficient to be inclusive in diverse settings. She emphasizes that the only way to build equitable educational systems is to develop multiple multilingual programs that acknowledge the use of hybrid languages as a resource for engaging students cognitively and socially, In order to enable a better understanding of this variety, Pryzmus (2016) suggests that youth identities can be described as emergent bilinguals (English language learners (ELLs)), recursive bilinguals (Spanish heritage speakers), and dynamic bilinguals (English heritage speakers) and argues that TWI educators need to acknowledge all these identities in their practices

Freeman (2000) found that in her study of an urban middle school in Philadelphia planning to implement a dual language program, students in the school used multiple discourses as well as code-switching practices in their everyday lives. She recommends that TWI programs need to better understand the discrepancies between 'ideal' policy and actual practice of target populations in a specific context, that is, 'How do members of social groups use and evaluate language? What prejudices against non-standard forms of language underlie teachers' perceptions of pedagogies?' (2000: 219).

Researchers have also urged educators to look through the lenses of the multiple discourses found in students' neighborhoods as well as the impact of technology in forming identities and constructing discourses. Higgins (2015) suggests that secondary students can examine their community environments for examples of hybrid language on posted signs that combine one or more languages to make new words or phrases. As De Costa and Norton (2016) note, the digital revolution has shifted our understanding of time, space, and our place in the world. Students no longer have to travel 'abroad' to be immersed in language. In this new digital space, students have many options for creating and choosing identities according to their social context. They also assert that narrative inquiry, both oral and written, helps students to see how identities can be shaped by social, cultural, and historical conventions. In keeping with this concept, Waller *et al.* (2016) suggest that tasks can be designed to make students experts who can draw on their culture and educational resources to experiment with academic identities. They suggest using students' language knowledge to discuss contrastive rhetoric choices and to explore the use of grammar in their own language. Another idea presented was to use mind maps to see how language changes with students' differing roles in their community. Although these studies did not take place in secondary TWI programs, they illustrate practices that can easily be integrated into a TWI program.

Equity and social justice

Using and recognizing the validity of multiple discourses in the classroom are ways to address the inequities in a TWI classroom. There may, indeed, be a need to add a fourth goal to TWI programs. Cervantes-Soon *et al.* (2017) state that there is increasing evidence that TWI programs are not living up to their ideal to provide equal access to educational opportunity for transnational emergent bilingual students. They encourage a framework for creating a more equitable and integrated multilingual learning spaces that incorporate a 'fourth goal' of critical consciousness that uses critical, question posing pedagogies (Cummins, 2000; Freire, 1970) as well as border pedagogies (Giroux, 1988) that legitimize the multiple discourses transnational students bring to the TWI classroom. This fourth goal could work well with an emphasis on cultivating the third goal (Feinauer & Howard, 2014; de Jong & Bearse, 2008) where the integration of self, culture, and sociopolitical contexts meld to form adolescent identities.

Conclusion

Our review of the literature on secondary TWI programs show that, following results from elementary TWI programs, secondary TWI students generally perform as well as or outperform peers in reading and math. The picture for other content areas (science, social studies) is more mixed but underscores the added value of continued participation in the program. We also highlighted that current research does not often consider alternative outcomes measures (drop-out/graduation rates, advanced placement, college attendance) or include measures in the partner language.

Paralleling research on elementary TWI, cultural outcomes are the least studied, particularly from the perspective of identity construction through classroom practices. We argued that questions of language use, multiple discourses, and identity development are particularly relevant and pertinent to the study of secondary TWI programs. Adolescents face issues of rapid change as to their identities and these identities are complex, multifaceted and influenced and shaped through social practices including technology-driven practices. If TWI programs wish to meet their long-term language and academic goals, we argue, TWI educators need to pay attention to identity investment and its role in students' motivation to continue to learn and use the partner language in support of on-going bilingual development. Sizemore (2011) suggests that high school is more about social belonging and post-high school career planning or college exploration. This understanding has implications for TWI program models and practices. Effective secondary TWI programs create spaces to affirm student identities, build community connections and consider relevant and real-life purposes to use the language that enable grammar to be taught in context (Lindholm-Leary, 2015). Explicit attention to students' discourses and identities need to become part of successful and more equitable programs at the secondary level. Embracing multiple discourses and equitable programming are areas where additional research could pave the way for more innovative TWI programs at the secondary level.

References

Arnot-Hopffer, E.J. (2007) Las tres amigas: A study of biliteracy from kindergarten through adolescence. Unpublished dissertation. University of Arizona, Tucson, AZ.

Baralis, C.L. (2009) The long-term effects of a K-5 dual language program on middle school student achievement and biculturalism. Unpublished doctoral dissertation. Hofstra University, Hempstead, NY.

Bearse, C.I. (2005) *The Sky in My Hands: Accelerating Academic English through the Writing Process*. Cambridge, MA: Language Learning Innovations, Inc.

Bearse, C. and de Jong, E.J. (2008) Cultural and linguistic investment: Adolescents in a secondary two-way immersion program. *Equity and Excellence in Education* 41 (3), 325–340.

Block, N.C. (2012) Perceived impact of two-way dual immersion programs on Latino students' relationships in their families and communities. *International Journal of Bilingual Education and Bilingualism* 15 (2), 235–257.

Cazabon, M.T. (2000) The use of students' self-reporting in the evaluation of the Amigos two-way language immersion program. Unpublished doctoral dissertation. University of Massachusetts.

Cazabon, M.T. (2008) Two-way students become medical interpreters. Paper presented at the 2-way CABE Conference, Newport Beach, CA. Boston, MA.

Cazabon, M., Nicoladis, E. and Lambert, W.E. (1998) *Becoming Bilingual in the Amigos Two-way Immersion Program*. Santa Cruz, CA: National Center for Research on Education, Diversity, and Excellence.

Cervantes-Soon, C.G., Dorner, L., Palmer, D., Heiman, D., Schwerdtfeger, R. and Choi, J. (2017) Combating inequalities in two-way language immersion programs: Toward critical consciousness in bilingual education spaces. *Review of Research in Education* 41 (1), 403–427.

Cobb, B., Vega, D. and Kronauge, C. (2006) Effects of an elementary dual language immersion school program on junior high school achievement. *Middle School Research Journal* 1 (1), 27–47.

Conrad, T.R. (2000) An exploration of transformative intercultural and intracultural interaction among middle school students of a dual language Spanish/English class. Unpublished doctoral dissertation. Indiana University of Pennsylvania, Indiana, PA.

Cruz, G.I. (2000) Learning in two languages: A case study of a two-way bilingual education program at the middle school. Unpublished doctoral dissertation. State University of New York, Albany, NY.

Cummins, J. (2000) *Language, Power, and Pedagogy: Bilingual Children in the Crossfire*. Clevedon: Multilingual Matters.

Darvin, R. and Norton, B. (2015) Identity and a model of investment in applied linguistics. *Annual Review of Applied Linguistics* 35, 36–56.

De Costa, P.I. and Norton, B. (2016) Identity in language learning and teaching: Research agendas for the future. In S. Preece (ed.) *The Routledge Handbook of Language and Identity (Routledge Handbooks in Applied Linguistics)* (1st edn) (pp. 586–601). London: Routledge.

de Jong, E.J. and Bearse, C. (2011) The same outcomes for all? High school students reflect on their two-way immersion program experiences. In D.J. Tedick, D. Christian and T.W. Fortune (eds) *Immersion Education: Practices, Policies, Possibilities* (pp. 104–122). Bristol: Multilingual Matters.

de Jong, E.J. and Bearse, C.I. (2014) Dual Language programs as a strand within a secondary school: Dilemmas of school organization and the TWI mission. *International Journal of Bilingual Education and Bilingualism* 17 (1), 15–31.

DeMatthews, D. and Izquierdo, E. (2017) The importance of principals supporting dual language education: A social justice leadership framework. *Journal of Latinos and Education*, 1–18.

Dorner, L.M. (2010) English and Spanish 'para un futuro' – or just English? Immigrant family perspectives on two-way immersion. *International Journal of Bilingual Education and Bilingualism* 13 (3), 303–323.

Durán, L. and Palmer, D. (2014) Pluralist discourses of bilingualism and translanguaging talk in classrooms. *Journal of Early Childhood Literacy* 14 (3), 367–388.

Dworin, J. (2011) Listening to graduates of a K-12 bilingual program: Language ideologies and literacy practices of former bilingual students. *Gist Education and Learning Research Journal* (5), 104–126.

Erickson, E.H. (1968) *Identity, Youth, and Crisis*. NY: W.W. Norton and Co., Inc.

Feinauer, E. and Howard, E.R. (2014) Attending to the third goal: Cross-cultural competence and identity development in two-way immersion programs. *Journal of Immersion and Content-Based Language Education* 2 (2), 257–272. John Benjamins Publishing Co.

Forman, S. (2016) Interests and conflicts: Exploring the context for early implementation of a dual language policy in one middle school. *Language Policy* 15 (4), 433–451.

Freeman, R. (2000) Contextual challenges to dual language education: A case study of a developing middle school program. *Anthropology and Education Quarterly* (31) 2, 202–229.

Freire, P. (1970) *Pedagogy of the Oppressed* (M. B. Ramos, Trans.). New York: Continuum.

García, O. (2009) Education, multilingualism and translanguaging in the 21st century. *Social Justice through Multilingual Education*, 140–158.

García, O., Flores, N. and Chu, H. (2011) Extending bilingualism in U.S. secondary education: New variations. *International Multilingual Research Journal* 5 (1), 1–18.

García, O. and Wei, L. (2014) Translanguaging and education. In O. García and L. Wei (eds) *Translanguaging: Language, Bilingualism and Education* (pp. 63–77). London, UK: Palgrave Macmillan.

Garcia, A. (2017) Building a bilingual pipeline. Portland public schools and Portland State University dual language teacher partnership. www.newamerica.org. See https://na-production.s3.amazonaws.com/documents/FINAL_SupportingVisionELEquity.pdf

Giroux, H.A. (1988) *Teachers as Intellectuals: Toward a Critical Pedagogy of Learning*. Santa Barbara, CA: Greenwood Publishing Group.

Hernandez, Y. (2008) Peer capital: A network of support in dual language settings. Master's Thesis. University of Texas at El Paso.

Higgins, C. (2015) Intersecting scapes and new millennium identities in language learning. *Language Teaching* 48 (3), 373–389.

Hsieh, J.Y. (2007) The perceived effectiveness of dual language programs at the middle school level. Unpublished doctoral dissertation. University of Southern California, Los Angeles, CA.

Howard, E.R., Sugarman, J. and Christian, D. (2003) Trends in Two-Way Immersion Education. A Review of the Research. Center for Research on the Education of Students Placed at Risk: Baltimore, MD.

Kibler, A., Salerno, A. and Hardigree, C. (2014) More than being in a class: Adolescents ethnolinguistic insights in a two-way dual language program. *Language and Education* 28 (3), 251–275.

Kohne, L.E. (2006) Two-way language immersion students: How do they fare in middle and high school? Unpublished doctoral dissertation. University of California Irvine, Irvine CA and University of California Los Angeles, Los Angeles, CA.

Lima, E. and Lima, M. (1998) Identity, cultural diversity, and education. In H. Trueba and Y. Zou (eds) *Ethnic Identity and Power: Cultural Contexts of Political Action in School and Society* (pp. 321–343). Albany, NY: State University of New York Press.

Lindholm-Leary, K.J. (2011) Student outcomes in Chinese two-way immersion programs: Language proficiency, academic achievement, and student attitudes. In D. Tedick,

D. Christian and T. Fortune (eds) *Immersion Education: Practices, Policies, Possibilities* (pp. 100–118). Bristol: Multilingual Matters.

Lindholm-Leary, K. (2015) Research and resources for English language achievement. Issue 12, *Secondary Dual Language Education*. San Jose State University. See http://www.lindholm-leary.com/resources/Publications/LindholmLeary2015Starlight_Secondary_English.pdf

Lindholm_Leary, K. (2016) Students' perceptions of bilingualism in Spanish and Mandarin dual language programs. *International Multilingual Research Journal* 10 (1), 59–70.

Lindholm-Leary, K.J. and Borsato, G. (2001) *Research Paper # 10: Impact of Two-way Bilingual Elementary Programs on Students' Attitudes Toward School and College*. Santa Cruz, CA: Center for Research on Education, Diversity and Excellence.

Lindholm-Leary, K.J. and Borsato, G. (2005) Hispanic high schoolers and mathematics: Follow-up of students who had participated in two-way bilingual elementary programs. *Bilingual Research Journal* 29 (3), 641–652.

Lindholm-Leary, K.J. and Ferrante, A. (2005) Follow-up study of middle school two-way students. In F. Salili (ed.) *Language in Multicultural Education*. Charlotte, NC: Information Age Publishing.

Lindholm-Leary, K.J. and Hernández, A. (2011) Achievement and language proficiency of Latino students in dual language programmes: Native English speakers, fluent English/previous ELLs, and current ELLs. *Journal of Multilingual and Multicultural Development* 32 (6), 531–545.

Lindholm-Leary, K. and Genesee, F. (2014) Student outcomes in one-way, two-way, and indigenous language immersion education. *Journal of Immersion and Content-Based Language Education* 2 (2), 165–180.

Martin-Beltran, M. (2014) 'What do you want to say?' How adolescents use translanguaging to expand learning opportunities. *International Multilingual Research Journal* 8, 208–230. DOI: 10: 1080/19313152.2014.914372

McCollum, P. (1999) Learning to value English: Cultural capital in a two-way bilingual program. *Bilingual Research Journal* 23 (2–3), 113–133.

McGee, E.A. (2012) Sheltered English immersion vs. two-way bilingual education: A case study comparison of parental attitudes and Hispanic students' perceived self-efficacy. Unpublished doctoral dissertation. Brigham Young University, Provo, UT.

Mc Kay, S.L. and Wong, C. (1996) Multiple discourses, multiple identities: Investment and agency in second-language learning among Chinese Adolescent immigrant students. *Harvard Educational Review* 66 (3), 577–608.

Markus, H. and Kitayama, S. (1991) Culture and the self: Implications for cognition, emotion, and motivation. *Psychological Review* 98, 222–248.

Merritt, S. (2012) Conflicting ideologies about using and learning Spanish across the school years: From two-way immersion to world language pedagogy. Unpublished doctoral dissertation. University of California, Berkeley, CA.

Montone, C.L. and Loeb, M.I. (2000) *Implementing Two-way Immersion Programs in Secondary Schools*. Santa Cruz, CA: Center for Research on Education, Diversity and Excellence.

Norton, B. (2013) *Identity and Language Learning: Extending the Conversation*. Bristol: Multilingual Matters.

Porter, J. (2014) The academic performance of English dominant students in the two-way immersion dual language enrichment classroom. Unpublished doctoral dissertation. Lamar University, Beaumont, TX.

Przymus, S.D. (2016) Challenging the monolingual paradigm in secondary dual-language instruction: Reducing language-as-problem with the 2–1–L2 model. *Bilingual Research Journal* 39 (3–4), 279–295.

Quintanar-Sarellana, R. (2004) Si se puede! Academic excellence and bilingual competency in a K-8 two-way dual immersion program. *Journal of Latinos and Education* 3 (2), 87–102.

Rodriguez, C. and Trueba, H. (1998) Leadership, education, and political action: The emergence of new Latino ethnic identities. In H. Trueba and Y. Zou (eds) *Ethnic Identity and Power: Cultural Contexts of Political Action in School and Society* (pp. 43–65). Albany, NY: State University of New York Press.

Rubinstein-Ávila, E., Sox, A.A., Kaplan, S. and McGraw, R. (2015) Does biliteracy + mathematical discourse = binumerate development? Language use in a middle school dual-language mathematics classroom. *Urban Education* 50 (8), 899–937.

Salcido, S. (2009) *'Se dice Pendiente' – Incorporating Academic Language and Culture in the Secondary Mathematics Classroom.* Bel Air High School, Ysleta Independent School District, El Paso, Texas. Soleado Newsletter Spring. See http://www.dlenm.org/index.php/resources/soleado-newsletters

Sánchez, M., García, O. and Solorza, C. (2017) Reframing language allocation policy in dual language bilingual education. *Bilingual Research Journal.* doi: 10.1080/15235882.2017.1405098

Sellards, R. (2015) Pedagogy and successful practices in dual language programs. Unpublished doctoral dissertation. Brandman University, Irvine, CA.

Senesac, B.V.K. (2002) Two-way bilingual immersion: A portrait of quality schooling. *Bilingual Research Journal* 26 (1), 85–101.

Sizemore, Cindy and Graduates of Del Valle H.D., TISD, El Paso, Texas. Ysleta ISD (2008) *Students Lead the Way with Secondary Dual Language Education.* p. 9. Soleado Newsletter, Fall. See http://www.dlenm.org/index.php/resources/soleado-newsletters

Sizemore, C. (2011) Planning for secondary dual language: Asking the critical questions. Soleado Newsletter, Fall. See http://www.dlenm.org/index.php/resources/soleado-newsletters

Stebner, M. and Ruiz, C. (2012) *Enhancing Literacy Instruction through Community Connections.* West Salem High School, Salem-Keizer Public Schools. pp. 1 and 12. Spring. Soleado Newsletter. See http://www.dlenm.org/index.php/resources/soleado-newsletters

Spindler, G. and Spindler, L. (1989) Instrumental competence, self-efficacy, linguistics, minorities, and cultural therapy: A preliminary attempt at integration. *Anthropology and Education Quarterly* 20, 36–50.

Stevenson, L.M. (2014) A comparison of English and Spanish assessment measures of reading and math development for Hispanic dual language students. Unpublished doctoral dissertation. The University of Iowa, Iowa City, IA.

Swanson, D., Spencer, M. and Petersen, A. (1998) Identity formation in adolescence. In K. Borman and B. Schneider (eds) *The Adolescent Years: Social Influences and Educational Challenges* (pp. 18–41). Chicago: University of Chicago Press.

Vega, L.D. (2014) Effects of an elementary two way bilingual Spanish-English immersion school program on junior high and high school student achievement. Unpublished doctoral dissertation. Colorado State University, Fort Collins, CO.

Vega deJesus, R. and Sayers, D. (2006) Bilingual youth constructing and defending their identities across borders, a binational study of Puerto Rican circular migrant students. *Multicultural Education* 14, 16–19.

Waller, L., Wethers, K. and DeCosta, P. (2016) A critical praxis: Narrowing the gap between identity, theory, and practice. *TESOL Journal.* DOI: 10, 1002/tsj/256.

7 Teacher Preparation for Dual Language Classrooms

Barbara Kennedy

Introduction

'Teacher quality has received much attention over the past five years, yet teacher preparation has stayed remarkably off the radar. States have made unprecedented changes in their teacher policies, but few have addressed the area of teacher preparation. However, … breathing new life into the teaching profession requires that we begin at the beginning, attending to who gets admitted to preparation programs and what kind of training is provided' (Greenberg *et al.*, 2013).

While the statement above targets educator preparation in general, it is arguably even more valid when applied to the area of dual language (DL) teacher preparation. Despite rapid growth in the popularity of DL education and the resultant proliferation of DL programs across the country today, there is no systematized approach to preparing teachers to serve in DL settings.

A handful of states have adopted educational policy that requires the identification of bilingual teacher competencies, establishment of bilingual teacher preparation standards and defined pathways to bilingual teacher certification that include assessment of content, pedagogy and skills in bilingualism and biliteracy. Still, the vast majority of states provide guidelines solely for the preparation and certification of teachers serving in English-only classrooms. Moreover, even in states that offer bilingual teacher preparation programs, the focus is on development of bilingual rather than DL competencies.

The lack of clear programmatic guidelines for provision of effective DL teacher preparation leaves leaders in higher education working in an ad hoc and uncoordinated fashion to meet increased market demands for teachers prepared to teach in DL settings. This challenge is further exacerbated by a long-standing national bilingual teacher shortage that makes it increasingly difficult to appropriately staff DL schools (Darling-Hammond, 2000; Kennedy, 2013).

This chapter aims to draw attention to the important issue of DL teacher preparation. It presents a brief yet comprehensive overview of the current landscape in this scantily researched field. The research identifying features of effective DL instruction and key competencies and skills required of an effective bilingual teacher will be reviewed in order to begin to define a DL teacher specialized skill set that points toward a DL teacher preparation curriculum that specifically targets development of these skills. Descriptions of four university DL preparation programs will be shared to illustrate how leaders in higher education today are working to develop DL teacher preparation programs in response to state initiatives and increased market demand. The featured programs range from mature to those still in the early stages of development. They represent an array of geographic, demographic, social and political contexts and include programs from California, Oregon, Texas and Minnesota. Their collective efforts to prepare DL educators for a growing number of classrooms, within social, legislative and political contexts that are not necessarily devised with multilingual and multicultural education identified as a priority, serve to paint an instructive picture for program leaders across the country to relate to and learn from.

The chapter closes with a summary of common themes that emerged across the four featured programs and a list of recommendations for education policy makers and university program leaders to consider as the basis for future investigation and research. As such, this chapter aims to fill the gap in current research by providing a brief yet comprehensive snapshot of the current state of affairs in DL educator preparation in the United States.

Literature Review

Researchers today agree: it is essential that schools provide high-quality core instruction in a student's native language and English as a crucial ingredient for academic and lifelong success (August & Shanahan, 2006; Collier & Thomas, 2009; Slavin & Cheung, 2005). The growing Hispanic English language learners (ELL) student population poses a 'demographic imperative' (Garcia & Jensen, 2009: 3) that challenges policy makers at the federal, state and local levels to develop and implement effective strategies for ensuring that bilingual teachers are adequately prepared, recruited into the schools and supported and retained through ongoing professional development. Garcia *et al.* (2009) called for a collaborative and well-funded effort to solve the nation's bilingual teacher shortage problem by expanding the teacher pool. One approach to addressing these challenges is to establish clear curriculum guidelines for university-based teacher preparation programs that are designed specifically to develop in aspiring bilingual teacher candidates the competencies and skills they need to effectively serve students in DL classrooms.

In bilingual and DL classrooms, teaching students academic content in two languages, combined with widespread adoption of rigorous content standards and inclusion of students from increasingly diverse populations, is a daunting task that requires a specialized educator skill set (Achugar

& Pessoa, 2009; Diaz Soto, 1991; Guerrero & Guerrero, 2009; Menken & Antunez, 2001). Preliminary work was done in the area of bilingual teacher preparation in California in the 1990s (Walton & Carlson, 1995). This was prior to the advent of standards-based instruction and high stakes testing in the wake of the No Child Left Behind (NCLB) Act of 2001 (No Child Left Behind Act of 2001). Since then, research in educator preparation has focused on the needs of teachers serving ELLs in settings in which English is the language of instruction, with a focus on sheltered English techniques (Echevarría *et al.*, 2010) and culturally responsive pedagogy (Gay, 2010). Despite wide recognition in the research of the importance of using native language in the delivery of highly effective ELL instruction (Thomas & Collier, 2012), little attention has been paid to the investigation of best practices in bilingual teacher preparation. In the area of DL teacher preparation, the research is even more scant.

The Guiding Principles for Dual Language Education, 3rd Edition – GPDLE (Howard *et al.*, 2018) provides a comprehensive overview of the fundamental features of an effective DL program. While the GPDLE does not address DL teacher preparation, Strand 3 (*Instruction*) delineates strategies that teachers should be prepared to implement on a routine basis in the DL classroom, namely the ability to: (a) integrate language, literacy, and content instruction in English and the partner language through the use of sheltering strategies; (b) demonstrate the language and literacy skills needed to provide rigorous literacy and content instruction in English and the partner language; (c) provide systematically designed opportunities for students to develop metalinguistic and metacognitive skills; (d) deliver instruction that is student-centered and maximizes opportunities for students to benefit from peer models; and (e) promote sociocultural competence through the use of diverse materials that reflect the various subgroups of the student population and via a variety of targeted strategies. These DL teacher competencies and skills provide a starting point for creating DL educator standards, which in turn could be used to drive the design of DL teacher preparation curriculum and development of DL teacher certification requirements and assessments.

Another potential source for guidance on the design of DL teacher preparation curriculum is the extant research focused on the preparation of teachers to serve in Spanish bilingual programs. Findings indicate that coursework needs to target the development of academic language proficiency in Spanish (Guerrero & Guerrero, 2009); understanding of linguistics and second language acquisition theory (Menken & Antunez, 2001); knowledge of the Hispanic culture (Walton & Carlson, 1995); diversity awareness and skills in culturally responsive teaching (Gay, 2010; Walton & Carlson, 1995), including the adoption of a non-deficit attitude toward bilinguals and bilingualism (Achugar & Pessoa, 2009; Diaz Soto, 1991); effective multicultural parent communication and education strategies (Diaz Soto, 1991); and specially designed delivery of the content in English, such as sheltered instruction techniques (Echevarría *et al.*, 2010). While these recommendations for Spanish bilingual teacher preparation may require modification in order to align with the needs of DL teachers and teachers with a partner language other than Spanish, they likely serve as a viable starting point for DL teacher preparation curriculum development.

Program Case Studies

The four featured programs were identified via convenience sampling as the result of an internet search of university-based bilingual programs as well as through networking at professional DL conferences. Information was gathered via an electronic survey that included a variety of qualitative and quantitative question types designed to inform a program description in terms of age/phase in program development, size, purpose, design and curriculum, as well as to identify specific successes and challenges faced. Additional program information was gleaned from documents submitted by program leaders as well as program web sites. Program descriptions were drafted, with all identifying information redacted, and sent for review to each program leader.

California. California has long been a leader in bilingual education and educator preparation and boasts a number of established programs that prepare teachers to serve in bilingual and DL classrooms with Spanish being the most commonly supported program partner language.

The featured program is housed at California State University San Marcos (CSUSM) in San Marcos, California. CSUSM offers a longstanding face-to-face program that provides credit toward a Master's degree to prepare current and aspiring K-12 educators for the California Bilingual Authorization. In addition, they are in the initial implementation stages of a DL certificate program targeting K-12 teachers in California and elsewhere in a fully on-line format. This program offers graduate credits or may be completed as a stand-alone certificate program.

While compliance with State requirements drives the Bilingual Authorization pathway program at CSUSM, market demand and an anticipated rapid increase in the need for DL teachers provided impetus for the new on-line DL certificate program. The bilingual program offers coursework delivered in Spanish, but the on-line DL program is conducted entirely in English to reach a wider audience of potential participants. Field experience placement in bilingual classrooms is a requirement in the bilingual program only, as the DL program serves teachers who are already credentialed. Bilingual program participants demonstrate language proficiency on a State-generated language proficiency assessment as part of the credentialing process, but no such requirements exist in the DL program.

Even with two programs in place, the program leader reports she does not anticipate being able to meet the demand for DL educators, citing a need for expansion of efforts to reach out to wider communities in order to expand the pool of potential candidates. With the passage of California Proposition 58 in November 2016, which allowed non-English languages to be used once again in public schools, and the revocation of Proposition 227, the need for appropriately prepared and certified DL teachers is certain to grow. Currently, participant demographics are generally traditional graduate students with the majority being female and representing a balance of races and ethnicities.

The DL program curriculum, according to the website, prepares participants to 'understand, analyze, and reflect on the major concepts, principles, theories, and research related to DLE through: (1) content instruction in the primary and second language to native speakers and English learners; (2) curriculum development, program assessment, and inclusion of students with special needs or struggling learners; (3) data-informed instruction and assessment of linguistically diverse students; and (4) cross-cultural competence for students and implications for educational leadership in diverse societies.' As such, the program curriculum shows strength in the areas of curriculum design, linguistically and culturally appropriate instructional practices, knowledge of program structure, and communication and family engagement. In the area of assessment, the program leader identified a need for more targeted preparation in analysis of partner language assessment data to inform instruction.

The program leader celebrated many program successes, stating, 'Our local districts prefer to hire our candidates due to their high level of qualification in the field of education, knowledge of current standards, [and] methodology/strategies, particularly in bilingual settings.' When asked about issues and concerns faced in implementing the DL program, the program leader cited the need to 'articulate more with other college disciplines (e.g. linguistics department, foreign language education) in order to create pathways for new students into education programs (recruitment) and also to build support classes to maintain/expand skills in the target language (e.g. Spanish) for teacher candidates.'

Oregon. The State of Oregon has a long history of bilingual and DL education. However, until recently, these programs were concentrated in a few areas within the state. Currently, Oregon is experiencing a surge in DL program growth and commensurate demand for appropriately trained DL teachers. According to Oregon Public Broadcasting, 'Oregon has 70 schools with dual-language programs, with more on the way. Demand is booming,' in part because of research showing that students in the process of learning English are more successful in dual-language programs than English-only programs (Manning, 2014). Martha Martinez, formerly in the State's Education Equity Unit, underscores this point, predicting that 'the demand is only going to increase ... because these programs are just exploding, not just in the state, but nationwide' (Manning, 2014). In response, educator preparation programs across the

State are working hard to develop programs to prepare teachers to serve in DL classrooms.

As is typical in Oregon, Oregon State University Corvallis (OSUC), located in Corvallis, Oregon, has an established program to prepare teachers in English for Speakers of Other Languages (ESOL) that has also served to prepare bilingual teachers. Approval was gained in January 2018 to offer an online program to prepare currently practicing teachers for serving in Spanish-English DL classrooms. Coursework includes topics in biliteracy conducted in English and Spanish, racial and cultural harmony, multilingual linguistics and ESOL theory and methodologies. The program requires 90 hours of field placement with extensive instructional experience in Spanish. In the past, the university's teacher candidate pool has been predominately female and White/non-Hispanic. Program leaders are committed to diversifying the teacher education pipeline and recruiting more bilingual candidates. The DL licensure specialization is new to Oregon, and to become accredited, each university will need to include assessment measures for candidates' partner language proficiency. While OSUC's program aims to produce 10–15 DL specialized teachers per year through the program, it is anticipated that this will not be a sufficient number to meet current market demand.

Still in its initial stages of program implementation, the program leader listed a number of early signs of promise and potential success, including the existence of 'high levels of interest across potential students, districts, and faculty; two successful implementations of biliteracy courses (over two summers); recent faculty recruitment and hires at our university (supported by the College and university); momentum is building for the urgency and need for Dl [Dual Immersion] programs and research; State initiatives to develop and support DI programs.'

At the same time, concern was expressed surrounding successful implementation of the DL specialization program with regard to appropriate university program staffing, both for instruction and recruitment. The new DL program will require significant Full-Time Employment (FTE) to achieve success. An additional challenge is the provision of much-needed 'supports, mentorship, and financial assistance to keep bilingual teachers moving forward toward success and completion.'

Finally, the program lead called on policy makers at the State and Federal levels to increase funding to assist prospective DL teachers in paying tuition and fees and to make 'changes in testing of teachers for licensure [and] to value the second language and not just the ability to pass numerous tests in English' in order to expand the DL teacher pool and make entry into the profession more enticing and manageable. The program lead also identified the need for funding to create 'online repositories for DL research and working papers' to support implementation of quality DL teacher preparation programs in Oregon and across the nation.

Texas. Texas has long provided native language instruction to its diverse population of largely Spanish-speaking English learners. The State has a clearly articulated pathway to bilingual teacher certification that includes a rigorous language proficiency and literacy test in Spanish (Bilingual Target Language Proficiency Test – BTLPT) that assesses academic Spanish and its use in PK-12 bilingual school settings (State Board for Educator Certification, 2010). Texas also has a set of bilingual teacher competencies and an aligned assessment system for bilingual teacher licensure (State Board for Educator Certification, 2011). Nonetheless, this clearly articulated preparation and assessment system is designed for the certification of bilingual teachers but no specific guidelines are provided for DL educator preparation.

The University of Texas Rio Grand Valley (UTRGV), located in South Texas near Mexican border, is a new university (starting in 2016–17) that resulted from a merging of two universities, UT Pan-American in Edinburg and UT Brownsville. The information provided here is based on the UT Pan-American program, a mature program that offers a Bachelor's and a Master's degree in Bilingual Education and graduates approximately 350 pre-kindergarten and elementary teachers annually, as well as about 250 secondary teachers.

The UTRGV program provides coursework in Spanish and prides itself in offering a preparation curriculum strong in the areas of curriculum design, linguistically and culturally appropriate instructional practices, knowledge of bilingual education theory and program structure, and communication and family engagement. Areas cited by the program lead as in need of improvement include identification of assessments in the partner language, data analysis of partner language assessment outcomes, partner language literacy development (including making cross-language connections) and strategies to elevate the status of the partner language. Program quality is a pride point, however, particularly with regard to the Master's program. The program lead shared: 'Many of our students become the movers and shakers in their districts. Thanks to many of our Master's students, their districts have moved from transitional bilingual education to dual language education.' The community context, which is reported to not be particularly supportive of dual language education, stands in contrast to the aspirations of program leaders at UTRGV to produce educator advocates for dual language education.

With regard to program participants, UTRG serves a combination of non-traditional and traditional commuter students. Program participants are primarily female and White/Hispanic, with about 15% reported as fully bilingual and biliterate in English and Spanish. About half of the program participants are fully fluent and literate in English and partially so in Spanish, with the remaining participants either fluent in an additional partner language (15%) or monolingual English speakers (20%).

The program lead identified development of English and Spanish language and literacy skills among its program participants as posing a significant challenge.

With regard to meeting market demand, the program lead shared: 'There is a big demand for bilingual teachers in the state of Texas, and we do not produce enough teachers to fill this demand. Even though our university prepares the greatest number of bilingual teachers in the State, most of our students are not willing to relocate to other parts of the State where the demand is high.'

When asked to share concerns, the program lead identified inadequacies in the State teacher certification exams, which were not viewed to accurately measure DL educator quality. She also cited difficulties with regard to field placement, as aspiring DL teachers typically experience only one semester in a DL classroom setting and spend the other two semesters of their field-based preparation in early-exit transitional bilingual classrooms, largely due to scarcity of available program options in the local community. Despite these challenges, the program at UTRGV serves as a model for large-scale bilingual and DL teacher preparation.

Minnesota. Minnesota has an established record of providing language immersion education for its diverse student population. The University of Minnesota – Twin Cities (UMTC), located in Minneapolis, Minnesota, offers two programs designed specifically to prepare DL teachers for service in a variety of multilingual education contexts, including one-way second/foreign language immersion, two-way immersion, developmental bilingual, and Indigenous language immersion classrooms. Both programs are offered at the graduate level, with one catering to the needs of teachers who are already certified (in-service) and the other preparing teachers for initial certification (pre-service).

The more established of the two is the in-service program that targets certified teachers currently serving in a variety of PK-12 multilingual education contexts. On average, the majority (about 65%) of participants in this certificate program work in PK and elementary classrooms, while about 15% serve at the secondary level. The remaining 20% serve in other roles such as administration, coaching, and program coordination. The 15-credit certificate program takes 2.5 (5 semester terms) years to complete and, at the time of this writing, approximately 100 participants had completed the program. Because the program is online, participants represent many states within the U.S. as well as several countries outside the U.S. The in-service program is growing in popularity and fills a critical need, as explained by the program leader: 'The reason is to provide practicing Dual Language and Immersion (DLI) teachers with the requisite knowledge base and pedagogies to be able to work effectively in DLI contexts. The vast majority was prepared in generic teacher education programs and has not received DLI-specific preparation. The certificate program is designed for them.'

UMTC also has in development a pre-service program that will focus on the preparation of new-to-the-profession elementary DL teachers. The goal is to create a cohort of 25–30 bilingual teacher candidates every 2 years. The licensure program is open to currently practicing teachers working on a waiver who need an initial license in elementary education. It also welcomes bilingual paraprofessionals and other bilingual individuals who already hold an undergraduate degree and are interested in a career in dual language and immersion teaching. The program will infuse DL-specific knowledge and skills throughout the 30 credits of licensure coursework, and completion of two additional DL-specific classes (one on biliteracy development and one on language-focused instructional practices) leads to a master's degree.

According to the program coordinator, Minnesota offers DLI programs in 8 languages (Dakota, French, German, Hmong, Korean, Mandarin Chinese, Ojibwa). To best serve this diverse group of candidates, the pre-service program offers coursework in English only to ensure accessibility to a wider audience. The program will require practicum experience in DLI classrooms as well as English-medium classrooms.

The in-service program attracts primarily White/non-Hispanic teacher candidates, with some exceptions, but the pre-service program is attracting very diverse teacher candidates (Hispanics, French-speaking Africans, Chinese internationals, Native Americans). Beyond Spanish, other languages in which in-service program participants are fluent currently include French, German, Indigenous language (Ojibwa), Japanese, Mandarin Chinese and Portuguese. The program coordinator indicated that market demand is not currently being met, but the hope is that implementation of the new program will alleviate the problem. She emphasized: 'Finding qualified teachers who are highly proficient in instructional languages remains one of the biggest challenges facing our DLI programs.'

UMTC program strengths include a strong curriculum that focuses on development of the specific skills DL teachers need in order to be successful. Participants indicate that 'this is the best professional development they have ever received,' according to the program coordinator, who further explained: 'They comment on how many of the experiences and assignments … have helped them to transform their classroom practices. Also, they comment on how much they learn from having participants from different contexts (types of programs, geographical contexts) – the diversity of levels, languages, program models and geographic contexts make the online courses very rich.' Curricular areas identified for growth by the program coordinator included 'issues related to cultural competence and language, culture, and identity. It would also be ideal if there were some way to build in teaching teachers ABOUT the languages they teach in – most lack a strong base in grammatical knowledge about the partner language and English.'

Finally, when asked to share recommendations for policy change, the coordinator stated: 'I think that state licensure requirements should include a proficiency measure for non-native speakers. I also think that they should require some type of endorsement that is specifically about DLI education. So many teachers are in DLI who have never received any DLI-specific preparation or professional development. The state should acknowledge that DLI teaching is different from teaching through the medium of English – that it requires a unique knowledge base and pedagogical skill set.'

Common Themes

From this chapter's exploration of four DL teacher preparation programs there emerged several common themes.

- DL teacher preparation comes in a variety of formats, including: undergraduate degree, undergraduate minor, graduate degree, licensure, certificate, face-to-face and on-line.
- The majority of programs prepare teachers to serve in elementary (rather than secondary) DL classrooms, and target the development of teachers in Spanish-English DL programs.
- Many programs offer flexible programming (pre-service, in-service) in order to meet the needs of aspiring as well as current practicing DL teachers.
- There is widespread recognition that DL teachers have preparation needs that are distinct from ESOL teachers and traditional bilingual teachers (partner language proficiency, specialized skill set).
- There is recognition of the need to identify, align and systematize DL teacher preparation standards, DL preparation program curriculum and DL teacher licensure requirements.
- There is general agreement that it requires a comprehensive and coordinated effort among policy makers, university leaders, school district leaders and community stakeholders to effectively address the DL teacher shortage.
- State initiatives and state policy are important drivers in preparing teachers to deliver effective DL instruction, but funding, research and research dissemination are required in order to actualize policy in the field.
- Program participants in most programs are female, traditional undergraduate and graduate students, and are White (Hispanic and Non-Hispanic), possibly indicating a need for increased efforts to recruit a more diverse pool of DL teacher candidates.
- Program curriculum is generally perceived as strong but improvements in the areas of assessment, native language literacy development and cultural competence are needed.
- Despite strong efforts, universities continue to struggle to meet high market demand for DL teachers.

Recommendations

The following list of recommendations is designed to guide policy makers and leaders in teacher preparation as they collaborate in devising programs that will effectively prepare an expanded pool of DL educators to serve in our Nation's schools:

- fund research efforts aimed at identifying best practices in DL educator preparation;
- fund the creation of national DL educator standards, aligned curriculum guidelines and resources, DL teacher assessments (to evaluate content knowledge as well as partner language proficiency), DL teacher licensure recommendations, and DL teacher evaluation systems;
- fund a portal that houses research reports and tools and resources for effective implementation of DL teacher preparation programs.

Conclusion

This chapter provided a snapshot of current research on DL educator preparation and featured four university preparation programs striving to fill the need for appropriately trained and certified educators to serve in the growing number of DL classrooms across the country. It is hoped that increasing awareness around this issue will result in policy makers and institutions of higher education adopting policies and practices that alleviate the DL teacher shortage and increase the capacity for DL teachers to be effective in the classroom.

References

Achugar, M. and Pessoa, S. (2009) Power and place: Language attitudes towards Spanish in a bilingual academic community in Southwest Texas. *Spanish in Context* 6 (2), 199–223. doi: 10.1075/sic.6.2.03ach

August, D. and Shanahan, T. (eds) (2006) *Developing Literacy in Second-Language Learners: A Report of the National Literacy Panel on Language-Minority Children and Youth.* Mahwah, NJ: Lawrence Erlbaum Associates.

Collier, V.P. and Thomas, W.P. (2009) *Educating English Learners for a Transformed World.* Albuquerque, NM: Dual Language Education of New Mexico Fuente Press.

Darling-Hammond, L. (2000) *Solving the Dilemmas of Teacher Supply, Demand, and Standards: How can we Ensure a Competent, Caring, and Qualified Teacher for Every Child.* New York: Columbia University, National Commission on Teaching and America's Future.

Diaz Soto, L. (1991) Teacher preparation and the linguistically diverse young child. *Education* 111 (4), 487–490.

Echevarría, J., Vogt, M.E. and Short, D.J. (2010) *Making Content Comprehensible for English Learners: The SIOP Model* (4th edn). Boston: Allyn and Bacon.

Garcia, E. and Jensen, B. (2009) Early educational opportunities for children of Hispanic origins. Social Policy Report, XXIII(II), 3–19. See http://www.srcd.org/spr.html

Garcia, E., Jensen, B. and Scribner, K. (2009) The demographic imperative. *Educational Leadership* 66 (7), 8–13.

Gay, G. (2010) *Culturally Responsive Teacher: Theory, Research, and Practice*. New York, NY: Teacher's College Press.

Greenberg, J., McKee, A. and Walsh, K. (December, 2013) National Council on Teacher Quality. Teacher Prep Review: A review of the nation's teacher preparation programs. Downloaded May 17, 2016. See http://www.nctq.org/dmsStage/Teacher_Prep_Review_2013_Report

Guerrero, M.D. and Guerrero, M.C. (2009) El (sub)desarrollo del español académico entre los maestros bilingües: ¿Una cuestión de poder? *Journal of Latinos and Education* 8 (1), 55–66. doi:10.1080/15348430802466795

Howard, E.R., Lindholm-Leary, K.J., Rogers, D., Olague, N., Medina, J., Kennedy, B., Sugarman, J. and Christian, D. (2018) *Guiding Principles for Dual Language Education* (3rd edn). Washington, DC: Center for Applied Linguistics.

Kennedy, B. (2013) A qualitative case study of the bilingual teacher shortage in one Texas school district. Unpublished dissertation.

Manning, R. (July 11, 2014; updated February 18, 2015) Oregon educators prioritize bilingual education. Portland State. Downloaded May 17, 2016 from: http://www.opb.org/news/article/bilingual-education/

Menken, K. and Antunez, B. (2001) *An Overview of the Preparation and Certification of Teachers Working with Limited English Proficient (LEP) Students*. See ERIC database: Clearinghouse on Teaching and Teacher Education.

No Child Left Behind Act of 2001, Pub. L. No. 107−110 115 § 1425 (2002).

Slavin, R.E. and Cheung, A. (2005) A synthesis of research on language of reading instruction for English language learners. *Review of Education Research* 75 (2), 247–284.

State Board for Educator Certification (2010) The Texas examinations of educator standards (TExES): Preparation manual 190 bilingual target language proficiency test (BTLPT). See http://cms.texes-ets.org/texes/prepmaterials/texes-preparation-manuals/

State Board for Educator Certification (2011) The Texas examinations of educator standards (TExES): Preparation manual 164 bilingual education supplemental. See http://cms.texes-ets.org/texes/prepmaterials/texes-preparation-manuals/

Thomas, W.P. and Collier, V.P. (2012) *Dual Language Education for a Transformed World*. New Mexico: Fuente Press.

Walton, P.H. and Carlson, R. (1995) Preparing for a more diverse student population. *Thrust for Educational Leadership* 24 (5), 36.

8 Making Space for Dual Language Education: The Role of Policy

Donna Christian

Introduction

As the popularity of dual language education grows, with more frequent media coverage (Harris, 2015; McInerny, 2016), and more research attesting to its efficacy (Christian, 2016; Lindholm-Leary, 2016), educators and communities around the United States are exploring the possibilities for establishing and expanding dual language programs. As they do so, they must take into account local conditions, our current knowledge base and a set of external policy contexts that expand or limit the possibilities for the programs. Because these programs are language-focused, they are subject to both education and language policies at every level of government, from local to national. Further, the policies come in many forms – laws, regulations, budget appropriations and judicial decisions, among others. This chapter will examine the interaction between various policy contexts and the implementation of two-way dual language education and discuss implications for program planning and advocacy.

Dual language programs are in a unique intersection of policy areas. All education programs must respond to many levels and types of policies related to education, in the form of compulsory schooling for children of certain ages, graduation requirements, and teacher qualifications, to name a few – but dual language education, by involving multiple languages, is also heavily influenced by the language policies and politics, overt or covert, in the sociolinguistic context of the program that are embedded in views of immigration, diverse cultures, and other social issues. Possibilities for the approach to succeed are, for better or worse, affected by the sociolinguistic reality of attitudes, beliefs and ideologies about language and education, that are sometimes independent of research-based evidence. They relate to the broader issues of power, access, opportunity, and inequality. In fact, among others, Joshua Fishman has lamented 'Why are facts so useless in this discussion?' (cited in May, 2008: 30) as he reminded us that discussions of bilingual education must always keep in mind the wider social and political context, including the positions and possible agendas of the commentators themselves. The debate about bilingual education in the United States is a classic example of this tension, where research on the outcomes of education using various bilingual approaches has routinely been dismissed by those who oppose bilingual education, because they do not 'believe' it.

Part of the sociolinguistic reality that must be acknowledged is the multilingual nature of the United States and most societies in the world. Historically, language policy and planning has largely followed the concept of the nation-state with a single language (Spolsky, 2009). In this age of mobility and shifting political borders, the one nation, one language standard has all but disappeared. The concept of 'super-diversity' has been introduced to capture this new reality, but the history of monolingual ideologies and intolerance persists (Wiley, 2014). This is the backdrop for our discussion of policy contexts for dual language education.

Policy Contexts

The approaches within the full range of dual language education (Christian, 2011) cut across somewhat distinct, though related, areas of the ideological and policy universe.

- *One-way (foreign) language immersion* sits in the sociolinguistic arena of society's beliefs about and interest in learning languages other than the so-called 'majority' or perhaps official languages. Motivators include usefulness for diplomacy, commerce, national security, personal enrichment and so on.
- *Heritage language immersion* connects to attitudes and beliefs about immigration, immigrants and their benefit to society. An appreciation of cultural and linguistic diversity and beliefs in language rights play a role here, as well as the concern for expanding national language resources for diplomacy, security and so on.
- *Indigenous language immersion* plays into the attitudes and beliefs about indigenous communities and their rights, including language rights. Support can come from an appreciation of cultural and linguistic diversity, as well as a concern for endangered languages.
- *Two-way dual language education* cuts across these ideologies by involving both groups – majority language speaking students and immigrant or indigenous speakers of another language. As a result, it can, and does, tap into all of the sources of support and tension mentioned above.

All models, of course, benefit from policies and attitudes that specifically recognize the benefits of multilingual approaches to education and the personal enrichment of knowing more than one language. This is the ideal – but the ideal is not often realized. This broad ideological frame serves as the setting for the formulation and implementation of policies that have a bearing on dual language programs.

As mentioned above, policy is formulated, overtly and covertly, at all levels of government and institutions, from macro to micro. In the United States and elsewhere, policy exists at many levels – federal, state, local, school, program, classroom – and may be codified and written or may be simply a matter of accepted and expected practice. Governmental policies at the federal, state, and local levels tend to be codified, often in law or regulation. Beyond overt statements, other government actions set policy, such as through judicial decisions and appropriations choices (i.e., a type of program may be authorized by law, but if no funding is provided, the program will not be able to operate). Every dual language educator can think of ways in which these factors have influenced their program.

Federal level

One of the most basic national level language policy decisions is the choice of one or more official language for the country. Many things follow from this, including the default language of instruction in schools. While the United States has no official language declared at the federal level despite attempts to make English the official language, English remains the main language in the curriculum, and as de Jong (2016) observes, 'much of our formal language-in-education policies that address linguistic diversity are firmly grounded in a monolingual mindset' (2016: 378). Other federal laws and regulations, including those related to education, civil rights, and national security, contribute to the overall policy context for schools. For two-way dual language education, federal policy related to civil rights plays a significant role, as it frames education for English learners with a Supreme Court decision (*Lau v. Nichols*) as a foundational element (Boyle *et al.*, 2015).

State level

In the United States, education is primarily the responsibility of the states, with some federal influence and involvement. State education policy sets the parameters for curriculum, testing, teacher requirements and other dimensions of education practice. Some states formulate overt language policies, including the designation of official languages. For example, the state of Hawaii made Hawaiian one of its official languages and gave support to the beginning of the Hawaiian immersion program. Naturally, states also gain power as the major source of education funding.

Local level

Local school districts operate within federal and state policies to determine how their system is organized, what kinds of programs they offer, and how funds are allocated to individual schools. At the local and school level, it falls to individuals to enact language and education policies, what Menken and García (2010) call 'agency in implementation.' They note that 'just as a policy statement can either open up or restrict "ideological and implementational" spaces (Hornberger, 2005), so too can educators either carve out or close off these spaces' (2005: 4). They argue that educators in the schools make choices as they implement policies, bringing their own perspectives and experience to their practice. As a result, policies in practice are far from uniform, and the top-down imposition of policy is met by the more 'bottom-up' actions in schools and districts. de Jong (2016: 379) describes this as '…the centrality of agency of individuals within their own situational context who make sense of and negotiate top-down policies within their own localized context and their own beliefs, values, and identities.' At the school level, for example, educators determine what language(s) will be used in daily announcements, a policy choice that communicates the value placed on the languages spoken by the students.

It can be exhausting to think about all the overlapping policy dimensions that play a role in making dual language programs possible, but potentially relevant policy factors come from many sources.

Finding Implementation Spaces

The notion of 'implementation spaces' articulated by Hornberger (2005) and others is helpful in thinking about how policy affects practice. These are 'agentive spaces in which local actors implement, interpret, and perhaps resist policy initiatives in varying and unique ways' (Hornberger & Johnson, 2007: 509). Then, policy can be seen as framing the implementation space, determining how big and open it is, or conversely, how limited. This conception also recognizes the role of local actors – teachers, administrators, community members and so on – as they are the 'agents' within these spaces. In the case of dual language education, the question becomes: What policy environments allow 'implementation spaces' for local programs and how can we work toward better environments or work within what exists?

The influence of policy on implementation space can be scaled, as shown in Figure 8.1. Policies can, individually or in combination, have an effect on dual language education from requiring it to forbidding it. While the extremes are rare, the areas between them, from encouraging to discouraging, are readily found. For example, the Utah state government has instituted a variety of incentives and supports to encourage dual language

POLICY
*prohibits dual language
*discourages dual language
*allows dual language
*encourages dual language
*requires dual language

Figure 8.1 How policies influence dual language education

education, policies that include funding for programs and teacher professional development. They have also removed some barriers to implementation, such as by expanding the pool of qualified teachers through special programs for teachers from abroad. These policies create space by encouraging dual language programs. Most policies are neutral, having little direct effect. Others have a discouraging effect, such as those that limit the offering of education in languages other than English to certain students (i.e., referenda enacted in Arizona and several other states). Policies that are seemingly unrelated can have a dampening effect on dual language education as well. For example, policies that limit magnet programs or charter schools can restrict the ability of districts to bring together students who are speakers of particular languages to participate in dual language education, such as a Chinese-English dual language program when the Chinese-speaking students are dispersed around the district. In fact, it is more likely that policies not specifically addressing dual language education will affect its implementation space, since policies specifically about those programs are rare. The constellation of more and less relevant policies defines the space available, and systemic support is needed for dual language education to flourish, with all policy points lined up, from language education to graduation requirements to budget appropriations for materials and beyond.

Policy contexts and the growth of dual language education

In the 1960s, the so-called 'quiet evolution of language and cultural relations' between Francophone and Anglophone communities was going on in Canada. One outcome was the adoption of policies to affirm the equal status of French and English, including the federal Official Languages Act. At that time, Anglophone parents in Montreal came together to advocate for a French immersion program for their children. Their goal was for their children to become bilingual in their home language, English and the predominant language around them, French. They believed that this would give their children better opportunities for education and jobs in the future. Although the federal government was not responsible for education, its movement toward the official language policy expansion, along with public support for learning French at the local level, provided the implementation space for these local actors. Immersion, a form of dual language education, was a local response to the need for language skills. It was allowed and perhaps even encouraged by the national and provincial language policies, enabled by the local school board, and clearly responded to the sociolinguistic context. As documented by collaborating researchers from McGill University, the program was also effective in reaching academic and language goals (Lambert & Tucker, 1972).

At the time the Canadian immersion program got underway, some policy makers and educators in the United States were becoming concerned about the nation's lack of capacity in languages other than English. These concerns had emerged after experiences in World War II and the launch of Sputnik by the then Soviet Union, which underscored the security, diplomatic, and economic disadvantages of insufficient language resources. Elementary and secondary schools were not producing individuals with language competency to enter the pipeline into postsecondary education and careers that involved using languages other than English.

After a visit to Montreal, Dr. Russell Campbell, professor of applied linguistics at UCLA, felt that the immersion approach would benefit U.S. education:

> ...on returning from a visit to the St. Lambert French immersion program and after extended consultation with students, parents, teachers, school officials, and McGill University participants in that program, [I] approached Culver City, CA Unified School District authorities to suggest the possible replication, with only minor modifications, of the St. Lambert program in an American setting. (Campbell, 1984: 115–116)

The Culver City school district agreed to try the model, with the help of researchers from UCLA. In this case, there was no U.S. national language policy that supported the initiative, but national and state policies at the time did not get in the way, and the local school district supported the program. The language of the immersion program was Spanish rather than French, reflecting the sociolinguistic characteristics of Southern California. Most of the students were monolingual speakers of English, and the goals of dual language education – bilingualism, biliteracy, and academic achievement – were set for them. Immersion gained attention, and research results demonstrated the effectiveness of the approach in the United States as well as in Canada (Campbell et al., 1985) giving evidence for continuing the programs. Subsequent research reassured schools considering the innovative dual language education model, and the number of programs grew.

This 'one-way' dual language (second/foreign language immersion) model expanded to other languages and other variations on the model not long after it was introduced in this country. Its original site in Culver City celebrated the 40th anniversary of immersion in 2011, with a program at two elementary schools, in two languages (Spanish and Japanese), and with continuation courses at the secondary level. As in many districts, there are more applicants than spaces in the immersion programs, a sign of their popularity with families. These schools join hundreds of others in the United States, and many more around the world, in the immersion enterprise.

Like the original St. Lambert program in Montreal, most immersion programs have been local initiatives (with some states being more active recently). Unlike Canada, however, the United States has no official language policy or even strong federal policy encouraging the learning of languages other than English. Federal and state policies have generally allowed such programs (for native English speakers in particular), assuming language learning would not interfere with students meeting general education requirements, but they haven't particularly encouraged them. As a result, in many places, implementation spaces were open for local agents to work within, but not necessarily inviting.

As the one-way dual language (foreign/second language immersion) model spread around the world, it extended to heritage and indigenous language contexts, in many cases with a goal to rejuvenate an ethnolinguistic minority community language that had declined in use among the younger generation. A prime example is the Hawaiian Immersion Program which has been a key component of the successful revitalization of Native Hawaiian (Wilson, 2014). In Hawaii, policy support came from all governmental levels. The declaration of Hawaiian as an official language of the state of Hawaii in 1978 helped create the environment for the establishment of the Hawaiian immersion program, and various federal laws, including the Native American Languages Act, established basic policy support for Native American languages. But in Hawaii, as in most places, local grassroots activities were key to making the program happen, with parents and communities advocating for the program from pre-school through the university.

Finally, extension of the early dual language model has brought together students from two different language backgrounds in two-way programs (two-way immersion). A U.S.-government-sponsored research center based at UCLA (the Center for Language Education and Research or CLEAR) was funded in the mid-1980s to examine, among other things, the ways in which bilingual education for English learners could be integrated with foreign language education for English-background students. It drew on the experience of programs with such integration that had earlier evolved from bilingual education (including the Coral Way school in Florida, where native Spanish speakers and native English speakers were being educated together). CLEAR researchers documented two-way dual language as a way to achieve this combination of models and worked with local school districts who wanted to try the approach (see Christian *et al.*, 1997).

During the 1990s, the number of two-way dual language programs grew steadily (see Center for Applied Linguistics, n.d.), particularly with federal policy as a stimulus when the Department of Education's bilingual education office provided discretionary funding designated for developmental bilingual and two-way programs and supported technical assistance efforts for local and state educators. Later, a small amount of federal funding became available for states and schools through the Foreign Language Assistance Program, with two-way programs considered to be an innovative approach to language education, but that funding stream was eliminated in the 2012 federal budget (Office of English Language Acquisition, 2014).

Given the state and local responsibility for education in the United States, policies at those levels are critical for program implementation. For one thing, two-way dual language programs are voluntary, so other educational policies need to be in place to make them a viable option for families. Similar to other immersion programs, programs often began as magnet programs or as a strand within a school so that parents could choose the program for their children or not. Also, with two-way programs drawing from both foreign language education and bilingual education arenas, local and state policies from both areas are at play; typically, two-way programs would be 'housed' in either the foreign language or bilingual education office, with more or less communication between them, and would be governed by the policies that applied to that domain.

As experience was gained with dual language education and research pointed to its potential (Genesee *et al.*, 2006), the model became more widely known as a high-quality educational alternative, with long waiting lists for entry. A particular motivation was the possibility of improving academic opportunity for Hispanic students who had a proportionately higher dropout rate and incidence of academic difficulty, making it an approach that could also address civil rights concerns. Thus, support for two-way dual language has come from those who seek more language education for all students as well as those who are concerned about the success of English learners. While most programs continued to involve Spanish and English, the languages of instruction diversified somewhat, though limited by demographic factors, since native speakers of the language are needed in sufficient numbers to populate half of the classrooms, to include Mandarin, Korean, French, Japanese and others.

Federal education legislation has remained a major factor in the space for dual language education, particularly the series of Elementary and Secondary Education Acts (ESEA) that have been passed. While early versions of the legislation incorporated the Bilingual Education Act (1968) that explicitly included bilingual forms of education, later versions, including *No Child Left Behind Act* in 2001 and *Every Student Succeeds Act* in 2015, emphasized English achievement through program and assessment requirements. While education through languages other than English is not prohibited, implications of various provisions of the laws have served to discourage it. Other statements of federal policy have been more welcoming, such as a 2015 statement on early childhood programs for dual language learners that focuses attention on children learning two or more languages and recommends increased awareness of the importance of home language development (U.S. Department of Health and Human Services & U.S. Department of Education, 2015).

In the next section, we will look briefly at several cases of two-way dual language programs and their implementation spaces.

Finding spaces for dual language programs

Arlington, Virginia, a diverse community near Washington, DC, began its two-way dual language program in the fall of 1986 with a first-grade class (Christian *et al.*, 1997). At the time, school district policy did not include bilingual education; it was an 'all-ESL' county, with a strong ESL program. Through CLEAR, the research center mentioned earlier that might be considered an example of federal policy through funding, the Center for Applied Linguistics (CAL) began working with Francis Scott Key Elementary School and arranged for a team of educators, including the principal, to visit the bilingual programs in Hartford, Connecticut. Following that visit, the principal pursued a model for his school that would provide bilingual education for Spanish-speaking ESL students and would add a second language for English speakers. He opted to begin a two-way program the following fall. One of the earlier implementers, Key School has gone on to become a whole school program, and the Arlington schools have created a two-way immersion path from kindergarten in several elementary schools through high school graduation. Local policies along the way supported this development, including the fact that the district organized schools in clusters so that parents could opt into the two-way program or another elementary school in their cluster. This is a good example of a non-language policy facilitating the implementation of dual language education as an opt-in program.

The policy context above the local level was essentially neutral at the time other than the federal support for the research center that allowed CAL to provide technical assistance. Federal language education policies were still reacting to the debates about bilingual education of the 1970s and 1980s, though the early years of the program coincided with the short period of time when the Department of Education offered funding for developmental bilingual education, including two-way programs, and later the district received a grant in 1991 (Christian *et al.*, 1997). The state, Virginia, did not require any form of bilingual education for English learners, but it did not restrict use of languages other than English in instruction. Further, the Arlington program was administered through the foreign language supervisor's office, so it escaped some of the controversy around bilingual education.

Other local stories show similar policy contexts – federal and state levels allowing dual language, but much of the action occurring in the local district. The Inter-American Magnet School in Chicago was another early adopter of two-way dual language, using the district magnet school policy as a basis for bringing Spanish speakers and English speakers together. In this case, parents were the spark for beginning the program, which started as a preschool offering in 1975, became a school-within-a-school, and expanded through the grades to its current preK through grade 8 whole-school program (Christian *et al.*, 1997). State-level policy was also supportive as the program grew, since Illinois's State Board of Education required schools to offer bilingual instruction if they have 20 or more English learners from the same language background. As two-way dual language programs emerged, they satisfied this requirement.

The Windham, CT, schools followed a similar path to implementation of two-way dual language education, with school administrators approaching the local Board of Education in 1992 in a state context that required bilingual instruction for English learners. According to an account of that process, one concern involved logistics (Romano, 2010). A pilot program was approved, but, since it was open to the whole district, transportation became an issue. Working with the school bus vendor, the administrators were able to accommodate children on bus routes as parents signed up. The program became established and added one grade per year. In the expansion through elementary grades, all funding was state and local. As the program reached the end of the elementary level, federal funding was received, bringing in the federal incentivizing role to extend the program beyond elementary school. Later, in 1999, the state adopted a policy to limit English learners to 30 months of bilingual education, but it exempted two-way dual language programs and, in fact, directed schools with transitional bilingual programs to 'investigate the feasibility of establishing two-way bilingual programs starting in kindergarten' (Tuhus, 1999). In a similar fashion, state lawmakers in Massachusetts, following a public referendum, eliminated bilingual education for English learners in the state as had California and Arizona not long before, yet exempted two-way immersion programs (Eaton, 2012). In both cases, the states, by exempting dual language from a restrictive policy, protected space for the programs. It is interesting to note that both California and Massachusetts have since reversed their policy, California by referendum in 2016 and Massachusetts by legislation in 2017, actions that restored bilingual instruction as an option for English learners.

The case of French-English dual language programs in New York City is interesting because it draws on both the local district's encouraging policies toward multilingualism in schools, the French government's support for French in U.S. schools, and U.S.-based French-American cultural organizations (Jaumont, 2011). In particular, the FACE Foundation works with the Cultural Services of the French Embassy to sponsor the French Dual Language Program in New York City Schools to serve French- and English-speaking families who want their children to attend bilingual schools, providing resources for students, teachers, administrators, and parents.

Finally, one more example illustrates the powerful role that state policy can play in the establishment of dual language education. In recent years, several states have initiated dual language programs, providing funding streams and support structures that incentivize schools to start programs. Utah has been a leader in this regard. In 2008, the Utah Senate passed legislation that included funding for 'dual language immersion,' including two-way and one-way programs in Chinese, French, and Spanish, setting a target of 100 schools and 30,000 students by 2015. According to the state's website, 195 schools participated in the 2017–2018 academic year, and Portuguese, German and Russian have been added to the languages offered (Utah State Board of Education, 2018). In addition to annual funding for schools, the state education office has been very active in helping schools with teacher recruitment, professional development, curriculum and materials. For example, they have made agreements with other countries, including China, Brazil and Mexico, to send teachers to work in Utah schools for one to three years (Pascopella, 2013), developing policies that allow them to address the significant challenge of staffing for dual language programs. Other states have undertaken similar efforts, including North Carolina, Delaware and Georgia (Boyle *et al.*, 2015). This level of support and encouragement in state policy and action creates a vibrant implementation space for dual language education and promotes success for programs that begin.

Promising Strategies to Improve the Policy Climate

Overt policy actions by state and local governments can be helpful if they directly promote dual language education, such as the Utah state legislation. Other policy-related activities can help create positive environments for building strong dual language programs even if they do not specifically address the educational program. The most obvious examples are those that reward or facilitate high levels of language learning as an outcome of the educational system. A few such activities will be mentioned here to illustrate.

Incentives

In 2011, California became the first state to offer a *Seal of Biliteracy* option on high school diplomas. In order to earn the Seal, students must demonstrate academic proficiency in English and at least one other language. This concrete marker of language proficiency serves as a goal for students to work toward, lends external approval to developing home language skills for English learners, and gives a tangible indicator for employers and higher education of the abilities of a high school graduate. Because of these beneficial outcomes, the policy also stimulates attention to language development in the schools for both English speakers and English learners and often leads to community advocacy for stronger programs, including dual language education. According to Californians Together, who promoted the Seal of Biliteracy credential in California and have assisted other states and school districts in developing their own seal, as of 2018, 33 states have instituted the policy, others have it 'under consideration' and a few other states have local districts that use it even though it is not official policy at the state level (see Seal of Biliteracy, 2018). Where the Seal of Biliteracy policy is in effect, the implementation space for dual language education becomes more open and welcoming.

Broader frameworks

Dual language education can also become attractive as part of a larger plan to increase language proficiency in a state or city, and the adoption of such a plan signals a more positive policy environment. An example is a 'language roadmap,' a component of a U.S. federal initiative to 'promote and support the study of foreign languages and cultures' (The Language Flagship, 2013). The U.S. Department of Defense's National Security Education Program oversaw the initiative, which was funded by Congress and co-sponsored by the Departments of Commerce and Labor. The first group of states to develop language roadmaps in 2007 included Oregon, Texas, and Ohio. Their plans illustrate the promise of forthcoming policies that would encourage dual language education. The Oregon Roadmap, for example, recommends that a new state office of language acquisition '...provide leadership and coordination for the expansion of *dual language* programs and international exchanges, while providing support and guidance for proficiency development and assessment, state proficiency goals, world language teacher licensures, and professional development' [emphasis added]. The Texas roadmap highlights successful dual language programs already in the state and recommends, among other things, a broad partnership of educators, parents and business to recommend an appropriate language program for all students beginning in preK.

These early implementers were followed by Utah (2009), Rhode Island (2012) and Hawaii (2013). Among its recommendations, Utah's roadmap seeks to 'Encourage the expansion of dual immersion programs to additional schools in multiple languages… Encourage elementary teacher preparation programs in higher education to graduate students who are certified to teach in dual immersion programs.' Rhode Island's plan even suggests a mechanism for increasing funding for this purpose by forming 'a consortium of supportive companies who pay dues into a fund managed by the Rhode Island Foundation. Schools can then apply for funding to put in place a sequence of bilingual education in their schools.'

Cities have also conducted Language Summits that lead to roadmaplike plans, including Salt Lake City and Austin. All roadmaps include intensive forms of language education, often one-way and two-way dual language, in their recommendations. With a policy framework like this for guidance, the space for dual language is made more evident, and the chances increase that policymakers will be more mindful of dual language education as they make policy and funding decisions.

Working with professional associations

In the United States, professional associations can influence policy by making policymakers aware of the benefits of particular approaches and community sentiments. To affect the policy context for dual language education, it is useful to align with groups and individuals who share similar goals in order to push for better implementation spaces through promoting policies that support the programs or, if necessary, opposing policies that interfere.

The Joint National Committee for Languages (JNCL) is a national policy organization concerned with language and international education. The National Council for Languages and International Studies (NCLIS) is its public advocacy arm. Each year, JNCL/NCLIS holds a Language Advocacy Day in Washington, DC, during which representatives of member organizations visit Members of Congress and their staffs to discuss issues important to language professionals. The JNCL website features information about the current policy environment and alerts visitors to actions and proposals that are significant for language issues, providing sample letters and other helpful tools.

Other professional associations also organize advocacy events and offer similar kinds of materials, designed to help educators and local communities be more effective in presenting the case for particular language and education policies at all government levels. Educational associations, including The American Council on the Teaching of Foreign Languages (ACTFL), National Association for Bilingual Education (NABE) and TESOL International Association have resources for advocacy on their websites, including alerts about current issues and positions the organizations have taken. ACTFL features a Legislative Action Center with current updates on issues for the language teaching profession. TESOL sponsors an annual Advocacy & Policy Summit in Washington, DC where members can learn about current policy issues and meet with Members of Congress to discuss those issues. In addition to the broadly based language organizations, there are also a number of groups that focus specifically on dual language education and engage in policy discussions and action, including the Association of Two-Way and Dual Language Education and Dual Language Education of New Mexico. These national level groups, and many organizations at the state and local level, can be important sources of information and allies in working toward better policy contexts for dual language education.

Policy Challenges

Even when implementation spaces appear to accommodate dual language education, other policy challenges need to be faced. A number of educational policies can limit two-way dual language initiation or continuation. A few will be mentioned here.

Teacher requirements

States report that staffing is one of the greatest challenges for dual language programs (Boyle *et al.*, 2015) since they need teachers who are fluent speakers of the program languages who also meet credential requirements for their grade and/or subject. There is both a need for appropriate policy to ensure qualified teachers in programs and a need for assistance in preparing teachers to be certified who have the necessary language skills. States set certification and other qualification requirements within federally-set general parameters. Few states have specific requirements for dual language program teachers, but many have credentials or endorsements for teachers working with second language learners. To improve the supply of qualified teachers, districts rely on in-service professional development or recruit personnel internationally or domestically with appropriate language proficiency and help them satisfy credential requirements with some states establishing alternative certification routes (Boyle *et al.*, 2015).

Articulation

For students to achieve the benefits of dual language programs for language learning and academic achievement, extended learning sequences are needed in order to develop academic language proficiency (Hakuta, 2011). While programs extending through elementary school are common, contexts are less conducive at secondary and post-secondary levels, particularly for articulated and cumulative language development, since most of those offerings are geared to students without previous language study. Some districts have adopted alternative programs such as the International Baccalaureate that can serve as the follow-on to an elementary dual language program (Montone & Loeb, 2000). Policy incentives such as the Seal of Biliteracy will also encourage better articulation to promote high proficiency in multiple languages. As the number of dual language programs grows, this issue will increasingly confront higher education institutions as well.

Assessment

The language and process of testing is another policy area that may restrict the dual language education implementation space. Aside from some limited exceptions, federal policies require assessment of students in English, and most states follow suit. Such policies have long caused concern, particularly in so-called 'high-stakes' testing, because English learners may not have the language skills needed to perform to their potential (Wiley & Wright, 2004). In addition, in dual language programs, English-only testing puts pressure on programs to increase the amount of English used for instruction in order to prepare students for the tests. Some states adopt language proficiency standards and assessments for languages of instruction other than English, including several states that require annual assessment of the language paired with English in state-funded dual language programs (Boyle et al., 2015). National assessments, such as the National Assessment of Education Progress, are also only in English. In general, these policies for testing only in English communicate the relative values assigned to the languages of instruction and detract from the goals of dual language education.

Concluding Thoughts

The achievement of the goals of dual language education requires support from policies at all levels (federal, state, local) to foster the ongoing development of first and second language and academic learning in all ways possible. Attention to policy should encompass not only legislation, but also regulations, guidelines and funding appropriations that are made. It is essential that a systemic approach be an objective – legislation will not make a difference without implementing regulations, appropriations, and court decisions that move in the same direction. In recent years, federal policy support for language education in the United States has been somewhat stronger in higher education than at the elementary or secondary levels, but it remains far from robust even there. Recent federal elementary–secondary education laws are silent on the use of languages other than English in education. They require that English proficiency and academic outcomes be measured for non-native speakers, and neither prohibit nor encourage native language development. Policies on the use of languages other than English for instruction are left to states and local districts to set. There has been some encouraging leadership from the U.S. Defense Department, such as the Language Roadmaps project mentioned earlier, but also funding for some K-12 programs, and in early childhood education.

Support for dual language education ideally would come from a broad and consistent orientation, if not a policy, that encourages and/or requires all students to become proficient in two or more languages and that provides supports and incentives for some students to develop very high levels of proficiency with an awareness of the personal and social benefits that will come. Then, all policies that could be supportive of that orientation would be aligned with it, including the following:

- encourage high-quality, well-articulated K-12 school-based programs such as two-way dual language that build on the heritage languages in local communities and promote second language learning for all students along with academic content, followed by postsecondary programs that build on those skills;
- include proficiency in languages other than English among core areas of achievement that are measured and accounted for, both locally and in national assessments;
- give credit and provide incentives for students who achieve high levels of proficiency in English and another language, such as the Seal of Biliteracy;
- include in standards for teacher preparation for ALL teachers the understanding of language learning, awareness of the value of language proficiency, and knowledge of ways to support heritage and second language development;
- expand availability of high-quality teacher preparation programs to prepare dual language teachers to increase the availability of effective teachers in a wide variety of languages.

In conclusion, it is useful to return to the notion of implementation spaces made available within the policy context. Following Figure 8.1, if policy contexts prohibit or discourage dual language education, action is needed in working with policymakers to change the orientation. Policies that allow, or even better, encourage dual language education can be thought of as in the 'implementation zone' and local educators and communities can make the most of them. Local agents can then fill these implementation spaces with two-way dual language and other highly effective language and academic programs, in synchrony with the local sociolinguistic reality, to give all students the opportunity to learn additional languages to high levels of proficiency and receive the intellectual, cultural, and economic benefits that can result.

Policies are needed at all levels, local to national, that create implementation spaces that will support a system where dual language is not only allowed, but encouraged and supported. As Menken and García (2010) recommend, educators should seek to understand their own sociolinguistic profiles and those of their students, the school, and the community and learn about the societal language and education policies and the school's language education policy, so that they can 'remain critical and aware of language education policies' (2010: 267) and how they play out in their classrooms. With active local agents and positive policy environments, dual language education could fulfill its potential of providing an affirming and effective education for all students learning two languages.

References

Boyle, A., August, D., Tabaku, L., Cole, S. and Campbell, A.S. (2015) *Dual Language Education Programs: Current State Policies and Practices*. Washington, DC: American Institutes for Research.

Campbell, R.N. (1984) The immersion approach to foreign language teaching. In California State Department of Education, *Studies on Immersion Education* (pp. 114–143). Sacramento, CA: California State Department of Education.

Campbell, R.N., Gray, T.C., Rhodes, N.C. and Snow, M.A. (1985) Foreign language learning in the elementary schools: A comparison of three language programs. *Modern Language Journal* 69 (1), 44–54.

Center for Applied Linguistics (n.d.) Growth of TWI Programs, 1962-Present. *Directory of Two-Way Immersion Programs in the United States*. Center for Applied Linguistics, Washington, D.C. See http://www.cal.org/twi/directory/twigrow.htm

Christian, D. (2011) Dual language education. In E. Hinkel (ed.) *Handbook of Research in Second Language Teaching and Learning* (pp. 3–20). New York, NY: Routledge.

Christian, D. (ed.) (2016) Special issue. Dual language education: Current research perspectives. *International Multilingual Research Journal* 10 (1). See https://tandfonline.com/toc/hmrj20/10/1

Christian, D., Montone, C.L., Lindholm, K.J. and Carranza, I. (1997) *Profiles in Two-way Immersion Education*. Washington, DC and McHenry, IL: Center for Applied Linguistics and Delta Systems Co. Inc.

de Jong, E. (2016) Afterword: Toward pluralist policies, practices, and research. *Language and Education* 30 (4), 378–382. DOI:10.1080/09500782.2015.1114632

Eaton, S. (2012) Have we learned our language lesson? See http://www.onenationindivisible.org/wp-content/uploads/2012/06/ONIstory4LanguageLessonV4.pdf

Genesee, F., Lindholm-Leary, K., Saunders, W.M. and Christian, D. (2006) *Educating English Language Learners: A Synthesis of Research Evidence*. Cambridge: Cambridge University Press.

Hakuta, K. (2011) Educating language minority students and affirming their equal rights. Research and practical perspectives. *Educational Researcher* 40 (4), 163–174.

Harris, E.A. (2015) Dual-language programs are on the rise, even for native English speakers. *The New York Times*, October 8, 2015.

Hornberger, N.H. (2005) Opening and filling up implementational and ideological spaces in heritage language education. *The Modern Language Journal* 89 (4), 605–609.

Hornberger, N.H. and Johnson, D.C. (2007) Slicing the onion ethnographically: Layers and spaces in multilingual language education policy and practice. *TESOL Quarterly* 41 (3), 509–532.

Jaumont, F. (2011) French language education programs in New York City's public schools. *French Embassy Report 2011*. See http://ps110k.org/wp-content/uploads/2012/09/FrenchEmbassyReport2011_FR.pdf

Lambert, W. and Tucker, G.R. (1972) *Bilingual Education of Children: The St. Lambert Experiment*. Rowley, MA: Newbury House.

Lindholm-Leary, K. (2016) Bilingualism and academic achievement in children in dual language programs. In E. Nicoladis and S. Montanari (eds) *Bilingualism Across the Lifespan: Factors Moderating Language Proficiency* (pp. 203–223). Washington, DC and Berlin: American Psychological Association and Walter de Gruyter GmbH.

May, S. (2008) Bilingual/immersion education: What the research tells us. In J. Cummins and N. Hornberger (eds) *Bilingual Education* (pp. 19–34). Volume 5, Encyclopedia of language and education. New York: Springer.

McInerny, C. (2016) Dual language programs continue to grow around state. StateImpact Indiana. See http://indianapublicmedia.org/stateimpact/2016/06/15/dual-language-programs-continue-grow-state/

Menken, K. and García, O. (2010) *Negotiating Language Policies in Schools: Educators as Policymakers*. New York: Routledge.

Montone, C.L. and Loeb, M.I. (2000) *Implementing Two-way Immersion Programs in Secondary Schools*. Santa Cruz, CA: Center for Research on Education, Diversity and Excellence.

Office of English Language Acquisition (2014) *Foreign Language Assistance Program (SEA)*. U.S. Department of Education. See https://www2.ed.gov/programs/flapsea/index.html

Pascopella, A. (2013) Utah's languages of opportunity. *District Administration*, November 2013.

Romano, J. (2010) *Transitions in Connecticut: Bilingual Education in the Windham Public Schools*. Bloomington, IN: iUniverse.

Seal of Biliteracy (2018) *State Laws Regarding the Seal of Biliteracy*. See http://sealofbiliteracy.org/index.php

Spolsky, B. (2009) *Language Management*. Cambridge: Cambridge University Press.

The Language Flagship (2013) *Language Roadmaps*. See https://www.thelanguageflagship.org/content/language-roadmaps

Tuhus, M. (1999) *Law Supports Bilingual Education*. The New York Times. See https://www.nytimes.com/1999/07/11/nyregion/law-supports-bilingual-education.html

U.S. Department of Health and Human Services and U.S. Department of Education. (2015). Policy statement on supporting the development of children who are dual language learners in early childhood programs. See https://eclkc.ohs.acf.hhs.gov/hslc/tta-system/cultural-linguistic/Dual%20Language%20Learners/toolkit/docs/dll-policy-statement-final.pdf

Utah State Board of Education (2018) *Welcome to Dual Language Immersion*. See https://www.schools.utah.gov/curr/dualimmersion

Wiley, T.G. (2014) Diversity, super-diversity, and monolingual language ideology in the United States: Tolerance or intolerance? In K.M. Borman, T.G. Wiley, D.R. Garcia and A.B. Danzig (eds) *Language Policy, Politics, and Diversity in Education* (pp. 1–32). Review of Research in Education, Volume 38. Thousand Oaks, CA: SAGE Publications and American Educational Research Association.

Wiley, T.G. and Wright, W.E. (2004) Against the undertow: Language-minority education policy and politics in the 'Age of Accountability.' *Educational Policy* 18 (1), 142–168.

Wilson, W.H. (2014) Hawaiian: A Native American language official for a state. In T.W. Wiley, J.K. Peyton, D. Christian, S.C.K. Moore and N. Liu (eds) *Handbook of Heritage, Community, and Native American Languages in the United States: Research, Policy, and Educational Practice* (pp. 219–228). New York: Routledge and Center for Applied Linguistics.

Conclusion: Taking Stock: Lessons on Dual Language Education

Fred Genesee

The publication of CAL's volume on *Profiles of Dual Language Education in the 21st Century* marks an auspicious time to take stock of what has happened and what we have learned about dual language education. The publication of the current volume in 2018 marks over 20 years since the Center for Applied Linguistics published the first volume on *Profiles in Two-Way Immersion Education*; it is almost 55 years since Coral Way School opened its doors to bilingual instruction in Florida; and is has been 50+ years since the Lau versus Nichols case in San Francisco that spawned a revolution in education for minority language students across the country. Much has happened since these early years, and we have broadened and deepened our understanding of dual language forms of education considerably. Our insights and knowledge about what it takes to create and maintain successful dual language programs has been enriched remarkably by the experiences of on-the-ground professionals and the concerted efforts of researchers in the U.S., and beyond, since the inception of dual language programs in the mid-1960s. Coincidentally, bilingual forms of education for majority language students were also initiated in the mid-1960s. In the early years, following Coral Way and Lau versus Nichols, a great deal of time and effort was focused on simply establishing that instruction in two languages was not only feasible but also effective for young learners. This was not an easy task since, during the early years after their inception, bilingual programs were cloaked in controversy and claims and counterclaims regarding their effectiveness. Despite such a rocky start, there is compelling evidence now that dual language forms of education work. Recent meta-analyses of research on bilingual education programs, as well as individual studies, have all come to the same general conclusion – educational programs that provide academic instruction through two languages are as, and sometimes even more, effective than monolingual programs and this is the case whether students are from minority or majority language backgrounds (e.g., Genesee & Lindholm-Leary, 2013; Goldenberg, 2008; National Academies of Sciences, Engineering and Medicine, 2017). However, not all dual language programs are created equal; nor, for that matter are monolingual programs. Creating and sustaining effective programs requires commitment, insight, and a deep understanding of the parameters that make programs effective.

In this final chapter in *Profiles of Dual Language Education in the 21st Century*, I discuss what I think are important lessons we have learned about effective dual language programs and the professionals who create and maintain them. Before proceeding, clarification of terminology and points of reference are needed. By dual language programs, I am referring to early childhood and K-12 programs in which more than one language is used to provide substantial amounts of interaction with and/or instruction to participating children/students. I focus on K-12 dual language school programs since this is the focus of most chapters in this volume. However, it is important to note that there is a growing number of preschool dual language programs and they are gaining increased research, policy and public interest owing to the growing importance attached to the preschool years for children's long-term development. Lindholm-Leary (this volume) provides a thorough and useful synopsis of dual language early education programs and issues (see also National Academies of Sciences, Engineering and Medicine, 2017). Typically, the languages used in dual language programs are the national language of the community in which the school is located along with another language that may or may not be spoken by a significant portion of community in which the school is located. Since the modern inception of dual language forms of education in the mid-1960s, alternative forms of bi- and multilingual education have been implemented across the U.S. and around the world (see Genesee & Lindholm-Leary, 2013, for a description of alternatives in the U.S.). Dual language forms of education have also proliferated worldwide (see Mehisto & Genesee, 2015, for a recent compendium of case studies from around the world) as a growing number of communities strive to meet the challenges of globalization or respond to specific national linguistic realities – as in Canada or Spain which have more than one official language. Outside the U.S., dual language programs are almost exclusively designed for students who speak the majority language of the community in which they live. The U.S. is unique in its systematic implementation and evaluation of dual language education for minority language students. Because of the unique contribution that U.S. dual language programs make to our understanding of this form of education and because the focus of the chapters in this volume is largely on the education of minority language students, this chapter will likewise focus on dual language programs for minority language students. Lindholm-Leary (this volume) provides a useful description of dual language options for K-12 students in the U.S.

In the following sections, I discuss seven lessons I think we have learned about dual language education from research and experience; this list covers a range of issues from community context to school leadership to instructional practices:

1. Context matters
2. Planning and strong leadership are critical
3. Both languages should have equally high status
4. All children can become bilingual
5. Pedagogy matters
6. L1 can be a useful tool for L2 learning
7. Ongoing assessment is important

What follows is necessarily a personal perspective – not everyone will agree with my list of important lessons, or my point of view on each. My discussion of each lesson is also necessarily limited in scope to what a single chapter can cover. Finally, my commentary has a limited shelf-life – as our knowledge and experiences with dual language forms of education expand in the coming years, and they undoubtedly will, our existing insights and knowledge will also expand and change.

Lesson 1: Context Matters

From a global perspective and considering all forms of dual language education for the moment, what is perhaps most striking about the pro-liferation of dual language programs, aside from their growing number, is the diversity of program models that have evolved as well as the diversity of community and national contexts in which they have evolved (see Mehisto & Genesee, 2015, for a compendium of case studies from around the world). Undoubtedly, the two are inter-related – as global realities change and call for competence in more than one language, educational leaders around the world have developed alternative models of dual language education to respond to the multiple and unique char-acteristics of the communities in which they live. The importance of context is equally evident within states or even school districts. The importance of local contextualizing factors is identified in a number of the chapters in this volume. Valero and Makishima (Chapter 4) empha-size that a 'one-size-fits all' approach to program development is to be avoided as they recount how careful consideration was given to com-munity characteristics in order to identify which specific program models would be implemented in individual schools in School District U-46 in Illinois. Christian's chapter on The Role of Policy (Chapter 8) highlights the importance of educational and other local, state and national policies as contextualizing influences that should be considered when devising dual language programs: 'All education programs must respond to many levels and types of policies related to education, in the form of compulsory schooling for children of certain ages, graduation requirements, teacher qualifications, to name but a few – but dual language education, by involving multiple languages, is also heavily influenced by the language policies and politics, overt or covert, that are part of the sociolinguistic context of the program and that are embedded in views of immigration, diverse cultures, and other social issues.' Christian goes on to point out that the success of dual language programs is dependent on yet other contextual factors – 'possibilities for the approach to succeed are, for better or worse, affected by the sociolinguistic reality of attitudes, beliefs and ideologies about language and education' that, in turn are often related to '...the broader issues of power, access, opportunity, and inequality.' In their historical description of the development of programs in NYC, García and her colleagues (Chapter 3) also underline the importance of both policy and local attitudes and, in this case, how they can work against the effectiveness of programs: '... past policies have actually impeded DLBE programs from reaching their full potential in city schools'. They go on to argue that 'If dual language bilingual education programs are going to spread and grow throughout the city, some flexibility in implementation guidelines is needed', emphasizing further the importance of variability in community context within a school district.

Mehisto and Genesee (2015) propose a tri-partite framework comprising forces, mechanisms and counterweights for analyzing and managing '...the myriad of factors that can contribute to or hinder the development of successful bi- and trilingual education...' (2015: 2). Forces belong to the ideational realm and generally take the form of attitudes, beliefs, or principles – such as a belief in or distrust of bilingualism, that can fuel or hinder initiatives to create dual language programs. Forces are powerful because they can affect the actions and behaviors of people with respect to dual language programs and, thus, they require a great deal of attention when planning and implementing programs. In contrast, mechanisms are the tangible parts of a system, such as teacher training programs, policy documents and learning materials, that provide the structure for a dual language program. In and of themselves they are inert; they receive their energy from a force or a combination of forces. Counterweights are offered as a way of analyzing the inevitable tensions among mechanisms, among forces and between the two. They can serve as tools for keeping a dual language system in balance. For example, systematic and independent evaluations of a program (mechanisms) can serve as a counterweight to political beliefs (forces) that seek to derail or undermine a program. Case studies of dual language education from around the world are presented in Mehisto and Genesee to illustrate the relevance and usefulness of the framework; each case provides a wealth of information that can help inform other educators about the forces to be considered and mechanisms that are useful when planning programs as well as the counterweights that educators in other communities have undertaken to ensure the ongoing success of their programs.

Lesson 2: Planning and Strong Leadership are Critical

Planning and strong leadership are considered together in this section since planning is only possible if there is strong leadership. As Valero and Makishima (this volume) point out, a steering committee that includes representatives of important stakeholders is a feasible and effective way to both ensure that contextual factors are considered when planning a new program and, I would add, ensuring strong leadership by presenting all points of view on issues that must be considered when creating and developing programs. García and her colleagues likewise discuss the importance of district leadership to ensure a vision for dual language education that goes beyond and 'counter[s] monolingual U.S. schooling' and reflects the 'dynamic' realities of bilingual students and the communities in which they live. Arteagoitia's narrative description of the evolution of Escuela Key, one of the pioneering dual language schools in the U.S., since its inception 30 years ago, illustrates that strong school leadership is critical not only for starting up a new school program, but also for maintaining its effectiveness over time: 'Among the program's many attributes, some stood out .... First, the *strong leadership* (emphasis added by author) provided by the principal and the vice-principal and their commitment to the program's mission, vision and goals. Second, the support and dedication of the *World Languages supervisor* (emphasis added by author) to the DL program and her belief in it.'

Strong school leaders are important because they ensure timely, effective and ongoing school-wide planning that supports the work of everyone in the school – teachers, education specialists, students and support personnel. Strong leadership ensures coherence, continuity and collaboration among all members and components of a school so that it is maximally effective and able to change with changing times. For example, we know from many years of research that the benefits of dual language instruction take time to materialize (Genesee & Lindholm-Leary, 2012). This should not be surprising – language is the most complex skill humans acquire and it takes time to become fully proficient in a new language; it does not happen after one school year, or two or even three. For students to achieve high levels of dual language proficiency in school, educators must create developmentally sound learning environments that are integrated across grade levels. This calls for a common vision of the program, including a common understanding of the goals of the program and a shared commitment to work together to achieve those goals. It also requires timely, state-of-the-art and ongoing professional development (see Kennedy, this volume, for a discussion of the importance of professional development). Most schools, including dual language schools, operate with limited resources – human, financial and physical. Decisions need to be made about how to allocate existing resources and how to obtain new resources. None of this can happen without strong leaders and planning. Strong school leadership implicates not only the principal and vice principal but, as well, heads of departments within the school, education specialists who work in the school, and support staff who support the day-to-day functioning of the school.

People's thinking about bilingualism and teaching and learning in general are often colored by their own experiences as students or by common myths – like the notion that only high achieving students can thrive in dual language programs. Many of these ideas are not supported by current research and theory. If unchecked, these misguided or unsupported ideas undermine the effectiveness and long-term stability of a program. It takes strong school leadership to counteract these views and advocate on behalf of the program. In a related vein, dual language programs, such as innovative teaching in general, are often criticized by other teachers in the system, members of the community who do not see the value of other languages, or by parents whose children are not attending the program. Strong leadership is needed to counteract forces that might destabilize or weaken the program.

Getting the support of leaders in the community is also important because they can elevate the status of a program and help school leaders make a strong case for their program. Increasingly, business and other members of the community see the value of competent multilingual graduates, and many are likely to be keen to support efforts to promote dual language learning to remain competitive in the global marketplace. Business leaders in Indianapolis, Indiana, for example, provided considerable support for the creation of a new multilingual international school with a focus on English, Spanish and French. They saw the new school as a way of attracting experts from outside the U.S. to live and work in Indianapolis, home of a number of important international pharmaceutical companies. As Christian (this volume) points out: 'Dual language education can also become attractive as part of a larger plan to increase language proficiency in a state or city, and the adoption of such a plan signals a more positive policy environment.' The importance of state-wide leadership and its effects on planning and promoting dual language education can perhaps best be illustrated by the case of Utah which saw bilingual competence as an important goal of its school system in order to foster the state's, as well as its students', development and prosperity (see Christian, this volume, for more details).

Strong school and district leadership are essential for all these reasons.

Strong leadership also ensures that all staff in a dual language school has the professional development opportunities they need so that their thinking is informed by state-of-the-art research and professional opinion. However, as Kennedy (this volume) points out: 'the vast majority of states provide guidelines solely for the preparation and certification of teachers serving in English-only classrooms. In bilingual and dual language classrooms, teaching students academic content in two languages, combined with widespread adoption of rigorous content standards and inclusion of students from increasingly diverse populations, is a daunting task that requires a specialized educator skill set.' However, there is a 'lack of clear programmatic guidelines for provision of effective DL teacher preparation' and this 'leaves leaders in higher education working in an ad hoc and uncoordinated fashion to meet increased market demands for teachers prepared to teach in DL settings'. Bearse *et al.* (this volume) make a strong case for a greater emphasis on cultural dimensions in curriculum and professional development. This is especially important, they argue, at the secondary level '…given the central role that identity development plays for students at this age' (see also Gaudet & Clement, 2005) and because 'learning languages has a significant impact on identity development'. All of these demands and expectations call for strong district- and school-level leadership.

Lesson 3: Both/All Languages Should have High Status

In most dual language contexts, be it in the community at large or in the classroom, one language has more status than the other because it is viewed as the language with more status or power. Even in bi- and multilingual families, one language often has more status than the other. Immigrant children or children who speak an indigenous language can be reluctant or even embarrassed to use their home language because they perceive it to have low prestige in comparison to the high-status language of wider use in the community. This imbalance in status can create problems in schools and classrooms with a dual language focus because it disfavors use of one of the languages. As Arteagoitia (this volume) points out: 'Despite teachers' efforts at promoting Spanish and equity among groups, the NES students tend to dominate interactions and teachers are continually looking for ways to empower EL students and further challenge students who are above grade level.' The ethos of dual language programs is 'to use language is to learn language'. If students perceive one of the languages to have low prestige, they will be reluctant to use it. This can also affect teachers' language use. Teachers in dual language programs who believe that one language has more status and is generally more useful or necessary (to pass mandated state or local tests, for example) risk favoring the language and speakers of the language with high status (Valdés, 1997). Privileging one language over another can occur in ways that are subtle and go unnoticed because the school has always done things that way: for example, by posting notices around the school or sending notes home in the high-status language only; by making announcements over the PA system in the high prestige or majority language only; by organizing fun extracurricular activities in the high-status language only and so on. Young learners tend to be very pragmatic – if they perceive that one of the languages they are learning is valued in school more than the other, they will be hesitant to use and learn the 'less popular' language.

Thus, a central goal of dual language educators is to ensure that both languages have equally high status in the school. Initiatives in support of this goal are especially important so that students in the class who speak a low-status or minority language see the value of their language; so that they feel that they can learn the additional language without sacrificing the home language; and so that students from different language groups develop respect and admiration for one another. This might actually mean giving more status to the low-status language in order to level the playing field. Research shows that higher levels of bilingual competence are often associated with greater academic achievement and other general cognitive benefits (e.g., Bialystok, 2006; Lindholm-Leary & Alcan, 1991). Raising the status of low-status languages in dual language programs helps ensure higher levels of bilingual competence by encouraging respect for and active use of both languages. The benefits of dual language competence can be extended by highlighting the cultural values and customs of the communities and families who speak each language, as noted by Bearse and colleagues – again especially the minority language. This enables students who speak the majority language to become familiar with and comfortable interacting with speakers of the minority language, a critical component of dual language competence.

In brief, ensuring that both languages have high status and are worth learning creates an additive bilingual learning environment – an environment in which speakers of the minority language feel that learning an additional language does not mean giving up their home language and speakers of the majority language feel that there is real value in mastering the other language. Some school districts/states have sought to enhance the value of dual language education by offering bilingual certificates or seals of bilingual competence to students graduating from dual language programs (e.g., California, Texas, Indiana; see Garsd, 2015).

Lesson 4: All Children can Become Bilingual

It is often thought that it is not appropriate or advisable for some children to participate in dual language programs, or to become bilingual under any circumstances, because this would put them at enhanced risk of language difficulties and, as well, academic difficulty in school. These beliefs are often most evident when it involves a child who has or is suspected of having a language-related impairment, such as specific language impairment or reading impairment; but, is also evident when thinking about students who might struggle in school for non-clinical reasons – for example, children with below average academic ability, children who speak a non-standard variety of the majority language or who come from a minority ethnic group, or children from low socio-economic families and communities (see Genesee, 2015, for a discussion of common myths about early dual language learning). Children with these backgrounds, although not all, often underperform in school in comparison to other students, for reasons that are not well understood. Such restrictive attitudes can be particularly prevalent in monolingual communities where it is assumed that monolingualism is the norm and, therefore, normal. It is not only parents and educators who believe this; but many speech and language specialists, child developmental specialists, and even medical practitioners may hold this view (Marinova-Todd & Mirenda, 2016). To deprive these children of the opportunity to learn more than one language is unfair given global realities that put a premium on dual language competence and, in the case of children who speak a minority language at home, it can mean abandoning the home language and, as a result, compromise relationships in the family. It is critical that these kinds of beliefs be subject to scientific scrutiny.

Restrictive beliefs about dual language learning are starting to change as more and more scientific evidence demonstrates that most, if not all, children can become bilingual within the limits of their ability. For example, there is a growing body of research from around the world on children with developmental disabilities who grow up learning more than one language from birth or shortly after birth – what is referred to as simultaneous bilingualism. This research is important because it shows that young children's ability to learn language is so powerful that they are able to learn two languages despite their developmental disabilities. Most current research on such children during the preschool years pertains to children with specific language impairment, Down Syndrome, and Autism Spectrum Disorders (see Kay-Raining Bird et al. (2016) and Paradis et al. (2011) for reviews). According to these studies, children with such developmental disorders who are raised bilingually develop the same levels of competence in each language, given adequate exposure to each language, as children with similar disorders who are raised monolingually; in other words, bilingual exposure does not put them at greater risk.

Although these studies indicate that children with developmental disorders can become bilingual during the preschool years, provided adequate exposure to both languages, the question remains: how about children with learning challenges in dual language school programs? In educational research, these children are often referred to as students with special education needs. Students with special education needs have a wide range of learner characteristics that can put them at-risk for difficulty in school, including visual or hearing impairments, developmental delays, speech and language impairments, autism, intellectual disabilities and specific learning disabilities, among others. Only a limited number of types of special education students attending dual language programs have actually been studied to date and extant evidence on such children, especially English language learners (ELLs), is limited (see Fortune (2010); Genesee & Fortune (2014); and Paradis *et al.* (2011) for reviews). Extant evidence indicates that, like their preschool-age peers, these children can also become bilingual without putting their academic achievement at risk.

Myers (2009) examined the performance of both native English-speaking and native Spanish-speaking students in two-way immersion programs in the U.S. who had been identified as having special education needs related to learning disability, developmental delay, emotional disturbance, and other health impairments. They were participating in 50:50 two-way immersion programs and were compared to students with similar special education needs in monolingual English language programs. The students were in grades 3, 4 and 5 and were evaluated using criterion- and norm-referenced tests of reading, listening comprehension, writing, spelling, mathematics, science and social science in English. Myers found no significant differences between special-needs students in the two-way immersion programs and special-needs students in monolingual programs at any grade level. Thomas *et al.* (2010) examined the reading and mathematics achievement of 86 students in 90:10 two-way immersion programs who were receiving special education services. The students were in grades 3 to 8 in six North Carolina school districts. The majority (90%) of these students were identified with specific learning disabilities or specific language impairment. Using criterion-referenced and end-of-grade state assessments, they found that the special needs students in the dual language programs outperformed their peers who were not in these programs in both reading and math. Although the sample sizes in this study were relatively small, they are important because they corroborate Myers' results. Lindholm-Leary and Howard (2008) similarly reported that ELL students with special education needs who participated in dual language programs experienced significant positive outcomes by the upper elementary grade levels. They argued that ELLs with special education needs may be better served in dual language programs than in English-only programs because, although they may have less well-developed literacy skills in English than students without special needs, they are biliterate. In fact, some score average in Spanish reading achievement and this could give them an advantage when they enter the job market in comparison to ELLs who are competent in English only. Supporting the development of the home language in children with special education needs is also important for their overall social well-being and for maintaining strong relationships in the family (National Academies of Sciences, Engineering, and Medicine, 2017).

Although more research about these learners and about other clinically at-risk learners is needed, at present there is no scientific evidence to justify in policy or in practice exclusion of at-risk learners (Genesee, 2016). However, despite this, it is important that parents and educators take student's life circumstances into account when making decisions about specific children. In this author's opinion, every effort should be made to include children in dual language programs, where available, when knowledge of another language in addition to English is critically important, such as children living in bilingual families or in families where another language predominates. In contrast, careful consideration should be given to the challenges of including children for whom knowledge of an additional language is optional, such as children who have no immediate or obvious future need for the additional language, if the school district, the school itself and/or the child's parents are unable to provide the extra support that these children need to succeed in school (see Paradis *et al.*, 2011, on how to identify and support at-risk bilingual learners). Moreover, it is important to keep in mind that the results from these studies do not tell us that *all* at-risk children will become bilingual easily and completely as a result of dual language instruction. Adaptations need to be made to create learning environments in school that allow students who struggle in school to succeed in dual language programs, as is the case for students in monolingual programs. Thus, on the one hand, districts that offer dual language programs should be prepared to accommodate learners with a variety of learner profiles; on the other hand, if they do not have a full range of services for dual language learners, parents should carefully consider the advantages and challenges of placing an at-risk learner in a dual language program that is not prepared to provide additional support if that child has no immediate need for both languages.

Lesson 5: Pedagogy Matters

As noted earlier, research in the U.S., Canada, and indeed from around the world indicates that teaching substantial portions of the prescribed school curriculum through two languages is effective for promoting bilingual proficiency and academic achievement for a wide diversity of students living in diverse socio-cultural-political communities. At the same time, research that has examined the effectiveness of dual language programs in detail has taught us that pedagogy matters. For example, Stevens (1983) carried out an early study on alternative instructional strategies in dual language immersion programs in Canada that is instructive even now. More specifically, Stevens compared the second language outcomes of two groups of English-speaking students who were participating in immersion programs that provided curriculum instruction using their second language (French) beginning in grade 7. In one case, the students spent 80% of their school day immersed in French – all academic subjects, except English language arts, were taught through the medium of French. The other group, in contrast, spent only about half as much time – approximately 50% of their school day was spent in French – math, science, and language arts were taught in French. In brief, Stevens' results revealed that, despite the time advantage of the first group, they did not score consistently higher than the second group on a variety of second language measures – the latter group actually scored as well as the former group on measures of speaking and listening and almost as high on tests of reading and writing. Stevens attributed the impressive performance of her 50% immersion students to the fact that they participated in an individualized, activity-based program that gave them certain choices about what they would study and how they would meet curricular objectives. Of particular importance, they were given plenty of opportunities to use the language while engaged in self-selected and individually defined projects that often involved 'field work' – in the school or local library or community museums and, even literally, in the field if it was a biological project. In contrast, the full-day program was characterized by a group-centered approach in which all students studied the same topics according to the same timeline and curriculum guidelines. This study is important in indicating not only that specific instructional strategies are important but also that time alone is not always the most significant predictor of second language learning – the intensity of exposure and, most importantly, the nature and quality of student engagement are very important. The importance of student engagement for promoting learning is a theme that has been discussed quite extensively in general education although less so by dual language educators (e.g., Guthrie *et al.*, 2004). The issue is how to best promote engagement in dual language classrooms when all or some students are learning through a second language.

Pedagogically speaking, dual language forms of education can be characterized as having an instructional approach with a 'focus on meaning' in contrast to traditional second language pedagogical approaches that often have a 'focus on forms' (see Lyster, 2007, and Norris & Ortega, 2000, for more discussion of this distinction). Briefly, in the former, students are expected to learn the target language by using it for academic or other authentic communicative purposes; whereas in the latter, mastery of the formal structures and properties (rules) of the language are taught as pre-requisites to functional use of the language. Of course, there is considerable variation from program to program and even classroom to classroom. The rationale behind dual language education at its inception was to take advantage of children's natural ability to learn language which occurs during authentic, meaningful and significant communication with others. To this end, dual language educators were often discouraged from correcting students' second language usage for fear of discouraging them from using the language. Moreover, there were often no specific guidelines on when and how to provide explicit instruction in the target language during classes when academic subjects were the focus of attention or even when and how to correct students' errors. There is growing evidence that, despite the overall effectiveness of this approach, an exclusive focus on meaning or language use to the neglect of explicit language teaching is not optimal when it comes to developing students' linguistic competence. In particular, research on immersion programs in Canada has revealed that despite participation in immersion programs for many years, immersion students often fail to master important aspects of the target language, such as verb tense, pronouns, and prepositions (see Lyster (2007) for a review). There are reasons to believe that the same is true of dual language programs in the U.S. For minority language students, this may also be true in their first language insofar as it is not widely supported outside school.

Mastery of language – and not simply being able to get by in a language – is important in dual language programs because the second language(s) is used to teach academic subjects such as mathematics or science or literature. Language becomes increasingly important for learning in academic domains in the higher grades as academic subject matter becomes increasingly complex and language-dependent. Advanced levels of oral language competence is also the foundation for competence in reading and writing, again especially in the higher grades. Being able to use the second language correctly and idiomatically is also very important in the long run, after leaving school, if students go on to higher education or compete for professional positions where they will use that language with native speakers.

The role of dual language educators is to create learning environments that will maximize students' linguistic competence as much as possible while ensuring that they achieve high standards in all academic domains. Increasingly, researchers and educational professionals are calling for more systematic and explicit instruction of specific vocabulary, grammar and discourse patterns linked to students' communication needs in their academic subjects – mathematics, science and other areas of the curriculum. There is evidence that instruction that balances focus on meaning and focus on form can achieve the same academic outcomes and, at the same time, enhance second language competence (Lyster, 2007). The importance of systematic and explicit language instruction during both English Language Development classes and non-language subject classes (such as science or history) along with strategies for doing this have been highlighted by numerous researchers and educators (see Echevarria & Short (2010); Lyster (2007); Mehisto (2012); Saunders & Goldenberg (2010); Snow *et al.* (1989)). There is a need for considerably more investigation into how best to achieve this balance to good effect.

Lesson 6: The First Language can be a Useful Tool for Learning a Second Language

For many years, educators working in dual language programs were told that students' use of their first language should be avoided at all costs during classes when the second language was being taught or used as the language of instruction. Letting students use their first language, it was argued, would become a crutch – students would 'turn off' when their less proficient, second language was being used and wait until the teacher spoke their stronger language. As a result, teachers in dual language programs often tried to create monolingual environments in which everyone would use only the second language during second language classes and only the first language during time devoted to the first language.

There is some justification for this practice. If students do not use their second language, they will not learn it. Letting students use their first language during times when the additional language is the language of instruction or when complex new concepts and skills are being taught can make it difficult for students to acquire complex skills in the additional language and this, in turn, can make mastery of new non-language skills and knowledge in the higher grades difficult. However, this view conceptualizes bilingualism in essentially monolingual terms insofar as both languages are viewed as existing in isolation of one another. Evidence from the fields of neurolinguistics (e.g., Hoshino & Thierry, 2011), sociolinguistics (e.g., Jorgensen, 2008), cognitive psychology (Kroll *et al.*, 2014) and multilingual education (García & Li Wei, 2014) call for a different, more complex conceptualization of bilingualism, one in which there are multiple dynamic interrelationships between the languages of bi/multilinguals. For example, in the field of cognitive psychology, researchers have found that child and adult bilinguals and, in particular, simultaneous bilinguals are able to code-mix without violating the grammatical constraints of either language most of the time (e.g., Genesee, 2002). These findings indicate that bilinguals have access to the grammars of both languages simultaneously and automatically. There is also a great deal of evidence from educational research for significant and positive correlations between reading skills in one language and reading skills in another in bilinguals; the nature and extent of the interaction depends to some extent on the typological similarity of the languages and their orthographic systems (e.g., August & Shanahan, 2006). Research on the acquisition, comprehension and production of two languages and during proficient bilingual performance has revealed further that both linguistic systems are differentially accessible and activated at virtually all times (e.g., Gullifer *et al.*, 2013). The two languages of bilinguals share a common cognitive/conceptual foundation that can facilitate use of more than one language during communication, thinking and problem solving. Research also suggests that competence in two or more languages engenders the development of sophisticated cognitive skills for negotiating and minimizing cross-language competition (Kroll, 2008) and can result in other neuro-cognitive differences and even advantages (Bialystok, 2017). Findings from these lines of research reveal highly sophisticated, interacting systems of language representations, access and use.

An important consequence of this shift in our conceptualization of bilingualism is that, while in the past many educators viewed use of the home or first language as a source of interference that might impede learners' ability to learn and use the second language, we increasingly view competence in the first language as potentially advantageous to bilinguals' overall linguistic development, processing and communication (Canagarajah, 2011; Cummins, 2014; García, 2009; Gort & Sembiante, 2015). Specifically with respect to dual language education, these findings have opened the door to what has been referred to as translanguaging (e.g., García, 2009) and, more generally, as cross-language/linguistic pedagogies that use both languages during the same lessons or units of instruction (see García & Wei, 2014; Lyster *et al.*, 2009, for more detailed discussion of these issues). This new perspective raises important questions about how much, when and how both languages should be used to promote dual language learning.

At present, there is in fact relatively little empirical evidence about the actual effectiveness of cross-language or translanguaging strategies versus monolingual strategies. Nevertheless, it seems reasonable to argue that how much it is advisable for teachers and students to use students' home language when the second or additional language is the language of instruction and how it is used will depend on the status of the two languages. More specifically, if the first language is a minority language – as in the case of ELLs, then it needs more support than if it is a majority language. Let's take two different cases – one from Canada and the other from the U.S. In Canadian dual language or immersion programs, the students speak English, a majority language, at home; and they learn through French and English in school. Teachers teaching during the French portion of the curriculum in these programs resist using English for fear that that their English-speaking students will become lazy and use only English because they 'can get away with it'. Focusing on one language at a time makes sense in this context. Because the first language of Canadian immersion students is a high-status language that is highly valued and widely used outside school, it does not need to be supported very much in school, especially during those times of the day devoted to French. However, a different strategy makes more sense in the case of dual language programs in the U.S. for minority language students who speak Spanish outside school and are participating in developmental bilingual and two-way immersion programs. Despite its status as one of the most widely spoken languages around the world and despite its widespread use in the immediate community of many students, Spanish is a relatively low-status language among both native speakers of English and Spanish. In this case, encouraging students to use Spanish in order to learn new concepts being taught in English and to push their proficiency in English forward could be helpful. By drawing on minority language Spanish-speaking students' knowledge of their first language during instruction in English, teachers can not only reinforce their students' skills in that language, they can take advantage of the crosslinguistic facilitation that has been found for some aspects of English language development and, most notably, reading and writing (August & Shanahan, 2006; National Academies of Sciences, Engineering and Medicine, 2017). They can also elevate the status of that language in the eyes of both Spanish-speakers themselves and their English-speaking peers to create an additive bilingual learning environment. Similarly, when immigrant children or children who speak an indigenous language are being taught only through the majority language – English, allowing them recourse to the home language while being taught in the majority language reinforces their competence and pride in that language. In other words, use of cross-language approaches to instruction needs to take cognizance of the status of the languages involved.

In the absence of sufficient evidence on how best to use cross-language strategies, it makes sense that cross-language teaching be done selectively and strategically so that teachers avoid privileging one language over the other. Cross-language teaching should never be used just to make it easier for the students or the teachers (see Ballinger *et al.*, 2017, and Genesee and Hamayan, 2016, for more discussion of these pedagogical issues). It is not uncommon to find teachers in dual language programs, for example, having to resort to using English in grades 5 and 6 even during instructional time devoted to teaching in Spanish because students have insufficient competence in academic Spanish to perform the necessary instructional tasks. This situation arises most likely when teachers have not insisted on or promoted the use of Spanish for academic purposes in the lower grades. Permitting use of students' home language to make teaching and learning easier in the lower grades can ultimately make teaching and learning in that language more difficult in the higher grades.

This does not mean that cross-language pedagogies are not useful at all. They can be – if used with specific learning goals in mind. For example, the language awareness approach is one useful way for thinking strategically about why and how to use both languages (Dagenais *et al.*, 2008). In this approach, students are encouraged to draw on and compare linguistic knowledge stemming from all of the languages that they speak or have some knowledge of. Students do not need to use both languages to communicate their ideas about their languages; rather, during these activities, they may compare specific aspects of their languages (e.g., how to transform nouns and verbs into negative forms, or how to form questions in two languages) while maintaining use of only one target language. The language awareness approach has the additional benefit of being inclusive of all languages represented in the classroom.

Another use of cross-language pedagogy has been explored by Lyster *et al.* (2009) who have investigated how cross-language strategies can be used to make connections between languages during literacy instruction in dual language immersion programs in Canada. In their work, French and English teachers in French – English immersion programs used their respective languages for literacy instruction with the same students using a reading series that was available in both languages. Students read and discussed one chapter in English with the English teacher and the next chapter in French with the French teacher. During each reading, teachers encouraged students to see similarities and differences in the two languages – with respect to vocabulary, grammar and organization; in fact, students often observed similarities and differences without being prompted. In this way, students made connections between English and French but they and their teachers stuck to using each language during designated class times. This technique can be particularly useful in two-way dual language programs because it permits students from each language group to contribute equally – depending on the language used in a specific lesson; this, in turn, allows speakers of the other language to benefit from the contributions of their other-language peers.

A final example also comes from the domain of literacy. Students can create 'cognate word walls' or notebooks in which they note words in both instructional languages, or even in other languages that are spoken by other students in the classroom, that are orthographically similar and share meanings along with those that are false cognates. This could be done during each lesson or during bridging time when the teacher sets time aside at the end of a lesson or unit for students to do this (Beeman & Urow, 2012). This can be particularly useful for comparing specialized or technical vocabulary and subject-specific ways of using language in mathematics and science, for example, to ensure that students are acquiring academic terminology in both languages even when instruction in a given subject is being delivered in one language. All of these possibilities promote the recognition of connections between languages without favoring one or the other and ensuring that students have lots of opportunities to use both.

Judicious use of cross-language pedagogies can accomplish a number of important pedagogical goals: to instill respect for all languages spoken in the classroom, to reflect and give voice to the dynamic relationship between the languages of bilinguals, to encourage participation by students from both language groups in two-way dual language classrooms, and to promote dual language development by taking advantage of cross-linguistic interactions between the developing languages of bilinguals.

Lesson 7: Ongoing Assessment is Important

The topic of assessment is dreaded by many educational practitioners and administrators because it is associated with mandated, high-stakes standardized testing that has little to do with local schools and their particular goals and curriculum. However, assessment broadly defined is invaluable in enhancing program success. The importance of assessment in the form of systematic research is evident in Lindholm-Leary's chapter (this volume) on early childhood dual language programs. In particular, the research reviewed in this chapter extends our understanding of the effectiveness of dual language forms of education to include preschool age children. It was the very same kind of evaluation research of K-12 programs that paved the way to their expansion following their inception in the mid-1960s, noted earlier (see Lindholm-Leary, 2001, for an early overview of research on dual language programs in the U.S.). In a similar vein, Valerio and Makishima recount in Chapter 4 that 'research' was identified by School District U-46 in Illinois as one of the three key elements to consider when planning the design and implementation of its dual language programs. Kennedy (this volume) points out how the relative lack of relevant research on important issues, such as professional development, can leave serious gaps in our understanding of dual language education. Systematic evaluation by expert researchers can serve to validate dual language education in its various forms and can provide valuable guidelines with respect to general programmatic and classroom issues – such as the outcomes of programs that introduce the second language in different grades or of different amounts of time devoted to use of the second language, and whether dual language education is suitable for all students. Thus, research can shape the development of policies and influence program planning in significant ways, as noted by other chapters in this volume (Arteagoitia, García et al. and Bearse et al., this volume).

School-based and designed assessments, especially if done systematically and continuously, can contribute to the success of individual programs by providing valuable information that can be used to monitor, modify, and update programs, teacher competencies, curriculum, and instructional materials so that they are as effective as possible. Many published studies have pointed out the benefits of using student achievement data to monitor and enhance program effectiveness (e.g., August & Hakuta, 1997; Slavin & Calderón, 2001). Effective use of student achievement data to improve program outcomes is most likely when schools use assessment measures that are aligned with the school's vision and goals and its curriculum (Montecel & Cortez, 2002) – a deficiency of most state or federally mandated accountability assessments. In this regard,

Arteagoitia recounts how the long-term success and evolution of Escuela Key was built in part on a continuous analysis of program outcomes and annual assessments of students' English, mathematics and science achievement. Similarly, Valero and Makishima recount that 'a fair assessment framework was created in order to assess students' development of bilingualism and biliteracy' that was also consistent with standards-based instruction was part of the implementation plans in District U-46.

Equally important is assessment that is designed and carried out by individual teachers in their own classrooms. In these cases, assessment is not only about evaluating student outcomes for accountability purposes, but also includes evaluation broadly defined – the collection of information about instructional materials and activities to judge their effectiveness; about students' preferred learning styles, interests and backgrounds to ensure student engagement; about students' initial oral language and literacy skills when they enter a program and in each subsequent year in order to plan individualized instruction; and more. Student self-assessment can also play an important role in enhancing learning outcomes by helping students become autonomous and focused learners. Viewed from these multiple classroom perspectives, assessment entails more than testing as it is commonly defined. It entails a variety of assessment tools, including checklists, dialogue journals, learning logs, portfolios and even systematic observation (see Hamayan *et al.*, 2013, for practical discussions of alternative forms of assessment). By taking charge of their own assessments and by including students as partners in assessment, dual language teachers can base classroom-relevant decisions on their own empirical evidence.

Summing up

Our understanding of dual language programs has advanced enormously since the first volume on *Profiles in Two-Way Immersion Education* was published in 1997. Of particular importance, our understanding of children's capacity for learning language in dual language contexts is light years ahead of our state of knowledge in 1997. It is now well recognized and well substantiated by scientists that the innate capacity that young children have for language learning is not limited to one language. Countless studies of children during the 0 to 5 age range have indicated that learning two languages is as natural as learning one (e.g., National Academies of Science, Engineering and Medicine, 2017; Paradis *et al.*, 2011). In fact, young learners can acquire the same levels of functional proficiency in two languages that monolingual children acquire in only one language in the same time (e.g., Thordardottir, 2011). This has been documented for children with developmental disorders as well as typically developing children, emphasizing further the power of children's capacity for learning two languages. Despite early skepticism about the effectiveness of dual language forms of education, we also now know from many scientific studies that dual language forms of education are as, and often more, effective than monolingual programs for minority language students – both with respect to their academic outcomes and their acquisition of the majority language. At the same time, minority language students attain levels of proficiency in the home language that are substantially higher than those of similar students in monolingual English-only programs. That is to say, they become highly proficient bilinguals. Again, this has been documented even for students who often struggle in school (e.g., Genesee *et al.*, 2013). Becoming proficiently bilingual is important for all students because it affords them personal, social, cognitive and, in the global world, employment advantages that they might not have otherwise.

However, this is not to say that all children raised bilingually or all students educated bilingually become fully proficient in both languages or academically successful. As evidenced by a number of reports in this volume, the challenges dual language students face in achieving these goals are attributable largely to the quality of the learning environments they are provided. In other words, successful dual language programs depend on the success of educators, other professionals who care for dual language learners (e.g., medical doctors), parents and other child care providers at providing consistently high-quality learning opportunities. We can no longer argue that dual language programs are ill advised because learners are not capable of benefiting from dual language instruction or that they are put at-risk by dual language instruction. Now that research has indicated clearly that dual language learning is not a challenge for most learners, notwithstanding the challenges some students face due to developmental or other learning disorders, we can and should focus on how best to provide high-quality programs. This is indeed very encouraging and promising because it focuses attention where further advances can be made. We are beginning to see movement in this direction, as evidenced by enhanced research on: effective interventions for struggling dual language readers (e.g., Genesee *et al.*, 2013); identification and support for dual language learners with language impairment (e.g., Kohnert, 2010), and effective early childhood care programs (see California's Best Practices, 2013, for a review). To keep abreast of developments in these and other relevant domains, a third volume on dual language contexts will be needed within the next decade.

References

August, D. and Hakuta, K. (1997) *Improving Schooling for Language Minority Children: A Research Agenda*. Washington, DC: National Academy Press.

August, D. and Shanahan, T. (2006) *Developing Literacy in Second Language Learners. Report of the National Literacy Panel on Minority-Language Children and Youth*. Mahwah, NJ: Lawrence Erlbaum.

Ballinger, S., Lyster, R., Sterzuk, A. and Genesee, F. (2017) Context-appropriate cross-linguistic pedagogy: Considering the role of language status in immersion education. *Journal of Immersion and Content-Based Language Education* 5 (1), 30–57.

Beeman, K. and Urow, C. (2012) *Teaching for Biliteracy: Strengthening Bridges between Languages*. Philadelphia: Caslon.

Bialystok, E. (2006) The impact of bilingualism on language and literacy development. In T.K. Bhatia and W.E. Ritchie (eds) *The Handbook of Bilingualism* (pp. 577–601). Malden, MA: Blackwell Publishing.

Bialystok, E. (2017) The bilingual adaptation: How minds accommodate experience. *Psychological Bulleti* 143 (3), 233–262.

California's Best Practices for Young Dual Language Learners. Sacramento, CA: CDE Publications and Educational Resources.

Canagarajah, S. (2011) Translanguaging in the classroom: Emerging issues for research and pedagogy. *Applied Linguistics Review* 2, 1–28.

Cummins, J. (2014) Rethinking pedagogical assumptions in Canadian French immersion programs. *Journal of Immersion and Content-Based Language Education* 2 (1), 3–22.

Dagenais, D., Walsh, N., Armand, F. and Maraillet, E. (2008) Collaboration and co-construction of knowledge during language awareness activities in Canadian elementary schools. *Language Awareness* 17 (2), 139–155.

Echevarria, J. and Short, D. (2010) Programs and practices for effective sheltered instruction. In California Department of Education (eds) *Improving Education for English Learners: Research-Based Approaches* (pp. 251–322). Sacramento, CA: California Department of Education.

Fortune, T.W. (2010) *Struggling Learners and Language Immersion Education*. Minneapolis, MN: Center for Advanced Studies on Language Acquisition.

García, O. (2009) *Bilingual Education in the 21st Century: A Global Perspective*. Oxford: Wiley Blackwell.

García, O. and Wei, L. (2014) *Translanguaging: Language, Bilingualism, and Education*. London: Palgrave MacMillan.

Garsd, J. (2015) *On the High School Diploma: A 'Bilingual' Stamp of Approval?* NPR. See https://www.npr.org/sections/ed/2015/04/21/400173544/on-the-high-school-dip loma-a-bilingual-stamp-of-approval

Gaudet, S. and Clement, R. (2005) Identity maintenance and loss: A concurrent process among Fransaskois. *Canadian Journal of Behavioral Science* 37 (2), 110–122.

Genesee, F. (2002) Portrait of the bilingual child. In V. Cook (ed) *Portraits of the Second Language User* (pp. 170–196). Clevedon: Multilingual Matters.

Genesee, F. (2015) Myths about early childhood bilingualism. *Canadian Psychology* 56 (1), 6–15.

Genesee, F. (2016) At-risk learners and bilingualism: Is it a good idea? *Colorin Colorado!* See http://www.colorincolorado.org/article/risk-learners-and-bilingualism-it-good-idea

Genesee, F. and Fortune, T. (2014) Bilingual education and at-risk students. *Journal of Immersion and Content-Based Language Education* 2 (2), 165–180.

Genesee, F. and Hamayan, E. (2016) *CLIL in Context: Practical Guidance for Educators*. Cambridge, UK: Cambridge University Press.

Genesee, F. and Lindholm-Leary, K. (2012) The education of English language learners. In K. Harris, S. Graham and T. Urdan (eds) *APA Handbook of Educational Psychology* (pp. 499–526). Washington DC: APA Books.

Genesee, F. and Lindholm-Leary, K. (2013) Two case studies of content-based language education. *Journal of Immersion and Content-Based Language Education* 1 (1), 3–33.

Genesee, F., Savage, R., Erdos, E. and Haigh, C. (2013) Identification of reading difficulties in students schooled in a second language. In V.M. Gathercole (ed.) *Solutions for the Assessment of Bilinguals* (pp. 10–35). Bristol: Multilingual Matters.

Goldenberg, C. (Summer, 2008) Teaching English language learners: What the research does – and does not – say. *American Education* 8–44.

Gort, M. and Sembiante, S. (2015) Navigating hybridized language learning spaces through translanguaging pedagogy: Dual language preschool teachers' languaging practices in support of emergent bilingual children's performance of academic discourse. *International Multilingual Research Journal* 9 (1), 7–25.

Gullifer, J., Kroll, J. and Dussias, P. (2013) When language switching has no apparent cost: Lexical access in sentence context. *Frontiers in Psychology* 4, 248.

Guthrie, J.T., Wigfield, A. and Perencevich, K.C. (2004) *Motivating Reading Comprehension: Concept-oriented Reading Instruction*. Mahwah, NJ: Lawrence Erlbaum.

Hamayan, E., Genesee, F. and Cloud, N. (2013) *Dual Language Instruction: From A to Z*. Portsmouth, N.H.: Heinle and Heinle.

Hoshino, N. and Thierry, G. (2011) Language selection in bilingual word production: Electrophysiological evidence for cross-language competition. *Brain Research* 1371, 100–109.

Jorgensen, J. (2008) Poly-lingual languaging around and among children and adolescents. *International Journal of Multilingualism* 5 (3), 161–176.

Kay-Raining Bird, E., Genesee, F. and Verhoeven, L. (2016) Bilingualism in children with developmental disorders. *Journal of Communication Disorders*. http://dx.doi. org/10.1016/j.jcomdis.2016.07.003

Kohnert, K. (2010) Bilingual children with primary language impairment: Issues, evidence and implications for clinical actions. *Journal of Communication Disorders* 43, 456–473.

Kroll, J. (2008) Juggling two languages in one mind. *Psychological Science Agenda* 22 (1). See http://www.apa.org/science/about/psa/2008/01/kroll.aspx

Kroll, J., Bobb, S. and Hoshino, N. (2014) Two languages in mind: Bilingualism as a tool to investigate language, cognition, and the brain. *Current Directions in Psychological Science* 23, 159–163.

Lindholm-Leary, K. (2001) *Dual Language Education*. Clevedon: Multilingual Matters.

Lindholm, K.J. and Aclan, Z. (1991) Bilingual proficiency as a bridge to academic achievement: Results from bilingual/immersion programs. *Journal of Education* 173, 99–113.

Lindholm-Leary, K.J. and Howard, E. (2008) Language and academic achievement in two-way immersion programs. In T. Fortune and D. Tedick (eds) *Pathways to Bilingualism: Evolving Perspectives on Immersion Education* (pp. 177–200). Clevedon: Multilingual Matters.

Lyster, R. (2007) *Learning and Teaching Languages Through Content: A Counterbalanced Approach*. Amsterdam, NLD: John Benjamins.

Lyster, R., Collins, L. and Ballinger, S. (2009) Linking languages through a read-aloud bilingual project. *Journal of Language Awareness* 18 (3–4), 366–383.

Marinova-Todd, S. and Mirenda, P. (2016) Language and Communication Abilities of Children with Autism Spectrum Disorders. In J. Patterson and B.L. Rodríguez (eds) *Multilingual Perspectives on Child Language Disorders* (pp. 31–48). Bristol: Multilingual Matters.

Mehisto, P. (2012) *Excellence in Bilingual Education: A Guide for School Principals*. Cambridge: Cambridge University Press.

Mehisto, P. and Genesee, F. (2015) *Building Bilingual Education Systems: Forces, Mechanisms and Counterweights*. Cambridge: Cambridge University Press.

Montecel, M.R. and Cortez, J.D. (2002) Successful bilingual education programs: Development and the dissemination of criteria to identify promising and exemplary practices in bilingual education at the national level. *Bilingual Research Journal* 26, 1–21.

Myers, M.L. (2009) Achievement of children identified with special needs in two-way Spanish immersion programs. Unpublished PhD dissertation. Faculty of Graduate School of Education and Human Development, George Washington University. Washington, D.C.

National Academies of Sciences, Engineering, and Medicine (2017) *Promoting the Educational Success of Children and Youth Learning English: Promising Futures.* Washington, DC: The National Academies Press. doi: 10.17226/24677.

Norris, J.M. and Ortega, L. (2000) Effectiveness of L2 instruction: A research synthesis and quantitative meta-analysis. *Language Learning* 50 (3), 417–528.

Paradis, J., Genesee, F. and Crago, M. (2011) *Dual Language Development and Disorders: A Handbook on Bilingualism and Second Language Learning* (2nd edn). Baltimore, MD: Brookes.

Saunders, W. and Goldenberg, C. (2010) Research to guide English language development instruction. In California Department of Education (eds) *Improving Education for English Learners: Research-Based Approaches* (pp. 21–82). Sacramento, CA: California Department of Education.

Slavin, R. and Calderon M. (2001) *Effective Programs for Latino Learners.* Mahwah, NJ: Lawrence Erlbaum.

Snow, A., Met, M. and Genesee, F. (1989) A conceptual framework for the integration of language and content in second/foreign language instruction. *TESOL Quarterly* 23, 201–218.

Stevens, F. (1983) Activities to promote learning and communication in the second language classroom. *TESOL Quarterly* 17, 259–272.

Thomas, W., Collier, V. and Collier, K. (2010) *English learners in North Carolina, 2010.* Fairfax, VA: George Mason University. A research report provided to North Carolina Department of Public Instruction.

Thordardottir, E. (2011) The relationship between bilingual exposure and vocabulary development. *International Journal of Bilingualism* 14, 426–445.

Valdés, G. (1997) The teaching of Spanish to bilingual Spanish-speaking students: Outstanding issues and unanswered questions. In M.C. Colombi and F.X. Alarcon (eds) *La Eensñnanza del Espanol a Hispanohablantes: Praxis y Teoria* (pp. 93–101). Boston, MA: Houghton Mifflin.

Index

Made in the USA
Coppell, TX
11 February 2020

15717865R10105